# CLASSICS
# OF
# SEA POWER

The Classics of Sea Power series makes readily available, in uniform, authoritative editions, the key works of professional naval thought. Illustrating naval development over the centuries, these major original, book-length works relating to theory, strategy, tactics, operations, and important themes in naval warfare have been chosen for their eloquence and timelessness. The series is a companion to histories, anthologies, and other interpretive writings, providing a depth of understanding that cannot be had from reading secondary sources alone.

Philip Colomb's *Naval Warfare* is the work of a pioneer thinker who used the study of naval history as the basis for professional understanding of the role of naval power and as a guide to modern naval problems. Colomb, one of the few in his time to use manuscript sources in his research, saw the importance of linking broad concepts to the detailed narration of events. In America his ideas were overshadowed by the work of Mahan, whom he preceded. However, Colomb's examination of the concepts of a fleet-in-being, command of the sea, and the role of sea power in attacks against the land were influential in other navies. In this, his work is important to the history of naval thought and establishes a benchmark from which the work of his successors, Mahan and Corbett among them, can be measured.

Naval warfare is Colomb's subject. He makes no effort to structure naval theory. His rich historical examples are incidental to a grasp of strategic wisdom, yet they are detailed so that readers can place themselves in the minds of the actors. The refreshing absence of differentiation between policy, strategy, tactics, and technology reflects Colomb's belief that these are a seamless blend. Readers accustomed to getting naval history in predigested morsels will savor this chance to walk with Colomb on a grand tour of British naval history.

## SERIES EDITORS

**John B. Hattendorf**
Naval War College
Newport, Rhode Island

**Wayne P. Hughes, Jr.**
Naval Postgraduate School
Monterey, California

# Naval Warfare

Vice Admiral P. H. Colomb
(*Illustrated London News*, 21 October 1899,
Photo: Elliott and Fry)

VICE ADMIRAL
P. H. COLOMB
ROYAL NAVY

# Naval Warfare

## Its Ruling Principles and Practice Historically Treated

### VOLUME 1

With an Introduction
by Barry M. Gough

NAVAL INSTITUTE PRESS          Annapolis, Maryland

This book was originally published in 1891 by W. H. Allen & Co.,
London
A second edition appeared in 1895 and a third edition in 1899.

Introduction © 1990 by the United States Naval Institute,
Annapolis, Maryland

Library of Congress Cataloging-in-Publication Data

Colomb, P. H. (Philip Howard), 1831–1899.
Naval warfare, its ruling principles and practice historically
  treated / P. H. Colomb ; with an introduction by Barry M. Gough.
      p.     cm.
Reprint. Originally published: 3rd ed. London : W. H. Allen, 1899.
Includes bibliographical references.
1. Naval art and science.   2. Naval history.   I. Title.
V103.C7 1990
359—dc20                                                89-13389
                                                            CIP

ISBN 0-87021-777-1

Series design by Moira M. Megargee

Printed in the United States of America

The paper used in this publication meets the minimum requirements of
American National Standard for Information Sciences—Permanence of
Paper for Printed Library Materials, ANSI Z39.48-1984.

# CONTENTS

# NOTE ON SOURCES
# AND
# ACKNOWLEDGMENTS

I WISH TO RECORD my generous thanks to several fellow scholars who have assisted in bringing Admiral Philip Howard Colomb's *Naval Warfare* back into print after nearly a century. My first obligation is to Professor John B. Hattendorf of the Naval War College, Newport, Rhode Island. Professor Hattendorf suggested that I undertake this new edition, and with avuncular kindness and abundant good sense he has guided the work from concept to reality. I shall always be in his debt for his sound counsel and thorough knowledge of naval history and strategic affairs. My second obligation is to yet another member of the naval history college, Donald M. Schurman of Kingston, Ontario. Professor Schurman first saved Admiral Colomb's work from obscurity by writing of him in his chapter "Clio and the Admiral," which appeared in *The Education of a Navy: The Development of British Naval Strategic Thought, 1867–1914* (Chicago, 1965). For certain biographical particulars and an analysis of Philip Colomb's strategic thought in my introduction I have drawn heavily from Professor Schurman's trenchant, if brief, assessment. My third obligation is to Dr. Robert Waring Herrick of Annandale, Virginia. Dr. Herrick, an acknowledged expert on Russian and Soviet naval strategy, theory, and practice, is the author of *Soviet Naval Strategy: Fifty Years of Theory and Practice* (Annapolis, Md., 1968) and *Soviet Naval Theory and Policy* (Newport, R.I., 1988). The latter work demonstrates beyond a shadow of doubt the ongoing influence of Philip Colomb, if only as a base for discussion of how a continental and heartland power has had to contend with concepts of sea power. As Dr. Herrick shows, Russian and Soviet historian-strategists gave phenomenal attention to Philip Colomb's writings. As late as 1953 the classical thalassocratic arguments of command of the sea that Colomb derived from his study of history were being scrutinized by Stalinist critics. That Admiral Colomb's writings should have provided a battleground for cold war ideology and strategic analysis is a subject for considerable wonder. More than this, it demonstrates that the influence of history on sea power, to invert Alfred Thayer Mahan's concept, has enduring interest. Dr. Herrick's meticulous research and thought-provoking analysis demonstrates that the Soviets took Admiral Colomb's writings far more seriously than do twentieth-century western powers. By implication, we are reminded that a fresh look at *Naval Warfare* may revive some fundamental truths about the nature of strategy, sea power, command of the sea, and the characteristics of naval warfare.

I must also record my thanks to a number of institutes which have aided my research: the Royal United Services Institute for Defence Studies, Whitehall; the National Maritime Museum, Greenwich; the Liddell Hart Archives and the Library, King's College, and the Athenaeum's Library, all in London; the Royal Canadian Military Institute Library, Toronto; the Royal Military College of Canada Library, Kingston, Ontario; the Canadian Services College, Toronto; and the Library of Wilfrid Laurier University, Waterloo, Ontario. Despite an extensive search, I have failed to uncover any significant body of extant correspondence of Philip Colomb. Perhaps one day such a rich body of documentation will come to light, and when it does it will add significantly to what my colleagues mentioned above have written and what my own introductory analysis suggests. Even then, I hope Philip Colomb will here be given the attention he so richly deserves—as one of the classic theorists of naval power, one of the great expositors of maritime strategy, and one of the enduring historians of naval warfare.

In conclusion, a word is necessary about the choice of republishing the third and final edition of *Naval Warfare*. I have selected this particular edition because it is the most complete and the most satisfactory. It is the most complete because it contains a chapter Colomb added to the second edition, "Recent Illustrations of the Principles of Naval Warfare." This dealt with the civil war in Chile, 1891, and the Korean War, 1894–95. It also contains a chapter Colomb added to the third edition, "The Spanish-American War." The third edition is also the most satisfactory because it contains the author's commentary on and defense of his two earlier editions. That he "stuck to his guns" in defense of his scientific understanding of the principles of naval warfare as stated in his first edition is added evidence both of the strength of his convictions as a strategist and of his conclusions as a historian.

Barry Morton Gough

# INTRODUCTION

O N 26 APRIL 1891, Admiral Philip Howard Colomb, R.N.,
Great Britain's well-known contemporary authority on the
history of naval warfare, wrote to his celebrated American counter-
part, Captain Alfred Thayer Mahan, in tones of appreciation and
good humor for the appearance of the latter's resoundingly successful book *The Influence of Sea Power Upon History, 1660–1783*
(Boston, 1890; London, 1890):

> My book on "Naval Warfare" which was in course of publication
> when your fine book came out is now complete and will be published
> in a week or so. I have told the publishers to send you a copy with my
> compliments.
> They are endeavouring to make arrangements with Messrs. Put-
> nam & Sons to publish in your country.
> I hope you were satisfied with the reception your book received in
> this country. I think all our Naval men regarded it as *the* Naval book
> of the age, and it has had a great effect in getting people to under-
> stand what they never understood before. I had the great pleasure
> and privilege of reviewing you in one or two influential quarters and
> I hope may have helped to direct attention to the book.
> My book comes a long way behind yours in literary worth, for we
> have all been struck by the beauty of your style as much as by the
> force of your arguments. I have ventured to say in my preface that my
> book is in some respects the complement of yours. But written and
> printed as it was from month to month, and while, indeed, I was very
> unfit for writing, there are many blemishes. But still I think there is a
> good deal of useful matter in it.
> I am afraid we over here think your views are so sound that we
> only hope your countrymen may not adopt them, unless before you

do we may make a league to keep the rest of the world in order between us.[1]

It was with great good grace that Colomb greeted Mahan's book.
A man of smaller mind and greater ego would have taken exception
to it and endeavored to run across his rival's bow. Colomb wrote in
his own preface that Mahan's work was from "an abler pen and a
deeper thinker" on the other side of the ocean.[2] That may well have
been true. Yet it does not diminish the importance of Colomb's own
work, which, like Mahan's, was significant in that it cast an eye to
the future. The whole idea of *Naval Warfare* was that England's security rested with command of the sea, and on this theme and it
alone Colomb hammered away to convince politicians, statesmen,
leaders of opinion, and voters that if Britannia's might was to endure then the lessons of history had to be read. If Mahan emphasized the influence of sea power upon history, Colomb tended to reverse the order and to stress the role of history upon sea power.
History dictated that countries that would be strong must learn
from the past and control the ocean trades and ocean routes of the
world.

What lessons could history teach the student of naval warfare in
that age, as in ours? Colomb held to the opinion that laws of warfare at sea exist, and, moreover, that these laws should not be transgressed. These rules were enduring. The same was true yesterday as
today, he wrote in the preface to *Naval Warfare*. The scope of his
book was scientific, he wrote: it was a sketch of historical transactions and events, not an examination of personalities. Its object was
to search for the laws of naval warfare, what he termed the "ruling
principles" of war at sea. In this endeavor he took issue with the old
naval histories, including some from his own age: they tended to be
chronological in scope and to focus on individuals. These works, as
useful as they might be, were unconcerned with the causes of success or failure in naval war. Colomb was dreadfully serious about
his work, and sought not to entertain but to instruct, for on the lessons of history the whole British Empire's security rested. Colomb
believed that it would be a useful benefit to the British Empire if he
were to write a larger history of naval phases of war from the strate-

1. Quoted in Donald M. Schurman, *The Education of a Navy: The Development of British Naval Strategic Thought, 1867–1914* (Chicago, 1965), pp. 52–53.
2. All quotations from Colomb's *Naval Warfare: Its Ruling Principles and Practice Historically Treated* cited in my introduction are from the 3d edition (London,
1899) and are reproduced in full below.

gical perspective. He therefore set about his task with an eye to the future, to maintain Britannia's preeminence.

That Colomb was aware of the challenges facing Britain's naval strength at this time is abundantly clear from the experiences of his own career as a sea officer and his contributions as a technological innovator in an age of certain resistance to such things. Like Mahan he was not an armchair strategist but had the sea in his blood and knew the political intricacies of the navy. The senior service in which Colomb had served was one that had undergone a remarkable change in the near-century since the glories of Trafalgar.

In 1815 Britain had stood virtually alone and the master of all that it surveyed. But France and the United States were contending naval rivals, and by 1854 Russia had ended a peculiar interlude of peace in which the *Pax Britannica* had been exercised on the oceans with the assistance of carefully nurtured alliances with continental powers. Technological revolutions in shells, gunnery, and propulsion, in armor, weaponry, and communications had changed dramatically the nature of naval warfare. Blockade by steam vessels was altogether different from that by ships reliant on winds. The gunboat was a different warship from the ship-of-the-line or even the sloop-of-war. The torpedo and submarine mine, the torpedo boat and the submarine—all these indicated that the naval war of the 1890s and later would be significantly different in character from that of sail-driven fleets contending for the windward advantage and the opportunity to engage more closely when the opportunity best afforded itself. Moreover, wireless telegraphy indicated that ships-of-war would be deployed more speedily and more independently than heretofore. By the 1890s, naval architects were designing warships of ten thousand tons and more, carrying ten-inch guns. Within a decade the Dreadnought class had been designed, the most revolutionary vessel of its kind to date, and only exceeded in its historical significance as a revolutionary weapon of sea warfare by the nuclear-powered aircraft carrier and the Trident class submarine of our own times.

Colomb had lived much of the nineteenth century's change in naval technology and warfare.[3] Born in Scotland on 29 May 1831,

3. Colomb wants a biographer, but at present the absence of any known corpus of personal documents prevents that possibility. For biographical particulars I have relied on Schurman, *Education of a Navy*, p. 36ff.; J. K. Laughton's biography of Colomb in *The Dictionary of National Biography, 1st Supplement, Volume 2* (London, 1901), pp. 49–50; Frederic Boase's *Modern English Biography, Volume 4 (Sup-*

he was the third son of Lieutenant General George Thomas Colomb and of Mary King, daughter of Sir A. B. King, Bart., of Dublin. His elder brother (with whom he is frequently confused) was Sir John C. R. Colomb, formerly a captain in the Royal Marine Artillery, a member of Parliament, and author of the celebrated pamphlet on imperial defense "The Protection of Our Commerce and Distribution of Our War Forces Considered" (1867). Philip Colomb entered the navy on 6 February 1846 after being educated privately. In 1847 he served on the coast of Portugal, suppressing insurrection. In the following year, 1848, he was in the Mediterranean during the revolutionary epoch. For the next three years, 1849 to 1851, he was in China seas suppressing piracy and keeping the sea-lanes open for legitimate trade. He fought in the Burma War of 1852 and was involved in Arctic explorations in 1854 in search of Franklin's party. The Russian, or Crimean, War of 1854 found him engaged in the Baltic campaign, and on 3 February 1855 he was commissioned lieutenant. He now had a period of time ashore or near to shore: he was flag-lieutenant at Portsmouth from late 1857 to mid-1860, and during that time he devised a system known as Colomb's flashing signals, first adopted by the army. This system of signals was adopted eventually by the Royal Navy 12 February 1867 and came to be universally called the "Morse" system because of the notation involved. Colomb's insistent attempts to get the reluctant Board of Admiralty to adopt this system of signals cost him dearly, and his advance in career suffered accordingly.

During these years he advanced to the rank of commander (on 12 December 1863) and was eventually given command of the steamer *Dryad* on the East Indies Station in the suppression of the slave trade in the Indian Ocean, especially East Africa, from 1868 to 1870. It was during this period that he wrote his work on the attempted suppression of the slave trade by the Royal Navy, *Slave-Catching in the Indian Ocean* (London, 1873; reprinted, 1968). This was a large book with good, hard detail on the trade and a sober conclusion that even a total suppression of the trade on the seas would not stop the nefarious traffic on land. This book launched Colomb's literary career, and from that time onward he was much in demand by the learned and informed periodicals of the day to

*plement, Vol. 2)* (London, 1912), p. 46; *Who Was Who* (London, 1919), p. 150; and obituaries in the *Times,* 16 October 1899, p. 11, and *The United Service Magazine,* October 1899–March 1900, pp. 214 and 305–12.

write pieces on naval history, strategy, tactics, and imperial defense. He was one of the first to write on the naval lessons of the Battle of Lissa, 1866, the first fleet action between ironclads in history.

On 4 April 1870 he was advanced to the rank of captain, and for the next four years he was employed by the Admiralty preparing the *Manual of Fleet Evolutions,* which was officially issued in 1874. He went again to sea, this time in command of the *Audacious* on the China Station, 1874 to 1877, as flag-captain to Vice-Admiral Sir Alfred Phillips Ryder. In 1880 he commanded the *Thunderer* in the Mediterranean. From 1881 to 1884 he was captain of the steam-reserve at Portsmouth, and served as flag-captain to Sir Geoffrey Phipps Hornby in the shore establishment H. M. S. *Duke of Wellington.* About this time he produced the adopted system of interior voice-tubes in warships. On 29 May 1887 he was compulsorily retired because of his age and subsequently advanced on the naval list, becoming, in turn, rear-admiral on 6 April 1887 and vice-admiral on 1 August 1892. His study of how collisions at sea occur led to a number of manuals and articles on the subject. One such article, "Our Peril Afloat; or, Collisions and How to Avoid Them," was first published in *Naval Science* and reprinted from it, in pamphlet form, in 1879. His last work on this vitally important subject appeared in 1895 and was published by the Shipmasters' Society, an indication that his work was read widely not only in the senior service but in the merchant marine as well.

Upon his retirement Colomb settled down in Steeple Court, Botley, Hampshire, and lived there a gentlemanly life until his death from heart problems on 13 October 1899 at the age of sixty-eight. "Always a man of strong literary instincts," wrote Sir John Knox Laughton, the naval historian who knew Philip Colomb well, "in his retirement he devoted himself more and more to the study of history as a key to the many problems of naval policy and strategy which are continually arising." Laughton explained: "The science of naval evolution he had, theoretically, a complete mastery of, though hard fate of advanced age prevented him from combining practice with his theory, and thus his views did not always, among naval men, meet with that ready acceptance which many believed they were entitled to." The fact of the matter was that Colomb had an opinion on every naval topic of the day, and he wrote to the *Times* of London untiringly. Indeed, so voluminous was his correspondence that the famous naval reformer Admiral Sir John Fisher is reported to have called Philip Colomb "column and a half," an appropriate quip from one so trenchant with his language, so spare with his directions.[4] It was at the meetings of the Royal United Service Institution that Colomb found another platform for airing his strategical and tactical views. He spoke frequently and contributed numerous important papers to the R.U.S.I. *Journal*.[5] He never tired of writing on seemingly nuts-and-bolts issues. These included signals, ship's lights at sea, compasses, rules of the road, retirement, coastal defenses, and the torpedo. Taken together, his interests seem extraordinarily catholic and all-embracing, and if we include his pieces on tactics and strategy, plus his historical writings, an appreciation is gained for the breadth of the man's thinking. By any gauge his work measures as a major contribution to naval strategic and tactical thought.

Some of Colomb's essays from the R.U.S.I. *Journal* and elsewhere were published in a volume under the title *Essays on Naval Defence* (1893; 2d edition, 1896). This was Colomb's attempt to draw together some of the main themes of his writings during the years 1871 to 1889. He reasoned that the essays merited republication because up to that time no single book existed on the whole subject of naval defense "where the great principles of strategy and tactics are placed side by side with the material and personal conditions which either govern or are governed by them." In addition, he stated, the work had been published because the range of the subjects covered in his various essays "forms a record of progress of Naval ideas" and, more, that causes could be specified for results produced, and thus it was conceivable, in his words, "to forecast the results many years before they appeared."[6] Here is stated his deductive approach regarding practical questions of naval policy. To a certain degree, Colomb argued that history had lessons, and that the outcome of history was predictable. Many a historian would quarrel with these pronouncements about the didactic and predictable characteristics of history, arguing that Clio is a much more seductive muse and certainly nonreducible to the scientific equation. Nonetheless, we take Colomb for what he was attempting to do: provide rationale and order to the maritime defense of the United Kingdom and the Brit-

4. Quoted in A. J. Marder, *The Anatomy of British Sea Power: A History of Naval Policy in the Pre-Dreadnought Era, 1880–1905* (New York, 1940), p. 47, n. 6.

5. Thirty pieces by P. Colomb are listed in Robin Higham, ed., *The Consolidated Author and Subject Index to the Journal of the Royal United Service Institution, 1857–1963* (Ann Arbor, Mich., 1964), pp. 31–32. The first contribution was in 1863, the last in 1899.

6. P. H. Colomb, *Essays on Naval Defence* (London, 1893), p. iii.

ish Empire in an era of rapid technical change and of threatened British naval supremacy.

Colomb's interest in the predictability of history, and his interest in communications techniques, fleet tactics, and blockade, led him into war games, and he may be regarded as one of the pioneers of war-gaming of the nineteenth century. In 1879 he published his first literary contribution along this line, *The Duel: A Naval War Game*. In later years, when the chances of war became more acute, Colomb involved himself in the speculation of this age concerning Britain's preparedness for war, and the nature of warfare in the eventuality that such might occur. As a journalist, or, more correctly, a publicist of naval matters and especially senior service needs, Colomb was one of several eminent authorities who wrote about future warfare. He contributed to a narrative—really a collection of imaginary news releases or "reports from the scene of battle"—entitled *The Great War of 189-: A Forecast* (London, 1897). Colomb was joined in this enterprise by Colonel V. J. F. Maurice of the Royal Artillery, Captain F. N. Maude, Archibald Forbes, Charles Lowe, D. Christe Murray, and Francis Scudamore. We know nothing of the success of this work, or whether or not it fulfilled its contributors' and publisher's expectations. The aim was laudable: "to forecast the course of events preliminary and incidental to the Great War which, in the opinion of military and political experts will probably occur in the immediate future. The writers, who are well-known authorities on international politics and strategy, have striven to derive material for this description of the conflict from the best sources, to conceive the most probable campaigns and acts of policy, and generally to give to their work the verisimilitude and actuality of real war" (p. i). Colomb's contributions were reports from the North Sea and Baltic.

Colomb contributed a number of other works to naval literature. He edited the *Naval Yearbook for 1887*, wrote a book on the working of retirement schemes in the Royal Navy, and, as his last major historical work, compiled a biography, published in 1898, of his friend, the distinguished admiral of the Victorian Age, the Right Honorable Sir Astley Cooper Key.[7]

Of all his writings, *Naval Warfare: Its Ruling Principles and Practice Historically Treated* (1st ed., 1891; 2d ed., 1895; 3d ed., 1899) is regarded as the most significant. The book, Donald Schur-

7. A full list of his books, and their various editions, may be found in the *British Museum Library Catalogue*.

man writes, comprises a selection of his articles published in serial form in the *Illustrated Naval and Military Magazine*. Owing to its origin in a series of articles it lacked the organized symmetry of Mahan's *Influence of Sea Power upon History*. Nonetheless, as Professor Schurman has concluded, it "was the first reasonably sound, and yet far-reaching, British historical work on naval history."[8] It was the triumph of his career as a sailor and a historian.

The work's intention was to show the laws governing naval wars. The idea for this book, and indeed the characteristics of the mature Philip Colomb's naval thought based on history, had derived from the perils of his times. Upon his retirement Colomb had worked more eagerly than ever on defense matters, perhaps out of the necessity of maintaining his large family; but by this time, too, he was lecturing on a regular basis on tactics and strategy at the Royal Naval College, Greenwich. "There," as Professor Schurman puts it, "both the nature of his work and undoubtedly this contact with John Knox Laughton determined the firm commitment he now made to history as a determining guide for the study of modern naval problems."[9] Laughton was a keen historian and publicist of English naval history and, in addition to launching the Navy Records Society and being professor of Modern History at Kings College, London, was interested in the scientific study of naval history, on which he had published an important article in 1874. Doubtless Colomb picked up on this argument, and he had good reason to do so, for in an age when imperial federation was being widely discussed, when the defenses of British possessions overseas were under close examination by a national commission, and when the possibilities of a war with Russia were considerable, Colomb had every reason to join in the debate. Beginning in 1886 Colomb began to emerge as a hard-shelled navalist. He began to speak about imperial defense and federation, naval and military. He presented papers on convoys and blockade, the latter contributing substantially, as recent study has shown, to the character of British blockade theory down to 1905.[10] He began to assail the War Office and the Admiralty for neglecting commerce protection and for overestimating the possibilities of invasion. In 1888 he delivered a revolutionary paper on the naval defenses of the United Kingdom to the Royal United

8. Schurman, *Education of a Navy*, p. 52.
9. Ibid., p. 42.
10. M. S. Partridge, "The Royal Navy and the End of the Close Blockade, 1885–1905: A Revolution in Naval Strategy?" *The Mariner's Mirror* (May 1989), pp. 119–36.

Services Institution.[11] No longer could shore defense be thought of as a joint navy and army enterprise. Drawing from history, he demonstrated that there existed only two ways to keep England free from invasion. The first method, close blockade, was exhibited by Earl St. Vincent. The second, the defensive waiting-with-intact-fleet-method, was associated with the name of Lord Howe. His main and abiding point was this: unless Britain had the naval forces to maintain communications and command of the sea, fortifications were useless. This, then, was what came to be known as Blue Water thinking and the seminal idea of the Blue Water school. It shattered prevailing thought.[12]

The reader approaching the bulky substance of Colomb's *Naval Warfare* is advised that the book comprises several distinct but unequal parts.

Originally published in one volume, the book has been made into two volumes for this edition. Although the work is divided into chapters, it can be more broadly conceived in sections. However, it should be added, Colomb himself did not clearly identify these sections. Chapter 1 is introductory and deals with the nature of naval warfare in early English history, especially during the Elizabethan era. Chapters 2 through 4 can be taken together under the heading "Struggle for the Command of the Sea," the Anglo-Dutch wars being the focus. Chapter 5 stands alone. It concerns the differentiation of naval units, that is, the deployment of various types or classes of vessels in the varieties of naval warfare. Chapter 6 opens a four-chapter series on attempts to gain command of the sea with definite ulterior purpose. This brings the reader through a number of major battles of the eighteenth century and closes with Trafalgar.

Volume 2 opens with chapter 10, called "The Conditions Under Which Attacks on Territory from the Sea Succeed or Fail." This particular chapter forms an introduction to the latter half of the book as it appeared in its original edition. Here, in chapters 11 through 18—nine in all, including the preliminary one—the concern is with the use of naval forces in attacking fortifications and harbors and in blockading enemy shores. The last of this series, chapter 18, appropriately draws some conclusions from this section. Then follow two add-on chapters. The first, chapter 19, examines the Chilean War of 1891 and the Korean War of 1894—95, and the second, chapter 20,

11. P. H. Colomb, "The Naval Defences of the United Kingdom," *Journal of the Royal United Services Institution* (1888), pp. 565–601.

12. For extensive discussion of Colomb's 1888 paper, see Schurman, *Education of a Navy*, pp. 46ff.

the Spanish-American War in 1898. The work has no conclusions as such. As Colomb saw it, the conclusions were the rules of naval warfare themselves, and these, and the examples on which the argument is based, are given by the author immediately under each chapter's number and heading.

With the skeletal structure of the book now in place we can begin to fill in some of the detail of the various chapters. In beginning his book Colomb explains that a true naval war cannot be carried out without seaborne commerce, national business enterprise and wealth, and warships able "to keep the sea." The principles of this emerged, he argues, during the reign of Elizabeth I. The Spanish lack of understanding of these precepts was one of the reasons for the failure of the Enterprise of England. By the close of this Anglo-Spanish war the principles of naval warfare had been grasped by Sir William Monson and Sir Walter Raleigh. They understood that the primary aim of naval war is the command of the sea; and, as Colomb put it in concluding his chapter, "any other aim is an acceptance of the position of the inferior naval power, and the abnegation of all hopes of ultimate success." From these early examples Colomb derived the principle, already mentioned, of what some called the Blue Water school: that he who would command the broad common of the waters must be able to enforce completely his authority at sea.

How was this command of the sea to be acquired? and How was this struggle for command of the sea to be waged in naval warfare? "True naval war," Colomb says in opening his second chapter, "is established when there is sufficient property at sea to make its loss of serious importance to the State owning it; and when there are seakeeping warships to attack it." Campaigns against other warships or against merchant vessels may occur. Single-ship actions may also occur. But these cannot give command of the sea for any sufficient degree of time until the naval force defeated has also been annihilated. During the Anglo-Dutch wars, which figure in these three chapters, naval warfare was not fought to its logical conclusion. Rather, it was discursive in its characteristics and ineffectual in its ultimate results.

Colomb then moves in chapter 5 to look at the varieties of vessels-of-war employed in early naval history. What he and others called "the differentiation of naval force" shows that in early naval warfare, before the classic age of fighting sail, the "promiscuous [disorderly] system of fighting did not tend to the production of any particular classes of ship." However, as ships began to fight in line-of-battle, boards of admiralty and naval constructors began to develop ships capable of "standing in line," as it were, and to equalize their power in these sorts of ships, which were variously rated by guns carried—from the largest class, the first rates, down to the smallest class, the sixth rates. At the same time, commerce warfare necessitated the development of a lighter class of ship. Moreover, the necessity of having proper lookout vessels demanded yet a third. Tracing the evolution of these three classes of vessels down to 1813 Colomb argues that the type of naval war being prosecuted demanded the building of three classes of vessels: one for gaining and keeping command of the sea, another for undertaking discursive operations, and a third for maintaining communications.

Chapter 6 finds Colomb returning to his themes about the principles of naval warfare. Under his series of chapters entitled "Attempts to Gain the Command of the Sea with Definite Ulterior Purpose," he differentiates between an *end* and a *means* of naval warfare. Whereas the Anglo-Dutch wars showed that the attempts to gain command of the sea were the *end* of naval warfare, the Anglo-French wars demonstrated that attempts to gain command of the sea were the *means*. The events of 1690, the Battle of Beachy Head, show that partial command of the sea will not permit invasion, and that a partially beaten fleet is still a force to be reckoned with. The transactions of 1692 demonstrate the difficulties involved when a temporary command of the sea is attempted. Citing other examples, as his narrative progresses, Colomb, in chapter 8, looks at French sea power during the American War of Independence and after. France concentrated its naval power in the Channel, but this was ineffective against the nonetheless inferior British fleet. Again, in 1796, the same strategic mistake was made by France in what is generally known as the French and Napoleonic wars. France continued to waste its naval forces at the battles of St. Vincent and Camperdown. "I think we cannot have avoided observing," remarks Colomb in his opening paragraph of chapter 8, "how very marked is the difference between the attempt to gain the command of the sea as an end and as a means, when we have before us the practical effect as exemplified in the Dutch wars and these successive failures on the part of France." To this he added the telling remark that reverberates down to us through the years: "Looking back on the ground we have passed over, it does seem as if there were a possibility that had France thought nothing of invasion, but had devoted herself wholly, as Holland did, to wresting from us the command of the sea, she might always have maintained a

better naval position than she actually did. But wasting her energies on a double design, she fell more and more at the opening of
each war, into the position of an assuredly inferior naval power,
which could only look to better her position by some stroke of
fortune much more to be hoped for than expected." In other words,
France, being a continental as well as a maritime power, had to
develop a special, more effective naval strategy. As Colomb im-
plies, France failed to learn the lessons that each successive war
was demonstrating.

Moreover, Colomb understood that even gaining command of
the sea was insufficient in and of itself to direct the course of am-
phibious operations, destroy shore installations, reduce fortifications, and control the enemy's possessions overseas. Chapter 10 begins a book within a book, a nine-chapter series of analyses on the
conditions under which attacks on territory from the sea succeed or
fail. Colomb was aware, and here he was a precursor of other naval
historian-strategists, especially Sir Julian Corbett, that ultimate
command of the sea was not required to achieve every objective
against the enemy. In making attacks on enemy positions overseas
there were often two objects in view: ravage and destruction, or occupation and conquest. Colomb's early examples are drawn from
the West Indies and Caribbean, with a few sidelights on the Crimean
campaign, Chagre, and Grenada, 1779; the Spanish Armada, 1588;
and Ireland, 1689–91. Guadeloupe, Martinique, Goree, Brest, and
a number of other locations, including Cadiz, Louisbourg, and
Quebec, are looked at with a view to determining the principles
upon which sea power was effective against shore installations, harbors, bases, factories, and garrisons in the eighteenth century. Acre,
Lissa, and Charleston are three examples from the nineteenth century. The reader's patience will be rewarded in these chapters, for
they are meticulous renderings of the narrative histories of these
several attacks and assaults. As Colomb notes, at the end of chapter
16, a fortification's defenses are only as good as the range of its
guns, and those who would think defensively in these terms are
doomed to misunderstand sea power and to fail to see its effective-
ness. "Still," he sighs, "we seem to see that those who made our
history for us looked to their fortifications to serve the purposes of
delay only, and not really of defence." Again, the material means of
a nation's defense lay in its ability to command the sea and thereby
to influence the course of human affairs on the sea and in its an-
nexes. "These chapters," Colomb concluded (in what was his first
edition's last lines), "leave us under the inference that certain condi-

tions—command of the sea, sufficient and well-handled land forces, landings either away from the batteries, or after their fire has been temporarily silenced, proper appliances and small vessels—have always been necessary to secure the success of territorial attack, and that there is at least nothing in recent times, to show that the rule has in any way changed." His chapter on the Chilean, Korean, and Spanish-American wars offers but further illustrations of the principles of naval warfare.

*Naval Warfare* was well received by the critics of the day judging by the glowing recommendations that appeared in the second edition. "The book," wrote the reviewer in the *Times*, "is almost a pioneer of its class, for, strange to say, the literature of the greatest Naval Power in history has no authoritative treatise on the principles of Naval Warfare. . . ." The work, it concluded, "ought to have an absorbing interest to every Englishman who loves his country and cares for its history." "Admiral Colomb," opined the *United Service Gazette*, "does good service in breaking what is positively new ground, for no one before him has treated naval history in the unique manner he has done, nor made so scientific an attempt to draw useful and practical lessons therefrom." "The volume before us," said the periodical *Academy*, with insight, "may be described as a work on the philosophy of naval warfare, confined to its purely strategic aspect; and it has been written because our naval literature is almost a blank in this most important province."

Colomb's *Naval Warfare* continued to have a major influence on naval thought long after its publication. "It is hardly too much to say," wrote John Knox Laughton more generally of Colomb's work in his obituary of the great man in the *Times*, 16 October 1899,

> that there are very few departments of the naval service which have not felt his influence and been moulded by ideas of which he was the persistent and often, at the outset, almost the solitary exponent. There is no one man perhaps to whom the Navy of today owes so much as it does to Admiral Colomb. He was often regarded as a visionary by men who saw less far ahead than himself. He was often misunderstood by men who failed to appreciate the logical coherence of his thought and the comprehensive sweep of his mind, and the co-ordination of both in the practical bent of his genius. Men who were his equals, perhaps his superiors, in practical seamanship often derided him as a theorist. But they little knew how much of their practice was founded upon his theories, and how often ideas which originate with him had become the commonplaces of the service. His fault was often, perhaps, an exuberant originality, often far in advance of the thought and practice of his professional contem-

poraries, and a confidence in his own opinions, begotten perhaps of
the frequency with which those who at first opposed him were found
in the end to be following the very path in which his thought had
preceded them. (p. 1)

Admiral Sir Cyprian Bridge, himself a student of such matters and
the first Director of Naval Intelligence, gave this testimony dated
March 1907 to Colomb's *Naval Warfare:* "The study of naval warfare, as far as it can be carried with merely the aid of books, will
need lengthy treatises relating, explaining, and applying to modern
conditions the events of past campaigns. The late Vice-Admiral
P. H. Colomb showed us nearly twenty years ago the kind of thing
required." [13] But whether or not statesmen and politicians read the
lessons of history was another matter altogether. Sir Julian Corbett,
author of *Some Principles of Maritime Strategy* (1911; new edition,
with introduction and notes by Eric J. Grove, 1988), had pointed
the way for naval strategy for the first world war. However, strategy
was often deflected by politics. As a key British defense planner,
Lord Esher, put it unerringly in 1915, "Julian Corbett writes one of
the best books in our language upon political and military strategy.
All sorts of lessons, some of inestimable value, may be gleaned from
it. No one, except perhaps Winston [Churchill], who matters just
now has read it. . . . Obviously history is written for schoolmasters
and armchair strategists. Statesmen and warriors pick their way
through the dusk." [14]

In Britain Colomb's *Naval Warfare* went through three editions
in less than a decade, leading one to expect that it would have had a
substantial impact on naval thought, especially as the substance of
the book was extremely stimulating on the subject of how a future
war at sea ought to be conducted. However, it is not easy to judge
its influence on other peoples and powers. Clearly in the United
States the work was always in the shadow of Mahan's great work,
which was read widely and seriously by navy boards, politicians,
and statesmen. Continental powers, which had always been concerned about matters of British dominance of the seas, were undoubtedly interested in the work. Russian, Swedish, and German

13. Sir Cyprian Bridge, *The Art of Naval Warfare: Introductory Observations*
(London, 1907), p. ix.
14. Lord Esher to Sir Maurice Hankey (Committee of Imperial Defence), 15
March 1915; quoted in Schurman, *Education of a Navy,* p. 190, and in Barry M.
Gough, "Maritime Strategy: The Legacies of Mahan and Corbett as Philosophers of
Sea Power," *Journal of the Royal United Services Institute for Defence Studies*
(Winter 1988), p. 61.

editions of the work appeared. Continental powers held an abiding interest in the obvious fact that sea control had as its end the influence of events on land. But they were particularly aware of the value of *guerre de course,* that is, of operating small squadrons, even single ships, to prey upon enemy commerce. "If utilized in overwhelming strength," notes the American scholar Clark G. Reynolds, "this offensive function may assume the proportions of an effective commercial *counterblockade,* preventing vital war supplies from reaching the maritime enemy's homeland." [15] Moreover, continental naval powers such as Russia, Germany, and France were drawn to Colomb's close attention to the efficacy of attacking naval forces in coastal and inshore waters, an influence made stronger by steam propulsion, longer-range guns, and the various forms of blockade that Colomb had explained in *Naval Warfare.* Colomb's attention to naval actions against shore fortifications was sure to jolt from slumber the armchair strategist in Stockholm, St. Petersburg, or Potsdam.

Among all the powers, however, the Soviet Union was the recipient of the greatest and most long-standing gain from *Naval Warfare.* Robert Waring Herrick has explained this in great detail in his *Soviet Naval Theory and Policy,* and a full repetition of his analysis does not belong here. [16] Suffice it to say that Colomb's general concepts went unchallenged in tsarist Russia and, after 1917, in the Soviet Union. Not until 1948 did V. Andreyev, later an admiral, attack "the pseudo-scientific theory of Admiral Colomb." He argued that an overall, global predominance of sea power was impossible for any nation. Britain's intention to advance its primacy by sea was denounced, and so too was the strategic concept that command of the sea would allow Britain to undertake necessary naval missions elsewhere. Andreyev argued that a temporary command of the sea could be acquired by the Soviet navy in order to carry out its own limited objectives. In a word, Colomb's "thesis of the impossibility of achieving success in partial operations without gaining a general command of the sea was . . . pseudo-scientific." [17] By pointing out other examples from history, Andreyev showed that naval warfare in a theatre or region was never conducted to gain command of the sea as an end in itself; rather it was a particular means to a more

15. Clark G. Reynolds, *Command of the Sea: The History and Strategy of Maritime Empires* (New York, 1974), p. 14.
16. Robert Waring Herrick, *Soviet Naval Theory and Policy: Gorshkov's Inheritance* (Newport, R. I., 1988), *passim,* esp. pp. 192–200.
17. Ibid., p. 193.

general end. Colomb was criticized as minimizing the possibilities for smaller naval powers undertaking operations for more limited purposes. He was castigated for setting, or seemingly so, the army against the navy. Andreyev felt that ground forces could be credited with being able to gain command of the sea by occupying the littoral of a theatre of operations, a misguided and unproven statement. We may conclude this Soviet assessment of Colomb's work by quoting at length the distinguished and insightful analysis by Dr. Herrick:

> Colomb's basic flaw was said to have been his failure to give his studies of naval warfare a broader context: the development of the states involved; the bitter economic and political struggle between the belligerent powers; the underlying causes of the war; the general course and outcome of the wars he considered; and, lastly, "the general course of military operations on land" as well as at sea. In so doing, Colomb was said to have "followed in the footsteps of the reactionary ideologist of German militarism, Clausewitz." Clausewitz was said to have based his teachings on war solely "on . . . land campaigns without any of their ties with events at sea." Since this was precisely what the dominant Soviet military historians and theorists were doing at the time with regard to World War II, there is little reason to doubt that the Navy, through Andreyev, was esoterically voicing a strongly felt complaint.
>
> Andreyev continued to castigate Colomb by claiming that he had made the same major error with regard to sea warfare that Clausewitz had committed concerning land warfare. That is, Colomb concluded that all of the main forces had to be concentrated for one general engagement (or per Clausewitz, one simultaneous strike) rather than a number of successive operations. On the naval side, Colomb was correctly cited as also having mentioned blockade as the one approved alternative to a single great general engagement. These two forms of naval warfare also were duly noted as having been prescribed by Colomb as the sole methods of gaining command of the sea—and hence, the only methods for achieving the aims of a war at sea.[18]

Andreyev's critique and assault on Colomb's *Naval Warfare* and concepts of command of the sea and their influence on affairs on and over the seas formed part of a more general Soviet critique of Blue Water thinking. In the late 1940s Mahan and Corbett had joined Colomb as subjects of scrutiny; old-fashioned classical theorists of the tsarist and early Soviet navies were likewise assailed. By

18. Ibid., p. 195.

the time Admiral Sergei Gorshkov had pronounced the new Soviet naval doctrine in his *Morskaya moshch' gosudarstva'* or *Sea Power of the State* (1976) yet another phase of the revolution in state policy in regard to control of the seas had been announced. Moreover, Soviet naval construction and deployment indicated a more general extension of sea power than the likes of a Colomb, a Mahan, or a Corbett could ever have anticipated from a continental power.

For all its faults, and they are many, Colomb's *Naval Warfare* is a significant contribution to the study of war at sea and the objectives, efficacy, and limitations of sea power. First, it is important because it drew to the national attention of the British at a time of urgency and confusion the value of maintaining a fleet capable of fulfilling the necessary mandate of such a sea service: containing the enemy's sea forces, protecting lines of supply and communication, and allowing the holder of the trident of Neptune to enforce its will and deploy its forces as required in order to achieve the necessary ends. In that sense of awakening the British from their defensive posture the obituary of Philip Colomb that appeared in the *United Service Magazine* speaks volumes: "The British nation owes a deep debt of gratitude to the late Admiral for his unceasing exertions in rousing it to a sense of its naval necessities, at a time when the Navy was not in a fit state to meet the enormous requirements of the Empire" (p. 214). Second, Colomb's *Naval Warfare* is a vital contribution to the study of war at sea and its objectives because it was a historical narrative and analysis. A one-volume work on naval history from the seventeenth century to the end of the nineteenth, it was much more comprehensive and in places more detailed than Mahan's classic. It showed Colomb's compelling love for history, his interest in the sources of British naval history, English and continental, his good grasp of geography, and his willingness, never a failure, to tell a story and to make sense of it. In re-creating history, that is, in bringing the past to light, he fell short of the mark, because he distrusted the role of personality in events and the interplay of character and circumstance. Nonetheless *Naval Warfare* was and is an important work of historical scholarship. That Colomb, like Mahan and Corbett, came to the study of history after another professional occupation is a testament to history's lure and to the belief that it has important things to say for the present and the future. Third and last, Colomb's *Naval Warfare* is of significance to the study of sea power and its influence on human affairs because it demonstrates that the nation that holds the trident of Neptune wields power to a disproportionate degree when compared to the nation and its allies that do not have it. Critics of the Blue Water school will continue to quarrel with the degree of overarching influence that a preeminent navy will have on world affairs. Yet they will always have to contend with the fact that the leading naval nation will have a greater choice of strategic and tactical options, and a greater facility in the deployment of forces for whatever may be the intended use. Today one could not say that history has laws or that there is anything inevitable about the curious course of human affairs. But Colomb's attempt to place naval warfare within the limits proscribed by principles operating from the examples of history may not be far off the mark. As modern-day planners grope for new strategies and tactics in order to achieve their ends, and those of their allies, a thorough look at the words of Colomb will not likely lead them astray.

# Naval Warfare

# PREFACE TO THE THIRD EDITION

A THIRD edition of this work being called for, I have taken the opportunity of examining and discussing the events of the Spanish-American War of 1898, so far as they relate to those "ruling principles" of naval warfare which it has been the object of the book to set forth and elucidate.

Most of what can be said on the conduct of this war in relation to its larger aspects has been said in the chapter itself. But my conviction may here be emphasised that whatever rules can be legitimately deduced from the operations of naval warfare when it was conducted in reliance upon the propulsive power of the wind, are shown by this latest of steam-wars to be much less subject to variation than was the case in former days. I doubt if any one doing me the honour to read my examination of the war can avoid some surprise at the conclusiveness of arguments gathered from wars under such very different conditions.

As, in writing some earlier chapters I endeavoured to develop the extraordinarily defensive powers of fleets in protecting outlying territories otherwise liable to attack, and generally in preventing invasions not otherwise preventable, I became more and more struck with the almost mathematical action of that power, so, on the evidence of the Spanish-American War, I think we must certainly pronounce that steam fleets are more defensive of territory than ever sailing fleets were, or could have been. I suppose it is the calculated certainty of a steam fleet's progress, and the almost necessary suddenness of its stroke when it comes within sight of its quarry that makes it so impossible to move in the matter of invasion, or of any military operation conducted over sea, when there is even a possibility of such a stroke being struck.

Though the war was full of lessons, as I have endeavoured to

1

show, the unequalness of the contest has left many problems of which the naval world has longed for the solution, unsolved. This is particularly the case with all torpedo questions. With regard to these Admiral Sampson made a shrewd remark which requires to be kept in mind. It was to the effect that the non-employment of the torpedo would tend to set it back in naval estimation, but that such a frame of mind would be illogical, because the torpedo was really in the same position now as it occupied before the war was declared.

Perhaps my apologies are due to my friends and brother officers across the Atlantic for the extreme freedom of my criticisms, and for what may be called the coldness with which I have written a sketch history of transactions which in so many cases showed the fine qualities of the officers engaged in them. But I may be pardoned and excused if it is remembered that the scope of the book is scientific; and if in any cases it has fallen into personalities, it has by so much fallen short of its ideal.

Every historian of this war cannot but return his sincere thanks to the Government of the United States for the full and free publication of the official documents respecting it. There may be, possibly, something to be said against a practice which is almost peculiar to the great Republic, but I scarcely doubt its substantial wisdom. What is most required after the close of a war is not only right thinking in regard to it, but general right thinking. I suspect that by far the best way to obtain this is by free exposure of its history as soon as possible after it closes. When official documents are scarce and difficult to come by, great principles which are elucidated in them become missed or perverted, and there is seldom any means of correcting misapprehensions. But now, if, as is probable, I may mistake in anything I have said, an appeal to the publications of the United States can always be relied on to correct me.

Besides offering my thanks to Mr. F. E. Hesse of the Great Eastern Extension Telegraph Company, upon whose information I have based much of my view of the status of telegraph cables in war, I have to thank the English publishers—Messrs. Hutchinson and Co.—of Mr. Charles Morris' excellent sketch of *The American War with Spain,* for the use of some of his maps.

*June* 17, 1899

# PREFACE TO THE
# SECOND EDITION

THE FOLLOWING EXTRACT from the Preface to the First Edition so fully expresses the intention of the work, that I cannot do better than reproduce it here:—

In writing this book I have kept in mind the double object of showing that there are laws governing the conduct of naval war which cannot be transgressed with impunity; and that there is no reason to believe them abrogated by any of the changes of recent years.

I was induced to undertake it from observing, with some surprise, a widespread conception that either there never had been any laws governing naval war, or that if there had been such in the days of sailing ships, they had been entirely swept away and destroyed by the advent of steam, steel ships, armour, breech-loading rifled guns, and torpedoes. This belief appeared to me the more singular, as no one ventured to suggest that railways, the electric telegraph, breech-loading rifled ordnance, and small arms, had altered the well established rules of war upon the land. But in considering the existence of such antithetical ideas side by side, it appeared to me that the cause might not improbably be found in the differences of method pursued by writers of naval and of military history. There did not exist, I believed, in any language a book written with the object of discriminating between the possible and impossible, the prudent and the imprudent, the wise and the foolish, in the conduct of naval war. But books describing war upon land with these objects in view were abundant in all languages, and I had been much struck with a more recent and powerful contribution to such literature—Sir Edward Hamley's *Operations of War*. Yet even the title chosen for this work seemed to confirm my view, in apparently inferring the opinion that war upon the land was, if not the only war of consequence to the world, at least the only war which would bear systematic analysis and treatment.

I had long been aware that ordinary naval histories, especially

3

works in English near our own time, were, as histories, quite the most unsatisfactory productions existing. They all ran in two grooves; the one contenting itself in a mere chronological narrative of events, having no other connections but those of time and place; the other being written for the glorification or condemnation of individuals whose characters were judged from isolated and disconnected acts. Perhaps no stronger illustration of my meaning can be drawn than by mentioning that while James is the recognised historian of the French Revolutionary and Napoleonic naval wars, he did not think it necessary to furnish his volumes with more than a personal index.

Historians then had generally neglected to give any attention to the causes of success or failure in naval war; they did not connect the facts or events which were necessary for that purpose. Naval commanders, on the other hand, seem to have been so entirely convinced of the force of causes beyond their control, and so satisfied of their obviousness, that they seldom alluded to them. Of writers on naval strategy there were absolutely none; writers on naval tactics were few and far between; they generally wrote as if the tactics of manœuvring embraced the whole subject; and the elaborate simplicity of Clerk of Eldin got an extensive hearing because he stood almost alone as a writer in applying to the naval battle considerations which no writer could omit in treating of the battle on land.

I held this condition of the literature of naval war to be mainly responsible for the want of its study, which was common; and thus for the existing belief that nothing was to be got from it either in lessons for the present, or guidance for the future.

It was the conviction that no state of mind could well be more dangerous for this Empire, that led me to think I might usefully employ my very moderate powers in writing a study of some of the larger phases of naval war, from the strategical point of view. The book may, I hope, be a pioneer. It is no more than the study for what in abler hands might become a great picture. I have not pretended to rewrite the histories I have used. My original research has been but small, indeed the scope of the work did not admit of it. But I have trusted to create an interest by not only giving the narratives as I find them, but by endeavouring always to extract the reasons for each event, and to bring out the causes which here conduced to success, and there determined failure.

I have a firm belief that the great laws of naval war, which I have endeavoured to trace throughout the centuries in which England has been building up her power, would be absolutely dominant in any naval war which now arose; and that they may be depended on for forecasting its course and preparing for it. Not that I assume to have, in all cases, arrived at just conclusions, but rather that there are, in the history of the past, ample materials for forming them and acting on them.

4

In preparing the Second Edition for the press, a certain temptation to re-write portions of the work presented itself. It arose from two causes; namely, that here and there discussion on the subject had thrown new historical light upon it; and that the publication of the book having had the full effect expected from it, the public point of view may be said to have changed for the better on all that relates to the strategy of war on the sea, since it was written.

But I soon found that any re-writing would necessitate a change in the whole character of the work, and that I should present the public with a new work and not with the second edition of an old one. I have therefore been obliged to content myself with minor corrections, including misprints.

But there are two cases of possible re-writing, which are of sufficient importance to deserve special mention here. An article in the *Quarterly Review* for April, 1893, and Professor Laughton in the *Army and Navy Gazette* for May 21st, 1892, by appeals to new works and to original documents, have thrown fresh light on the Battle of La Hogue. Amongst other points, it seems to be made out that the whole of the ninety-nine ships given by the histories on which my narrative rests, were not present under Russell at the battle; some seventeen of them were, in all probability, absent refitting. The correction of the data has, however, no effect upon the general view taken in the text.

Far more important was the question of any alterations of text arising out of criticisms on my treatment of the strategical aspects of the Battle of Beachy Head. I restored in my text that which was unquestionably the English, and most probably the French, naval view of the transactions, and of the conduct of Torrington at the time, but which subsequent historians—and notably Macaulay—had thrust altogether aside. By a powerful body of critics, including, I understand, Captain Mahan, my views have been fully adopted, and Torrington's phrase "A fleet in being," has come into general use to denote what, in naval affairs, corresponds to "a relieving army" in military affairs. That is to say, a fleet which is able and willing to attack an enemy proposing a descent upon territory which that force has it in charge to protect.

In my narrative, adhering to the limitations mentioned in the last paragraph but one in the extract from my Preface given above, I followed Lediard in supposing that the French Government, in the event of the complete suppression of Torrington's fleet by de Tourville, intended it should be followed up by an advance up the Thames, and a descent with a substantial body of troops upon our southern coast. Lediard's account is written in the belief that the French regarded a rising to welcome them as the friends of King James to be certain. That is to say, he believed that the utterances of King William, and the proclamations and acts of the Court against definite conspiracies and against alleged conspirators who were named, rested on a basis of fact. I, on my part, in accepting Lediard and Entick committed myself to the belief that de Tourville's action was an attempt to gain the command of the sea with a definite ulterior object, and that his failure to annihilate Torrington's fleet was, if not the only cause, yet a predominating cause, in preventing the ascent of the Thames, the invasion of the south coast, and the insurrection of James's adherents. I did, in short, accept the view that Torrington and his naval supporters understood the real situation better than the English Statesmen of the time, and than most of the historians who subsequently wrote upon the subject.

A considerable body of critics have challenged my position generally; and some have challenged it in particulars.

Many, if not most of the former body, have seemed to me to speak under an entire misapprehension of the case I designed to make of the Battle of Beachy Head in relation to doctrine of "the fleet in being." It has been said in plain terms, for instance, that I use the occurrences in question as the foundation, almost the sole foundation, of the doctrine. This is an extremely perverted view of all that I have said on the subject. No rule of war could possibly rest on a single instance, and the doctrine of "the fleet in being" arises first from the reason of the thing, and secondly from applying the methods of agreement and difference to the actual occurrences of war, which show that while descents on territory are common when there is no "fleet in being," they are absent whenever there is a fleet capable of interfering. This general argument is confirmed when it is found that in what might be called doubtful cases, the descent or attempted descent is more political than military; when leaders undertaking such descents almost invariably express the conviction that any "fleet in being" must be put out of being before the descent can be made; and because each of the two notable attempts to invade in defiance of the doctrine were disastrously frustrated by the "fleet in being" which it was sought to ignore.

Hence Torrington's operations are no more, and can be taken as no more, than one of a great group of occurrences whose cumulative evidence proves the rule.

But what gave prominence to Torrington's action, and what has more than anything else concentrated the attention of critics on that part of my work, are Torrington's words. He has given us the first and the best definition of that rule of war which ought to determine the action of the inferior fleet when a descent on territory is threatened, including in it an expression of the defensive power which resides in even the inferior fleet in such cases, and which was so completely vindicated by the Austrian fleet at Lissa.

This sort of misapprehension, if it had arisen out of the text, might have demanded re-writing, but as it certainly arose in spite of the text, the latter can only be left to work its way in the end.

Far more important has been the friendly criticism expressing belief that my principal authority, Lediard (1735), has misled me into classing the events surrounding the Battle of Beachy Head amongst the "attempts to gain the command of the sea with definite ulterior purpose," when they should have been placed as an illustration of "the struggle for the command of the sea" pure and simple. It is thought by those friends, amongst whom my acknowledgments are due to Professor Laughton, that there was no intention, at any rate no definite intention, on the part of the French Government to follow up the anticipated success of de Tourville over Torrington, by the ascent of the Thames, and a landing of French troops. This view, if it is a correct one, would of course condemn Torrington as absolutely as his enemies did, and would justify Macaulay's judgment. If I had been brought over to it, I must have re-written the whole story. But the conclusion I have come to is that no sufficient grounds that are easily accessible exist for doubting that the Battle of Beachy Head was an "attempt to gain the command of the sea with definite ulterior purpose."

Professor Laughton justly lays great stress upon the evidence offered by Eugène Sue's *Histoire de la Marine Française,* published in 1845, which largely uses and quotes from original documents in the French naval archives. Many letters from de Tourville are given in full which relate to the Battle of Beachy Head and the subsequent operations, and it must be confessed that if negative evidence would suffice, the absence of all mention of ulterior objects might lead to the belief that there were none.

But an enquirer speedily finds that negative evidence in a matter of this sort goes a very short way. Lediard has no idea of Torrington's defence; not a single historian that I have consulted mentions it, except Entick, from whose folio I have disentombed it. Would it ever be supposed by any reader who had not Entick or Entick's documents before him, that Torrington's conduct was dictated by a firm belief that he had received dangerously mistaken orders?

7

But Eugène Sue gives proof in a memoir of de Tourville's, submitted to Louis in the early part of 1690, that he most thoroughly comprehended the doctrine of the "fleet in being," the power of such a fleet, and the necessity of leaving force enough to mask it before the descent could be undertaken. "If the enemy," he said, speaking of a possible descent on the coast of France, "had 30 ships of war more than your Majesty's fleet, he could effect his landing by leaving 10 ships of war with the transports, and coming with the rest of his fleet before that of your Majesty to engage it."

Nor did he, in his caution, make the absurd little demonstration against Teignmouth, without sending a squadron to cruise in the Straits of Dover to watch the Anglo-Dutch fleet.

Lediard bases himself on Boyer (Hist. of K. Will. III.), who published in 1702. Boyer is followed by Kennet, who published in 1719. Then there is Burnet and Tindal, who published in 1746. Entick is later than them all, publishing in 1757. Lediard simply copies Boyer's statements as to the designs of the French, and the other historians mentioned are full of the conspiracies that they suppose existed, and of the plots which hinged upon help from France by way of descent. It is perfectly certain that before King William left for Ireland he spoke distinctly of his knowledge of these things and of the men who were mixed up in them. The acts of the Queen in his absence were ostensibly based on her belief in proposed landings of the French. Tindal (Continuation of Rapin), quotes an intercepted letter from James about August 1689, speaking of "contraband goods ready to be shipped off in order to be run into such places where they might not be seized by the Custom House officers," which, thinks Tindal, "sufficiently discovered the design of invasion."

On the other side there is Ralph, who, publishing in 1746, condemns Kennet, Burchett, Boyer, Tindal, and other writers who, he declares, in the matter of conspiracies and prospective invasions, all adopted "the forgeries of a party." He seems to declare that the Court party supported the forgeries, if they did not propagate the false beliefs, for the purpose of putting their feet on the necks of their enemies. Obviously he must include the King in his charges, though in the face of his own words he exempts him, and says if he had had intelligence of these things, he could never have left the Queen to cope with them.

But Ralph is only attacking Tindal, who tells us that at the very time when, in his opinion, the fears of invasion and insurrection were justified: "All pretended discoveries were laughed at and looked upon as fictions of the Court, and upon this, the City of London was generally possessed with a very ill opinion of the King."

Yet again, on the other side, and more recently, Lord Wolseley quotes a letter from Marlborough, dated July 16th, 1690, expressing his belief that a force assembled at St. Omer ostensibly for reinforcing the Duke of Luxembourg, was really prepared for the invasion of England.

Lord Wolseley also quotes a MS. letter from James dated 10th–20th August, 1690, urging Louis to invade; asking for 10,000 troops for the attack on London, which had not more than 10,000—Lord Wolseley says not more than 7,000—available to defend it.

The French naval historian, Comte de Lapeyrouse Bonfils (1845), speaking of the preparations for the campaign of Beachy Head, says, "Pour l'exécution de ce plan, des troupes furent cantonnées sur les côtes de France."

I think I have probably said enough to show that unless and until some historian writes a fuller and more complete treatise to upset my original authority than now exists, I can only leave my text as it stands, and believe that I truly prove the case.

The chapter which I have added on the Chilian Civil War and the Korean War is necessarily a mere sketch, but I hope it is sufficiently full and sufficiently accurate to bring my subject up to date.

*May,* 1895

# CONTENTS

11

The power which is weakest finds it impossible to defend commerce and struggle for the command of the sea at the same time.—On the opening of the second war the Dutch give up the defence of commerce, and prohibit it.—The attack on both sides is concentrated and direct upon the naval force.—When command of the sea becomes at all secure, attacks on shipping in harbours follow, as at the Vlie, and in the Thames and Medway; and troops for landing are embarked.

Experience has taught that a superior commerce cannot be protected by only an equal fleet; and the Dutch, in the third war, still abandon commerce till greater strength is gained.—The direct struggle for the command of the sea is resumed at Sole Bay.—It is useless to prepare for making descents on the enemy's coast unless his fleet is first disposed of.—The embarkation of troops by the Allies is of no service. —The great powers of naval forces on distant expeditions if not met by like forces.

The promiscuous system of fighting in the early days of naval warfare did not tend to the production of any particular classes of ships.— The rise of the line of battle tended to increase the force of the ships forming part of it, and to equalize their power.—At the same time the pursuit and defence of commerce tended to develop a lighter class of ships.—The necessities of a fleet in having proper look-outs demanded a third class.—The results of these tendencies are traced down to 1813.

There is a difference between attempting to gain the command of the sea as an end, and as a means for achieving some ulterior purpose.— The best examples are the Dutch wars on one side, and the various attempts of France to invade England on the other.—But invasions are at least rarely planned in the absence of command of the sea, unless help is hoped for within the country to be invaded.—The transactions of 1690 show that partial command of the sea will not permit invasion, and that a partially beaten fleet is still to be reckoned with in such operations.—The transactions of 1692 show the difficulties of the attempts, and of the great risks that are run in seeking for a temporary command of the sea.

The consequences of failure to gain command of the sea for an ulterior purpose.—The attempt of the French in 1695 to pass an army over to England, and its collapse.—The attempt of 1744 hardly to be classed under the subject of the chapter.—Its daring and rashness.—Its absurd ending.—Mistaken strategy of France in 1756–59.—Countries unable to protect their own seaboard can scarcely hope to attack those of other countries.—Narrative of the operations of 1759, and the destruction of every attempt at invasion.—Causes of French failure to be found in false strategical principles.

The entertainment of an idea of gaining the command of the sea merely for a particular purpose tends to reconcile a nation to the place of the inferior naval power, and to make it unable to desist from attempts almost necessarily abortive.—So France renews in 1779 her old schemes, but in concentrating a great combined fleet in the Channel, fails to take advantage of the inferior British fleet which was opposed to her.—The same ideas begin to work in France as early as 1796, and either directly or indirectly govern the movements of the enemy's fleets till the close of the war.—The consequent waste of naval force at St. Vincent and Camperdown.—The openness of the invasion flotilla to attack from the sea.—The indefinite and abortive combinations and manœuvres up to the close of the war.

Preparation from 1803 to 1805 to gain temporary command of the sea.—The British defence.—Napoleon's plans and orders.—Invasion does not occupy the first place.—The early failures of 1805.—Villeneuve's West Indian Expedition, and Nelson's prevention of its success.—Varying and indefinite orders to Villeneuve.—Return of the British and French squadrons to Europe.—Villeneuve's failure and the final abandonment of the invasion scheme.—Doubts whether it was ever really intended.—Attempts to gain command of the sea too serious and difficult to be considered side by side with any other design.

## Volume 2
## X. The Conditions under which Attacks on Territory from the Sea Succeed or Fail

The gradations in completeness of command of the sea in relation to attacks upon territory.—Special state of West and East Indian waters on account of trade-winds and monsoons.—Powers of holding places supplied over a commanded sea.—Limits of these powers.—Two objects in attack: (1) Ravage and destruction; (2) occupation and conquest.—Time at disposal a measure of success in each over a doubtfully commanded sea.—An expedition must either be accompanied by overwhelming naval force, or else naval force should be absent.—Attacks without troops rare; confined to bombardment and forcing purposes.—System of citadels usual in fortification last century.—The philosophy of the system and its disadvantages to the power with superior naval force.—Superiority of naval defence.—Recapitulation.

The two most conspicuous examples of failure, the Armada and the Battle of Lissa are found at the beginning and end of naval history.—The Armada expedition described.—Causes of its failure parallel to those bringing about the failure of the Italians at Lissa.—And of Napoleon in Egypt.—Descents conducted over a doubtful sea must be expected to fail.—Descents upon friendly shores illustrated by those on Ireland in 1689, &c.—The commencement of the long series of captures and recaptures of the West India Islands in 1690, exhibits all the elements of success in commanded sea, and co-operation between army and navy on the understanding that the navy places the army in position and then takes but a minor share in the attack.

Capture of Marie-Galante in March 1691.—Landing at Guadaloupe.—Siege of the forts at Basse Terre abandoned hastily in consequence of neighbourhood of French squadron.—Contemporary errors as to Commodore Wright's strategic position.—Successful attacks upon Nova Scotia from New England across an indifferent sea.—Failure of attack on Quebec from delay and insufficient force.—Impossibility of territorial attacks over a doubtfully commanded sea, illustrated by the operations of Commodore Wren and Count de Blanac in the West Indies in 1692.—Failure of the attack on Martinique in 1693 and its causes.—Successes on West Coast of Africa and their causes.—Remarkable paradox as to Goree.—Failure of attack on Brest and its causes.—Russell's operations in the Mediterranean

Power commanding sea, 1708.—Spanish coast held and supplied from the sea base.—French making head at sea, hope to carry Sardinia by evasion of allied fleet, Sir John Norris drives them back with loss, 1710.—Capture and abandonment of Cette.—Capture of Port Royal, Nova Scotia.—Attack on Antigua prevented by appearance of naval force.—Raid on Monserrat interrupted by rumour of naval force approaching.—Failure of intended attack on Quebec under Sir Hovenden Walker, through wreck, season, and want of supply.—Attacks successful and unsuccessful on Leeward Islands in consequence of distance of naval force at Jamaica.—Duguay-Trouin's capture of Rio Janeiro.—Reflections on these occurrences.

Spain in 1718, being in command of the Mediterranean Sea, conquers Sicily.—Byng appears, and destroys the Spanish fleet.—Sea round Sicily commanded by the British, Sicily offers to surrender.—Case of Sardinia parallel to that of Sicily.—Spanish attempt on Ross-shire a failure.—Vigo raided by Mighells and Lord Cobham.—Capture of Porto Bello remarkable as the direct attack by ships.—Cartagena, in the West Indies, bombarded by Vernon.—Surrender of Chagres to simple bombardment.—Change in strategic condition of West Indian waters in consequence of arrival of Spanish and French fleets.—Misapprehensions of contemporary historians.—Arrival of Ogle and departure of French fleet reverses strategic conditions.—Cartagena attacked.—Incomprehensible failure.—St. Jago de Cuba.— Failure of attack from personal causes.

Commerce suffers when territorial attacks are in progress.—The policy carried out in the West Indies, 1742.—The quarrels of joint commanders a fruitful cause of failure.—Knowles fails in his attacks on La Guaira and Porto Cavallo, 1743.—Successful attack on Louisbourg, 1745.—The causes of success usual.—Second successful attack in the same form on Louisbourg, 1758.—Peyton loses the command of the sea in the East Indies, Madras falls in consequence, 1746.—Attempted revival of cross-raiding at Cape Breton and L'Orient; failure of both attempts, 1746.—The first capture of Minorca, 1756.—The siege and reliefs of Gibraltar, and fall of Minorca, 1780–81 and 1782.—Reflections.

The war of American Independence prolific in strategical lessons.—But in the methods of attack there is no difference.—Fewer lessons

Consequences to land operations in the Korea.—Parallel with Campaign of Vittoria.—Error of Chinese in method of reinforcing its Korean army.—Defeat of the Chinese fleet off the Yalu.—Japanese command of the sea confirmed.—Consequences: 1. Blockade of Chinese ports; 2. Territorial attacks.

XX. The Spanish-American War ......................... 518

Anomalous character of the war.—Naval force on each side.—Causes preventing privateering.—Captures of merchant ships.—Blockade.—Absence of attempts to watch or mask the enemy.—Resulting division of United States force.—Augmentation of American naval force.—Intelligence.—Control of naval movement from Washington.—Status of telegraph cables.—Attacks on territory by naval force alone.—Panic on United States coasts.—Naval attacks on shore batteries.—Dewey's operations at Manila.—Attack on warships at Cardenas.—Encounters with batteries.—Attack on San Juan batteries.—Effect of command of the sea.—Attack on Manzanillo.—Effect of the "fleet in being."—Naval bases.—Invasions: Santiago and Porto Rico.—Differentiation of naval force.

Index ................................................. 571

# LIST OF ILLUSTRATIONS

# CHAPTER ONE

UNLIKE ITS MILITARY CONGENER, of which the principles descend from times immemorial, naval warfare is of comparative modern origin. Sea fights there were, no doubt, in very ancient times, but sea fights do not of themselves constitute naval warfare. With possible exceptions here and there, in early Grecian or perhaps Roman days, the ancient sea-fights were the result of military expeditions by sea and not of naval considerations.

The operations of military warfare have at all times been conducted with a view to territorial conquest; the field of battle was struggled for by the combatants as a possession to be either temporarily held as a basis for further operations, or as part of the territory which was to be permanently occupied. The sea-fight of ancient times was but the contention of armies on the water, not to hold the field of battle and surrounding waters, but simply as the encounter of one army with another which was barring its way to the conquest of territory. Permanent occupation of the water, as of the land, was a thing undreamt of, because impossible to the trireme of the ancients, or to the galley of the Middle Ages. Nothing that was then built was what we now call a sea-going or a sea-keeping ship, and there was, in fact, nothing to call for such structures. It was not till the frequented water areas became greatly extended, and till the oar ceased to be a propulsive power in the ordinary ship, that it was possible to build her so that she should remain in permanent occupation of the sea.

And yet, if we look back to what may be called the early days of naval warfare under sail, we shall observe that there was little or no contention for occupation of, or command over, the sea, such as was exercised and claimed over territory on land. Neither riches, nor renown, nor any other advantages could be gathered directly

21

from the sea. Commerce was absolutely small, but relatively to the power of nations possessing sea coasts, even smaller. The advantage of the sea was its convenience as a medium of transport, and it seemed one common to two neighbouring nations at war. Coasts were open, and the small attacks capable of being organized were sudden, and could not well be prepared against. The great value of the sea was the easy means it presented for getting at the enemy's territory and ravaging it.

England had for a long course of years put in a claim for what she called "the sovereignty of the seas" surrounding her. But this was chiefly a civil claim, not a military one. It was as nearly as possible a claim to extend what are now our admitted rights in our territorial waters—a belt three miles wide from the shore—over very large water areas indeed.[1] The whole claim being solemnly denied by the Dutch, and the denial formulated by the learned writer Grotius, Charles I. employed Selden to write a counterblast, reasserting the claim, and for the first time fitted out a fleet to enforce it.

But the claim had to do with rights of fishery, rights of traffic, anchorages, and so on. It was apart from any ideas of water command for military purposes, even so late as Charles' days. At an earlier time the sea was regarded as a common highway for military expeditions, there being but little attempt to secure it for the use of one side only.

Out of this view of the sea grew what I have ventured to christen "cross-ravaging," a system of retaliatory expeditions attacking territory, destroying towns, burning property, and laying waste with fire and sword. This is a system to which we are early introduced, but which is not confined to very early dates. It is a system out of which not much advantage to either side has ever come; but down to the latest periods we can find it where there is no distinct aim of purely naval warfare, that is to say, no distinct aim on either side to assert and maintain a control over the water, such as in military warfare is asserted and maintained over the land.

Thus, in 1512, Sir Edward Howard crossed to Brest with a fleet from which forces landed and burnt Conquet. A reinforcement being sent out, the new fleet met and defeated the French fleet just as it came out of port. That operation finished a year's campaign;

---

1. The British seas, or the Four Seas, as they were indifferently termed, over which this sovereignty was claimed, began at the point where the 63rd parallel touches the coast of Norway. Then the boundary ran down all the coasts to Cape Finisterre; in that latitude to the meridian of 23° W. Then along this meridian, to the 63rd parallel and to Norway again. See *Burchett's Naval History*, p. 34.

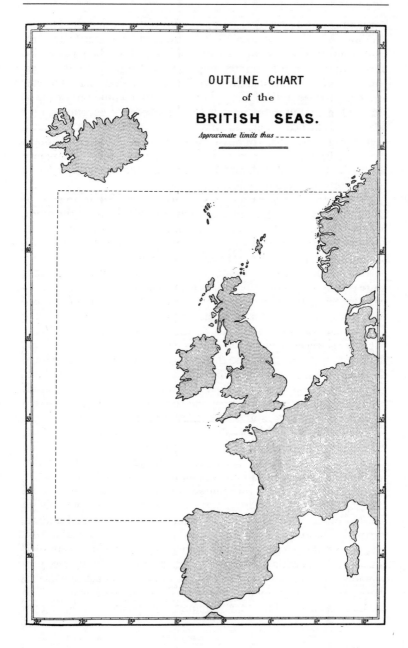

OUTLINE CHART
of the
**BRITISH SEAS.**
*Approximate limits thus* - - - - - - -

but next spring Howard again proceeded to Brest, and the French, pending the arrival of some galleys from the Mediterranean, remained in port, and permitted Howard to sail up the harbour, to burn and ravage the country opposite to Brest, but without attempting anything against the town itself, or the fleet there. The galleys then arrived at Conquet, where Howard, coming out of Brest, attacked them, but unfortunately lost his life in the encounter. Our fleet then returned home. But the French in their turn fitted out a fleet, ravaged the coast of Sussex and burnt Brighton. Sir Thomas Howard, brother of Sir Edward, fitted out another fleet before which the French retired, and he in his turn took an army over to Calais, and captured Terouenne and Tournay.

In 1522, the Emperor Charles V. joined Henry VIII. in an expedition to Cherbourg, which place, falling into the hands of the allies, became the base of operations for ravaging and destroying all the adjacent country. This done, the expedition returned to Portland. Sailing thence again, Howard took Morlaix by storm.

Next summer (1523), however, we meet a condition of things more closely suggesting the form which naval war was ultimately to take, for Sir William Fitz-William passed over to the coast of France with a fleet of thirty-six sail, for the purpose of intercepting a French fleet which was understood to be escorting the Duke of Albany back to his Regency in Scotland. He met and drove back this escort to Dieppe and Boulogne, and then Fitz-William, having thus gained the naval control of the surrounding waters, left a portion of his fleet to watch and mask the French in their ports, while he himself proceeded to ravage and destroy the coast as far as Tréport, where he burnt the suburbs, and all the ships in the harbour.

There were in our history no more expeditions by sea till 1544, when war broke out with Scotland, and then with France. King Henry landed an army at Calais, and marched to Boulogne, which fell into his hands after an investment by sea and land.

The French, in their turn, fitted out a fleet and made for St. Helens, where, after a partial action, rendered memorable only by the loss of the *Mary Rose* which preceded it, they landed and attempted to hold the Isle of Wight. Failing in this, they landed in Sussex, where they were repulsed with loss. Retiring to their own coasts, the French landed part of their army near Boulogne, presumably with the design of recovering it. But a change of wind either compelling it, or facilitating it, the French crossed again over to the English coast, where they were met and defeated by the English fleet. As a reply to this last attempt of the French, the English passed over to their coast and again burnt Tréport and thirty ships which were found in the harbour.[2]

In 1547, the French made an attack on Guernsey and Jersey, but ships and troops being sent from England, the attack was abandoned after the enemy had suffered considerable loss.

Calais fell to the French early in Mary's reign (1558), and not impossibly altered the general view of naval war by removing our last permanent foothold on the soil of France.

But our immediate reprisal was a projected attack on Brest, which, however, dwindled down ultimately to the re-burning of Conquet, and the ravaging of the adjacent coasts in the usual manner.

The whole system, it is readily seen, was one of military reprisals, always more or less open to interruption by the naval forces of the power attacked. There is hardly any idea present on either side of getting such a control of the sea as would prevent the other side from undertaking these ravaging expeditions. The reply to landing and ravaging on one side is generally the attempt at cross-ravaging on the other. The sea is a convenient medium for the transport of armies, and the sea-fight proper only comes in incidentally, as when the French fleet issues from Brest to meet a force proposing to land in the vicinity, or as when Henry VIII. collects his ships at Spithead to interrupt the French in their proposed capture of the Isle of Wight. Naval war this is not, and neither to facilitate the attack, nor to strengthen the defence, is direct possession of the sea sought.

Two things were wanting to alter this condition of military war carried on by water. On the sea itself was not to be found property of the enemy sufficient to make it an object of attack. Although sea-borne commerce was growing, it was not yet of a character or extent sufficiently important on any side to render its suppression a serious injury to the nation carrying it on. An hour or two's burning of a coast town probably offered greater prizes to the descending foe, and wrought greater distress in the nation attacked, than weeks or months of preying on the small and occasional cargoes which were to be found actually at sea.

The other want was ships capable of keeping the sea. If the sea was to be controlled, it was absolutely necessary that the ships as-

2. It is not necessary to quote authorities specifically for these early illustrations, as to which Burchett (1720), Lediard (1735), Berkley (1756), and Entick (1757) are all pretty well agreed. Lediard and Entick quote the original authorities, Burchett and Berkley do not. I have also consulted MM. Troude and Levot on the French side.

suming to control should be able to maintain their position at sea continuously. So long as it was necessary to return to port after a very short stay at sea; so long as ships were so mastered by the weather as to be continually driven back by it, with endeavours or intentions frustrated; it was always open to the enemy to reassume, if only for a time, that control of the sea which had been challenged. This condition was not reached by mere change of season. Winter voyages or cruises were forbidden to both sides for centuries, for neither had ships competent to face the dangers of winter weather. War by sea ceased in winter, just as it did upon land, and therefore neither side could gain an advantage until the summer came round again. But the summer gale which drove a fleet before it into the shelter of safe havens, might not be felt in the enemy's locality, or might help him over to his enemy's coast. If one fleet ran short of water, of provisions, or of munitions; or if its crews became sickly and demanded the recruitment of a stay in the quiet of harbour, it by no means followed that the other hostile fleet would be in the same condition at the same time. If they were in condition to put to sea when the first fleet was obliged to return to port, they were entirely free to use the water as the medium of transport, and to carry out their ravaging expeditions by its means. Miscalculations might occur; the fleet which had been compelled to retire into port, might be again ready for sea sooner than was anticipated, and there might be a sea-fight in consequence. But had the fleet which first retired into port been able to maintain its place at sea, or had it been at least understood to be ready to act at sea, the ravaging expedition could not have been carried out until the sea-keeping fleet had been in some way disposed of, or forced to withdraw.

The supply of both these necessary ingredients of naval war was gradual, and as a consequence the change from the practice of cross-ravaging over a theoretically free sea to systematic naval war with rules deduced from experience, and settled axioms which had become instinctive from continued and forced acceptance, was gradual too.

So far as this country is concerned, the sea-borne commerce question, either as one of defence or attack, did not come into material notice until the time of Elizabeth. But quite early in her reign, we begin to hear of the making of prizes in the Channel. Then we hear of French and Dutch privateers contemporaneous with, and perhaps, in cases, anticipating, the commencement of our partly legitimate and partly piratical war upon the rich commerce of Spain.

Thus Burchett[3] says, speaking of the years 1560–62, and of the Queen's efforts to increase and improve the naval force:

> In imitation of this laudable example of the Queen's, many of her wealthy subjects, who lived near the sea coasts, set themselves to building of ships, so that in a short time those of the Crown and of private persons were become so numerous as, on occasion of any naval war, might employ 20,000 men. The good effects of these preparations were shortly after seen in the war the Queen undertook in behalf of the Protestants of France, wherein, besides the land forces she sent over to Normandy to their assistance, her ships, scouring the seas, sorely distressed their enemies by taking great numbers of prizes from them, and at length totally interrupting their trade.

Lediard,[4] quoting earlier authorities, says that when in 1561 Elizabeth fitted a fleet out to intercept Mary Queen of Scots on her return from France, she gave out that it was intended to clear the sea of pirates; which indicates that a sea harvest was already beginning to be reaped.

Entick particularizes more closely, and says—quoting several authorities—that as the French Court commissioned privateers

> to prey upon our ships, Elizabeth was obliged to follow their example, and by proclamation she gave leave to her subjects to make reprisals; which was attended with such success, that one Clarke, with three frigates only, for his share carried into Newhaven, within a cruise of six weeks, eighteen prizes, valued at £50,000 sterling."[5]

From about this time, the attack and defence of commerce begins to take form and position as a regular element of naval war. The trade of England was pushing out in various quarters, under the auspices of the Company of Merchant Adventurers. Jenkinson opened it up with Russia and Persia; John Hawkins, using the trade in slaves as his instrument, drew the West Coast of Africa and the Western Indies together. The Portuguese and the Dutch were actively pursuing trade in the East Indies and in South America. Spain had a practical monopoly of commerce with the West Indies and the Pacific, which she was neither strong enough nor intelligent enough to hold.

An early indication of the advent of a regular system of naval war is offered by the attacks of Danish freebooters on our Russian commerce. In 1570 the Danes were worsted, and five of their ships cap-

3. Burchett, p. 343.
4. Lediard, vol. i, p. 138.
5. Entick, p. 208.

tured by the squadron of thirteen of the Merchant Adventurers' ships in the Baltic. A formal report of the action was made to the Emperor of Russia by Christopher Hodsdon and William Burrough, who commanded the English ships.[6] About 1573 the French Protestants, having taken to the sea as privateers or pirates, for the purpose of injuring their Catholic countrymen, extended their now lucrative operations so as even to include the ships of their English friends. And later, again, the Dutch, privateering ostensibly against the ships of their Spanish enemies, were in the same way tempted out of the legitimate line of their proceedings by the richness of possible English prizes. Under the pretext—which was very likely no pretext, but a truth, in some cases—that our ships brought supplies and succour to the Spaniards by way of Dunkirk, they fell upon our commerce to its serious detriment. Sir Thos. Holstock, who was then Comptroller of the Navy, was employed to suppress this loose piracy, and succeeded in both cases.[7]

But, perhaps, the real opening of the new phase, the source, as it were, from which the river of naval war was ever after to flow, was the treacherous attack by the Spaniards on Hawkins at St. Juan de Ulloa in 1567. All the world seems to have thereafter become alive to two things—the enormous value of sea-borne commerce to the countries which carried it on, and the tremendous risks attending its prosecution in war on the one hand, as well as the great advantages arising from its attack on the other.

As the growth of commerce can be inferred from the continued mention of its attack and defence, so the capacity of ships to keep the sea can be as well inferred from the numbers and length of the voyages now undertaken. English commerce had arisen before there were English ships to conduct it, and in the early part of the sixteenth century Candiots, Ragusans, Sicilians, Genoese, and Venetians carried English cargoes to and from London and the Mediterranean ports.[8] But there must have been a very rapid and complete change as the century drew on. For the service of the Queen, in repelling the Armada, the City of London, on its own account, fitted out 38 ships of the average tonnage as then counted, of 161 tons, and average crews of 71 men;[9] 197 ships, averaging 151 tons each,

6. Lediard, vol. i., p. 152; Berkeley, p. 307.
7. Burchett, p. 344; Berkeley, p. 312.
8. Hakluyt, quoted in Charnock, vol. ii., p. 7.
9. It is, perhaps, better to go by the number of men than by the tonnage as given. Monson gives tonnage as length × breadth × depth, which would give much more than the displacement. But if, as Mr. W. H. White thinks, the tonnage was the num-

and carrying on an average 89 men per ship, were got together on that occasion under the different leaders on the English side.[10] And as the voyages to the Coasts of Guinea, to the Levant, and to the ports of the Baltic were now freely prosecuted, it is obvious that there was an abundant shipping of sea-going capacity. As to size, amongst the war-ships of Elizabeth, Lord Howard of Effingham had under him the *Triumph,* of 1,100 tons and 500 men; the *White Bear,* of 1,000 tons and 500 men; the *Ark Royal,* of 800 tons and 425 men; the *Victory,* of the like tonnage and 400 men; the *Elizabeth-Bonaventure,* the *Mary Rose,* the *Hope,* and the galley *Bonasolia,* all of 600 tons and 250 men; besides six ships of 500 tons, and a considerable number of about 300 tons.

The change in the character of the ships, and their greater sea worthiness, must be left more to inference than to proof, as there is very little that is authentic as to how ships were really constructed, rigged, and armed before the reign of Charles I. and the era of the Petts. Accurate marine artists scarcely existed before the times of the Vandevelds, the father born in 1610 and the son in 1633. Yet it is probable that the ships of Henry VIII. bore a not remote resemblance to that given in the illustration, and if we compare it with the certainly authentic outlines of the *Speaker,* a Commonwealth ship of 1653, and suppose the change from the one type to the other to have been gradual, we can picture the intermediate types which occupied the field in the reign of Elizabeth.

So that, as the century approached its close, we had the two things necessary to establish purely naval war—abundant sea-borne commerce, and abundance of sea-going and sea-keeping warships. The inevitable result follows, that cross-ravaging from land to land falls into the back-ground; the sea is regarded more and more as a territory necessary to be held by the nation which desires to win in naval war; and it begins to be understood that if attacks on territory, to make which the forces must cross the sea, are to be resisted, the enemy must be met before he leaves the water.

But yet was it a new thing, and so considered for some scores of years, to have war upon the water alone. So new, that one of the chief actors in these times of change, writing long after the change had fully established itself, mentioned with something like con-

---

ber of butts or "tuns" which could be stowed, the tonnage was much less than the displacement. See Monson's *Naval Tracts,* Book iii., and *Manual of Naval Architecture,* First Edition, p. 89.

10. Entick, p. 261.

Ship of Henry VIII

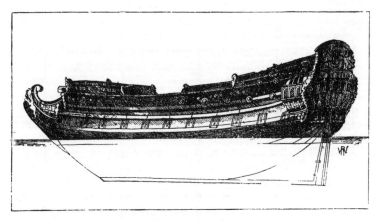

Hull of the *Speaker*

tempt, as "a mere action at sea," the dispatch of a squadron in 1590 under Sir John Hawkins and Frobisher, which, though it made no captures, stopped the whole trade from the West Indies to Spain in that year.

Yet, though the fact was not thoroughly perceived at the time, the vast amount of Spanish riches which were afloat forced the war with Spain and made it a naval one. The ravaging of Spanish territory by the English no doubt hurt Spain, but the capture of the Spanish galleons not only hurt Spain more, but enriched the captors and the nation to which they belonged. Spain, however, was even less conscious than England of the change which was being effected in maritime warfare. She attempted to work on the lines which had been possible three-quarters of a century earlier, in the absence of commerce and sea-going ships; and her grand and crowning error of the Armada was simply the embodiment of false notions as to the inevitable character of naval war.

It is curious and interesting to trace the form of naval war, emerging confusedly and gradually during the eighteen years that covered the struggle between England and Spain; but it is still more impressive to read the words of the chief actors in this struggle after it was over, and to observe how entirely they had accepted the new conditions and enunciated the line of policy, even in those early years, which successful naval war has ever since followed. I shall, therefore, run lightly through the principal incidents of the Spanish war, commenting as may be necessary while I proceed, and I shall then quote the emphatic language of Sir William Monson in 1640, when he was a retired officer, and of the unfortunate Sir Walter Raleigh during his twelve years' imprisonment in the Tower.

Drake's first expedition to the West Indies was in 1585, and this was entirely on the military reprisal plan, or on the system of cross-ravaging; so he sacked San Domingo, Cartagena, Santa Justina in Florida, and then returned home. But in 1587 we begin to see a change. Drake proceeds to Cadiz, not for the purpose of cross-ravaging, but to destroy the shipping which constituted the supply of the great armada preparing at Lisbon. Having succeeded in this enterprize, he fell somewhat back into the older grooves by assaulting certain castles on the coast of Spain; but, becoming aware of the real ineffectiveness of such proceedings, he steered for the Western Islands for the interruption of the enemy's commerce, then represented by an immense and valuable carrack expected from Mozambique. He succeeded in his object, and brought his great prize to England. Monson, not yet wholly alive to the real nature of naval war, but still in part comprehending, says of the first voyage:—

> And though this voyage proved both fortunate and victorious, yet considering it was rather an awakening than a weakening of him (the King of Spain), it had been far better to have wholly declined than to have undertaken it upon such slender grounds and with so inconsiderable forces.

Of the second voyage, the Admiral says:—

> This voyage proceeded prosperously, and without exception, for there was both honour and wealth gained, and the enemy greatly endamaged.[11]

The next year, 1588, was the Armada year, as to which nothing need here be said; but 1589 witnessed two expeditions, one under Drake, with land forces, as an attempt to replace the King of Portugal on his throne, which was of a wholly public character; and the other under the Earl of Cumberland, which was almost wholly an attack on the commerce of the Roman Catholic League against Henry IV., and of Spain. This was of the partly royal and partly commercial character which the state of the times favoured. Drake's expedition was a failure, due, it is said, to having wasted time in an abortive attempt on Corunna, or the Groyne, as it was then called. But it must be remembered that this was an entirely legitimate expedition, inasmuch as it was perfectly certain that the terrible defeat of the Armada had cleared the sea of Spanish war ships for some time

11. Monson's *Naval Tracts,* Book i.

to come. The Earl of Cumberland began by capturing three of the League ships in the Channel. Then he took £7,000 worth of spices belonging to Spain out of Portuguese ships off the coast of Portugal. Then he proceeded to the island of Flores, where he captured an outward-bound Spaniard. Then, in the Road of Fayal, he made prize of Spanish ships. Later, he took a French League ship returning home from Canada. Then he forced the little island of Graciosa to afford him provisions and refreshment. Off Terceira, he took a Spanish ship worth £100,000, and then, on his return towards the coast of Spain, he made two prizes, each worth £7,000, and a third he drew out from under the guns of the castle of St. Mary's, worth a like sum. The only thing this expedition undertook which was in the nature of cross-ravaging, but which was, in the absence of any possible interruption from Spanish ships, an act always found proper to be performed in like circumstances, was the sacking of the town of Fayal.

In 1590 was the expedition of Hawkins and Frobisher to the coasts of Spain and the Western Islands, to destroy the Spanish trade. This squadron was seven months at sea, and did not make a single capture of importance, and was what Monson characterized it, half in contempt and half understanding how completely it had fulfilled its mission, "a bare action at sea." Spain was recovering from the blow of 1588, and even got so far as to propose to meet the fleet of Hawkins and Frobisher at sea. But realising the disaster that would follow a second defeat, and not having force enough to make success certain, Philip recalled his ships and left the English fleet free to lie across the Spanish trade route and to hold it. But as the least of two evils, consequent on this position of his enemy, the King of Spain forbade the sailing of the ships from the West Indies, and so abandoned the whole of the nation's sea-borne foreign commerce for one year. This was really a blow of the heaviest character to Spain, and, as we shall see, is the penalty that must be paid by the weaker naval power. But in this case it was still worse for Spain, as, in the then unsheathed state of ships' bottoms, lying in tropical waters for a summer produced weakness of structure almost amounting to disablement, from the ravages of the worm. As a consequence, about a hundred of these detained ships were lost, with their rich cargoes, on the return voyage to Spain next year.

In 1591 Lord Thomas Howard took command of a fleet to the Western Islands, with the single intention of preying on Spanish commerce as before. But at this time the King of Spain had so far recovered himself as to send to sea a still larger and more powerful fleet than that of Lord Thomas Howard; this he did, and what took place is of the essence and being of naval war. In those days—though a change was even then understood to be necessary—Lord Thomas Howard's absence left the Channel uncovered, and had things been as they were, cross-raiding on English territory might have been effected by the Spaniards. But at what price? At that of the probable loss of the whole West India commercial fleet. Any damage that could possibly be done to the shores of England would have been paid for, over and over again, by the vast prize that would fall unguarded into Lord Thomas Howard's hands, while the loss to Spain by this great transfer of property would have been entirely uncompensated. Before any attacks on English soil could be thought of, Spanish commerce must be protected; and Don Alonzo de Bazan sailed to the Western islands instead of to the Channel.

Don Alonzo's fleet was greatly superior to that of Lord Thomas, and had the latter not been warned in time, all his ships might have suffered the fate of the *Revenge* with Sir Richard Grenville in command. Howard just escaped, and the Spanish Plate Fleet was saved. But so close was the issue, that had that fleet arrived at Flores one day sooner, or had Don Alonzo arrived one day later, Howard would have made the complete success he desired. But even though the main purpose of the expedition was a failure, Howard made sufficient captures in the course of his voyage to pay all its expenses, and Spain suffered not only to that extent, but also in the loss, already detailed, of the greater part of the rescued Plate Fleet on the way home, on account of the decayed condition of the ships.

In the same year, 1591, the Earl of Cumberland made a voyage to the Spanish coast, wholly intent on the attack on Spanish commerce. Slight tangible success alone attended his exertions, but while intelligence of Don Alonzo's preparations drove him home, the fact of the Earl's being on the Spanish coast enabled him to despatch that warning to Lord Thomas Howard which allowed him to draw off his fleet in time—all but the *Revenge*.

In 1592 Frobisher, in succession to Raleigh, took a squadron to the coast of Spain and to the Islands, but this broke up and acted more or less independently, some ships on the coast and some at the Islands. Don Alonzo de Bazan, on his part, being ordered to cover the West India fleet, by so much disobeyed his instructions as to allow captures to be made which he might have prevented. But he was at sea in superior force to the English, and they were perforce driven home.

The Earl of Cumberland, in 1593, repeated the practice which was now established of warring on Spanish commerce, first on the coast of Spain, and then, at the right season, amongst the Western Islands. Captures were made, of course, but Spain repeated her practice of appearing in superior force at the Islands, and necessitating thereby the retirement of the English.

This was now the third year, during which neither side had gained much advantage, and when the guard of Spain on her commerce had been nearly complete. Such proceedings were hardly of the essence of naval war, and might have progressed for an indefinite time. If Spain was able to show superior force at sea for three successive years, she should have pushed it farther. To get any advantage, she should have followed the English fleet up and mastered it. Then she would not only have protected her commerce, but would have been in a position to push her attacks closer home. The Spanish error was that they did not understand this; but possibly the question of season governed the Spanish naval policy to a greater extent than we can now easily realise.

The English, on their part, if they had rightly understood the position, would have acted with the sole purpose of mastering the Spanish fleet as a necessary preliminary to the destruction of her commerce. But probably no one then perceived what was axiomatic a century later.

Not improbably the failure to comprehend the exact position, however simple it may seem to us who have assimilated all past experience without knowing it, dictated the changed proceedings of the next few years.

The Spaniards had joined the Roman Catholic League, and in 1594 had ships in Brest, which was held in the interest of the faction. Three thousand English troops had been for some time operating in Brittany, in alliance with the troops of Henry IV., and Frobisher was now despatched with four ships to co-operate against the Spaniards, who at Brest were a threat to the security of the Channel. This operation was effectively concluded.

But cross-raiding was again uppermost in the English mind; for in the same year, 1594, Drake and Hawkins sailed for the West Indies with the intention of landing at Nombre de Dios, marching across to Panama, and possessing themselves of all the plunder which the sacking of that *entrepôt* for silver was likely to afford. This expedition was late in sailing, because a certain fear of attacks at home grew out of the presence of Spanish ships at Brest and on the coast of Brittany. But a home squadron being fitted out, Drake and Hawkins sailed.

The fears of cross-ravaging, though exaggerated, were not without foundation, for in this year four Spanish galleys ran over from France into Mount's Bay; their crews landed and burnt Penzance, Mouse-hole, Newlin, and a neighbouring church. Then they reembarked, and made off as suddenly and as secretly as they had come. Not a drop of English blood was shed, and all the historians agree that it was a mere piece of bravado, without sensible aim and object; and the galleys were seen by no one, either during their approach or on their retirement.

Before Drake and Hawkins sailed, news had reached England that a valuable Spanish carrack had put into Porto Rico damaged, and the Queen ordered them to make sure of this prize before attempting anything further. In this order, we had again a legitimate operation in the circumstances of the case. It was a worthy object; not requiring time to achieve, and therefore not liable to interruption from the sea. The march across to Panama required the occupation of Nombre de Dios and the security of their ships, not only to lie there, but to pass freely to sea laden with the spoils gathered from the shores of the Pacific. Clear ideas on such simple points were often wanting in those days, and even in the minds of Drake and Hawkins they could hardly have been present. The ships lingered at Guadaloupe, and allowed the Spaniards both information and time enough so to secure the treasure-ship that the English attack at Porto Rico was repulsed with loss, and Hawkins died, it is said, half of this trouble. Drake proceeded to Nombre de Dios, but found the march across impracticable, and he died, too, near hand, at Porto Bello.

That which was to be expected had meantime happened; and Baskerville, who succeeded to the command, only just escaped, after a partial action, the superior fleet which Spain had sent out to interrupt, in the only way possible, the operations of the English. Most probably, the failure of the march across the isthmus was the real saving of our fleet, which might otherwise have been caught half-manned at Nombre de Dios by the more powerful Spaniards.

Monson remarks on the risen sea-power of Spain since 1591, and how, in this year, she had secured herself by two strong fleets, one of twenty sail in the West Indies and another of twenty-four sail at the Western Islands. As a consequence, so far, her commerce passed in security, though the ships saw neither a friend nor an enemy before their safe arrival at Lisbon.

She was now really mistress at sea, and had she known what was proper to be done, she would have pushed up into the Channel with all her force before the English could have got out. By so doing she would have left her commerce and all her ports free behind her, for even if she failed to meet and beat the English in their own waters, her threat must have kept them at home. But if she could meet, and could beat them, it was impossible to limit the advantages to her which would immediately follow. She would have passed the period of naval defence, and would have been ready to take up the *rôle* of attack from the sea, which was secure behind her.

She was slow to read the lesson of the time, slower even than we were; and though thus really superior at sea, she left herself entirely open to the secret, sudden, and powerful attack which was made upon Cadiz by the Lord Admiral Howard in command of the sea forces, and of Essex in command of the land forces, yet with some joint commission, in this year, 1596.

The expedition did not sail till June 1st, and it was simply fatuous on the part of Philip, that with galleys raiding on our coast the year before, he should have had absolutely nothing by way of look-out, or *avant-garde,* to give him notice that a hundred and fifty ships were preparing to embark over seven thousand land forces, and that the Dutch were incorporating themselves in the grand design. But Spain was swelling with ideas of a repetition of her great cross-raiding designs of 1588. She was not in the least conscious that her breach of all the growing principles of naval war was the primary cause of her former failure, and would be, over and over again, the causes of her future failures as long as she continued them. She had been driving English fleets out of her own waters for four years running, and yet had not understood that water was water, and that if an English fleet fled before a Spanish one at Flores and off Cuba, the same fleet would be hard put to it off Plymouth or the Isle of Wight. But the thought was not in the Spanish Councils; they set out great ideas for the invasion of a heretic England, and the support of a rebellious yet orthodox Ireland, and they left the main body of their preparations open to the stroke of any one who chose to cross the sea to strike it.

Howard and Essex sailed, as I have said, on the 1st of June. They took the most singular precautions by means of widespread vi-dettes, which captured or detained every sail that was seen, so that early in the morning of the 20th June the vast fleet was off Cadiz, with nothing to prevent them sailing right up and making them-selves masters of the great assemblage of war and merchant ships that lay in unsuspecting tranquillity before them. But a day was lost in divided counsels, and notwithstanding the clearness of their instructions to master the ships in the first instance, and Monson's urgency as a leading naval adviser, it was not till night that the determination to attack the ships was come to. The result was that though many ships were taken, and many burnt to prevent them falling into our hands, the lesser value—the occupation of the town for fourteen days, and its ransom for 120,000 ducats—assumed the most golden hue, and the blow was not as complete as it otherwise might have been.

A point which is not cleared up in any of the histories before me, is the disposition of the Spanish fleet at this time. There were a considerable number of war-ships at Cadiz, no doubt, and some of the heaviest class. There was also at least a squadron at Lisbon, under Siriago, for six of them attacked a private expedition of the Earl of Cumberland off the Rock. But I do not gather whether the fleets of the previous year were guarding commerce this year in the West Indies and at the Azores. The English commanders knew some days before their arrival at Cadiz what ships they would find there, but it was not known to the home Government what the disposition of the Spanish fleet was, for the ascertainment of this was one of the duties enjoined upon the English commanders. Unless these had some knowledge that the sea was free behind them, they could hardly have made the serious attack they did, and would certainly not have remained as much as fourteen days in possession of the town of Cadiz.

It was a part of the Lords Generals' instructions to take the usual measures at the Western Islands for intercepting the Spanish trade, but disputes and discontents had arisen over the possible objections which might be taken at home, and no detachment westward was made. Essex was forbidden to attack Lisbon, and intelligence from Ferrol showed that no ships were there. So, as provisions were, as usual, running short, and there was no further operation open, the great fleet returned to England, arriving at Plymouth on August 8th.

Even this reverse at Cadiz, due as it was to a wholly mistaken naval policy, had no sort of legitimate effect on the Spanish mind, at least in the early part of 1597. The invasion idea was so far uppermost, that an assemblage in force began to be made at Ferrol, and the commerce at the Western Islands was left open. That could be protected only on the spot, or by a close threat in the Channel. An assemblage at Ferrol, which could hardly be in great force after the destruction at Cadiz, was not a strong threat, though in the rebellious condition of Ireland it certainly did require more notice than it had.

Essex took a fleet off the port, but having been very late in sailing—he only left Plymouth on August 17th—owing both to late preparations and to adverse weather, the Spaniards were amply secured against the simple raiding attack by part of the fleet, which was alone practicable. A determination was now come to which was only justified by want of full comprehension of what naval war necessitated. Essex sailed for the Western Islands, leaving it quite open to the Spanish fleet to follow him there, and perhaps fall on him at the least opportune moment, or else to deal such blows in our home waters as might be open to him. This move of Essex would have been entirely a false one had the English commerce been abreast of that of Spain in value, or near it, for then the Spanish ships might not only have fallen upon the English property at sea, and sent it securely into their own ports, but they were in a position to recapture the English prizes in returning to their home ports, if not to give battle to the returning war-ships in a presumably weakened state. The course taken was only less blamable, because English commerce did not approach the value of that of Spain.

But the operations suggested were open to the Spaniards, and they were at sea the day after Essex left.[12] Their plan was to use their local control of the sea in order to seize Falmouth or some western English port, and to use it as a base in which to rest and await the return of the fleet of Essex. Had their seamanship been equal to their strategy they might have done great things, and perhaps turned the tables on this occasion; but a heavy gale off Scilly dispersed the Spanish fleet when on its way to fulfil the mission, and the ships returned to their own ports, allowing Essex to bring home in safety the few prizes he had picked up to the westward.

We can easily trace the growing laws of naval war, unalterable and immutable if it is to be carried on with a view to the certain advantage of either side, and thereby to a speedy conclusion. We have seen Spain on her side able to guard and protect her trade by appearing in force at the point of attack; and we have seen her leave her chief port and source of greatness wholly open to the sudden attack of a fleet of whose approach she had no dreams. Now we see her making one forward step in advancing her base to Ferrol, and meditating operations in British waters. But as late as the middle of August, that is, when the season of naval operations is drawing to a

12. Berkley, p. 420.

39

close, the Spanish fleet has made no effort, and lies in its own port, masked by that of Essex. Only, therefore, by beating this fleet of Essex, or by some strategical error on the part of its commander, could the Spanish fleet have achieved its purpose. Meantime, unless there was a second fleet on the Spanish coast, and a third at the Western Islands, Spain is left open to attack by a second English fleet, supposing there was one, either on her commerce or on her territory.

But Essex commits the only error open to him. On the chance that he may do more damage to Spain in the Western Islands than Spain can do in the Channel, he sails away to that quarter, leaving everything open behind him. Because little or nothing was done on either side, we must not suppose that such breaches of plain law could be committed with impunity. It was only by error and mismanagement that Essex failed to possess himself of the whole of the Spanish West Indian ships at one *grand coup*. The attack on Falmouth would perhaps have been made, and all that was to follow it carried out, had it not been for the heavy weather which occurred so opportunely to save the credit of Essex.[13]

But the reason of the whole matter is simple, and can be simply put. Supposing that the English damage to Spanish trade, and Spanish damage in the Channel, were of equal moment to each of the nations at war, how was either to be advantaged if both damages were done, any more than if neither were done? Such cross-damaging can be of no force in bringing either nation to terms, and was much more calculated to exasperate and prolong the war. If Spain, then, committed the error of being too late in the Channel, and not in strength to have fought Essex fairly at sea, Essex should have held her fleet masked at Ferrol till the end of the season, and it would have been possible that a small detachment might have operated successfully upon the Spanish trade. The Spaniards were hardly wrong to have proceeded to carry out their intention of intercepting Essex on his return, rather than of following him to the Islands, though, as in former years, they might have secured their trade directly by the earlier despatch westward of the necessary force.

It would almost seem if these simple but great principles were now forcing themselves into men's minds as new light. For the Queen sent out no fleet next year (1598), and Spain made no move.

---

13. It may be stated that the English had the belief that the Spanish fleet would, as usual, fly to protect its trade, but in the later years of naval war no such belief would have been allowed to operate.

There was but a private raiding expedition of the Earl of Cumberland, which, after blocking, and so killing, the outward trade of Spain, made descents on the Canaries and Porto Rico.

The transactions of the year 1599 were of a nature to give further form and substance to rules and maxims which, though congealing in parts, were still soft and unstable.

I cannot write [says Monson] of anything done in this year of 1599, for there was never greater expectation of war with less performance. Whether it was a mistrust the one nation had of the other, or a policy held on both sides to make peace with sword in hand, a treaty being entertained by consent of each prince, I am not to examine; but sure I am, the preparation was on both sides very great, as if the one expected an invasion from the other, and yet it was generally conceived not to be intended by either; but that ours had only relation to my Lord of Essex, who was then in England, and had a design to try his friends in England, and to be revenged of his enemies, as he pretended, and as it proved afterwards by his fall. Howsoever it was, the change was not so great as necessary, for it was commonly known that the Adelentado had drawn both his ships and galleys to the Groyne; which was not usually done, but for some action intended upon England or Ireland, though he converted them afterwards to another use; for the galleys were sent into the Low Countries, and passed the narrow seas whilst our ships lay there. And with the fleet, the Adelentado pursued the Hollanders to the Islands, whither he suspected they were gone. This fleet of Hollanders, which consisted of 73 sail, were the first ships that ever displayed their colours in warlike sort against the Spaniards in any action of their own, for how cruel soever the war seemed to be in Holland, they maintained a peaceable trade in Spain, and abused us. This first action of the Hollanders at sea proved not very successful; for after the spoil of a town in the Canaries, and some hurt done to the Island of St. Tome, they kept the sea for seven or eight months, in which time their General and most of their men sickened and died, and the rest returned with loss and shame. Another benefit which we received by this preparation was, that our men were now taught suddenly to arm, every man knowing his command, and how to be commanded, which before they were ignorant of; and who knows not that sudden and false alarms in an army are sometimes necessary? To say the truth, the expedition which was then used in drawing together so great an army by land, and rigging so great and royal a navy to sea, in so little a space of time, was so admirable in other countries, that they received a terror by it; and many that came from beyond sea, said the Queen was never more dreaded abroad for anything she ever did.

Frenchmen that came aboard our ships did wonder (as at a thing incredible) that Her Majesty had rigged, victualled, and furnished her royal ships to sea in twelve days' time; and Spain, as an enemy, had reason to fear and grieve to see this sudden preparation.[14]

The armament consisted of nineteen Queen's ships under Lord Thomas Howard; they assembled in the Downs, but after a month there, the threat had presumably done its work, for the ships were recalled and dismantled.

But the assemblage, following on a year's inaction, and that again following on the experienced dangers of certain strategical operations, dangers which it does not appear were recognized before, would seem to indicate the working of a leaven which would ultimately leaven the whole lump, and fix in men's minds the nature of the inherent principles of naval war.

The year 1600 witnessed the founding of the East India Company, and the sailing of three of their merchant ships under the guidance of James Lancaster, and thus the further development of the strength of a maritime nation in peace and of its weakness in war. The only naval operation was the despatch by England of a small squadron to attack Spanish trade at the Western Islands, and its being driven off by the threat of a much larger Spanish squadron. The Spanish trade however avoided all chances of capture by pursuing a route altogether clear of the Islands, so that Sir Richard Lewson, who commanded the English squadron, saw not a hostile sail.

But the next year, 1601, again saw some relapse into the practice of cross-raiding, for while the English devoted themselves to assisting the Low Countries against the Spaniards, they left the sea so open that late in the year, when indeed, according to usage, fleets should be seeking their home ports, the Spaniards made for the port of Kinsale in Ireland with forty-eight ships and four thousand troops, and landed there.

But it cannot be said that this operation was a complete restoration of the practice of cross-raiding, for the Spaniards were in alliance with the rebel Earl Tyrone, and might plausibly adventure a flying column into what might prove a friendly country. Yet did the result yield its experience, and add to the accumulating evidence of the existence of rule in naval war.

Tyrone, on his side, failed to effect the junction which was sought. The Spaniards found themselves shut up in the town of Kinsale by the army of Mountjoy, which had already defeated Tyrone, while on the sea side they were blocked by Sir Richard Lewson. Yielding

14. *Naval Tracts*, Book i., p. 1599.

was a necessity, in the absence of all control of the sea, and the Spanish army was carefully conducted back to its own country, never again to illustrate their failure to apprehend the possible in conducting war with a maritime power.

But England, on her side, was more receptive of the lessons to be learnt. In March 1602, Lewson and Monson sailed "to infest the Spanish coast with a continual fleet." [15] and, with an interval of return, this "infesting" was pushed far into the autumn, and Monson did not quit the Spanish waters till the 21st October; a feat proving not only the capacity of the man, but his growing knowledge of the art of naval war, and the capabilities of the instruments for waging it. His attacks were wholly confined to shipping, and were very successful. The Spanish fleet was, however, much superior to his own; it was at sea, but never succeeded in coming into contact with this consummate seaman, who could think and act.

It was as if all the outlines of naval war had been marked when the Queen died next year (1603), for her fleet was prepared to start for the coast of Spain as early as February, and to remain there till November; a policy which would have held the naval forces of Spain in absolute check, unless she could have faced and beaten the English; while the latter would have had the free sea behind them either to prosecute their own commerce in peace or to stifle that of the enemy.

It had taken all these eighteen years to learn the lesson that nothing can be done of consequence in naval war till one side secures the control of the water area. But even then it was not clear to men's minds that this control must either be acknowledged by the side which has it not, and all its disabilities admitted; or else it must be fought for by all the naval strength either side is capable of putting forth.

Yet were the main principles partly apprehended and partly set forth by the two authorities, whose opinions I now quote in fulfilment of my promise at the beginning of the chapter. Thus writes Sir William Monson:—

> Whilst the Spaniards were employed at home by our yearly fleets, they never had opportunity nor leisure either to make an attempt upon us, or to divert the wars from themselves; by which means we were secured from any attempt of theirs, as will appear by what follows.

15. Ibid., p. 1602.

The Spaniards stood so much in awe of Her Majesty's ships, that when a few of them appeared on the coast they commonly diverted their enterprises—as, namely, in the year 1587, when Sir Francis Drake, with twenty-five ships, prevented an expedition that summer out of Cadiz Road for England, which the next year after they attempted in 1588, because not molested as the year before.

Our action in Portugal, following so quick upon the overthrow in 1588, made the King of Spain so far unable to offend, that if the undertaking had been prosecuted with judgment, he had been in ill circumstances to defend it, or his other kingdoms.

From that year to the year 1591 he grew great by sea, because he was not busied by us as before; which appeared by the fleet that took the *Revenge;* which armada of his, it is very likely, had been employed against England had it not been diverted that year by my Lord Thomas Howard.

And for four years together after this the King employed his ships to the Islands, to guard his merchants from the Indies, which made him have no leisure to think of England.

The voyage to Cadiz in 1596 did not only frustrate his intended action against England, but we destroyed many of his ships and provisions that should have been employed on that Service.

He designed the second revenge upon England, but was prevented by my Lord of Essex to the islands; which action of his, if it had been well carried, and that my lord would have believed good advice, it had utterly ruined the King of Spain.

The next year that gave cause of fear to the Queen, was 1599, the King of Spain having a whole year, by our sufferance, to make his provisions, and brought his ships and army down to the Groyne; which put the Queen to a more chargeable defensive war than the value our offensive fleet would have been maintained with upon his coast.

This great expedition was diverted by the fleet of Holland, which the Adelentando pursued to the Islands.

The following years, 1600 and 1601, there was hope of peace, and nothing was attempted on either side till the latter end of 1601 that he invaded Ireland; but with ill-success, as you have heard.

The last summer, 1602, he was braved by Her Majesty's ships in the mouth of his harbour with the loss of a carrack, and rendered unable to prosecute his designs against Ireland, for no sooner was Sir Richard Lewson returned but Sir William Monson was sent back again upon that coast, as you have heard, who kept the King's forces so employed, that he betook himself only to the guard of his shores.

It is not the meanest mischief we shall do to the King of Spain, if we thus war upon him, to force him to keep his shores still armed and guarded, to the infinite vexation, charge, and discontent of his subjects; for no time or place can secure them so long as they see or know us to be upon that coast.

The sequel of all these actions being duly considered, we may be confident that whilst we busy the Spaniards at home, they dare not think of invading England or Ireland; for by their absence their fleet from the Indies may be endangered, and in their attempts they have as little hope of prevailing.[16]

Surely I hold [says Sir Walter Raleigh] that the best way is to keep our enemies from treading upon our ground; wherein, if we fail, then must we seek to make him wish that he had stayed at his own home. In such a case, if it should happen, our judgments are to weigh many particular circumstances, that belongs not to this discourse. But making the question general, the position, whether England, without the help of her fleet, be able to debar an enemy from landing, I hold that it is unable to do so; and, therefore, I think it most dangerous to make the adventure. For the encouragement of a first victory to an enemy, and the discouragement of being beaten to the invaded, may draw after it a most perilous consequence.

Great difference, I know there is, and diverse consideration to be had, between such a country as France is, strengthened with many fortified places, and this of ours, where our ramparts are but the bodies of men. But I say that an army to be transported over sea, and to be landed again in an enemy's country, and the place left to the choice of the invader cannot be resisted on the coast of England without a fleet to impeach it; no, nor on the coast of France, or any other country, except every creek, port, or sandy bay had a powerful army in each of them to make opposition. . . . For there is no man ignorant that ships, without putting themselves out of breath, will easily outrun the soldiers that coast them.

"*Les armées ne volent point en poste*—armies neither flye nor run post," saith a marshal of France. And I know it to be true that a fleet of ships may be seen at sunset and after it, at the Lizard, and yet by next morning they may recover Portland; whereas an army of foot shall not be able to march it in six dayes. Again, when those troops lodged on the sea shores should be forced to run from place to place in vain, after a fleet of ships, they will at length sit down in the midway, and leave all at adventure.[17]

If we regard the utterances of these leaders of the Elizabethan era, and remember that what they wrote was not to set forth the principles of naval war in the abstract, but as they applied to the cir-

16. Ibid., p. 1603.
17. Raleigh, *History of the World.* Quoted by Creasy, *Fifteen Decisive Battles,* &c., p. 365. I only possess the abridgement of Raleigh's works published by his

cumstances of their own country at the time, we shall understand to some extent how far they went towards full comprehension, and where they stopped short of it.

Both laid stress on the paramount importance of operations by sea. In Monson's opinion it was only by transferring the war to the sea coasts of Spain that an advantage could be gained in attack; while Raleigh was clear that an attack coming over sea could only be met at sea. Neither leader gives any countenance to the old idea that the attack of one power on the territory of the other could be met by a counter attack of the same character. It follows that in both their minds the age of cross-raiding had passed away, and that the age of naval war as such, naval war absolutely on the sea, had taken its place.

In both their eyes, the policy of Spain must have been a mistaken one, unless she was driven to it by a clear sense of her inferiority at sea. But then, if she were clearly inferior at sea, both men would have held that all her attempted raids on territory were practically useless. If she was not absolutely inferior at sea, and Monson was clearly of opinion that she was not so from 1591 to 1595, then her course of policy was from Monson's own showing a wrong one, except upon the ground of the enormous superiority of her commerce to ours. "The King employed his ships to the islands, to guard his merchants from the Indies, which made him have no leisure to think of England." Quite so. But if English commerce offered as important a field of attack as that of Spain, when looked at from the point of view of national importance, a Spanish attack upon English commerce would have left England "with no leisure to think of" Spain.

But in any case, the appearance of Spanish fleets in the Channel must, in Monson's opinion, have had just the same paralyzing effect on the English fleets—as far as any attack on Spain was concerned—as the presence of English fleets in Spanish waters confessedly had on those of Spain. Monson must have been perfectly clear on this abstract proposition or he could not have urged, as he did, the importance of the English fleet's getting away for Spain as early as February. To be first in the field was the point. And the force that was first in the field must hold all the superiority of that position until it was beaten at sea.

---

grandson Philip Raleigh. But it is remarkable how completely that great man relies on ancient examples for modern guidance. The Roman and Greek experiences serve him continually with lessons for the English of James's time.

The control of the sea, or what I shall now and hereafter call by its established title, the "Command of the Sea," was henceforth to be understood as the aim of naval war. A power striving for anything else, such as evasions, or surprises of ports or territories, or merely defensive guardings of commerce, accepted the position of the inferior and beaten naval power, and could never hope, so long as she maintained that attitude, of seriously damaging her opponent.

# CHAPTER TWO

I N THE LAST CHAPTER I endeavoured to show how, in consequence of the presence of two requirements, large sea-borne commerce and war-ships capable of keeping the sea, naval warfare was settling into form at the close of the reign of Elizabeth. Its necessities, and the fixed rules arising out of those necessities, were becoming clear to English seamen who had full experience of the actualities surrounding and controlling it. But though knowledge of the subject had greatly advanced, it was probably the few and not the many who could look forward to a complete method in naval warfare.

Commerce, I have observed, was chiefly on one side in the Spanish war, and the side which owned it was that which had the least clear views of the right way to keep it and to defend it. The warships were still not of a wholly sea-keeping character, and the question of their supply was one which nearly always governed their movements and their capacity for keeping the sea.

In the peaceful years that followed through the reigns of James I. and Charles I. two things went on side by side, a wider distribution of sea-borne commerce, and a continual improvement in the character of the war-ships as well as of others. These were the things which governed the nature of naval war, and as they grew towards a standard of completeness they necessarily tended to define and harden the rules under which naval war would in future be carried on. Perhaps the best idea of these growths may be gathered from the perusal of a nearly complete quotation from the latter part of Raleigh's *Discourse of the First Invention of Ships, and the several parts thereof.*

> Whosoever were the inventers, we find that every age hath added somewhat to ships, and to all things else. And in mine own time the shape of our English ships hath been greatly bettered. It is not long

48

since the striking of the topmast (a wonderful ease to great ships, both at sea and in harbour) hath been devised, together with the chain pump, which takes up twice as much water as the ordinary did. We have lately added the Bonnet and the Drabler. To the courses we have devised studding-sails, topgallant-sails, spritsails, topsails. The weighing of anchors by the capstone is also new. We have fallen into consideration of the length of cables, and by it we resist the malice of the greatest winds that can blow. Witness our small Milbrooke men of Cornwal, that ride it out at anchor half seas over between England and Ireland, all the winter quarter. And witness the Hollanders that were wont to ride before Dunkirk with the wind at North-West, making a lee-shoar in all weathers. For true it is, that the length of the cable is the life of the ship in all extremities, and the reason is, because it makes so many bendings and waves, as the ship, riding at that length, is not able to stretch it; and nothing breaks that is not stretcht in extremity. We carry our ordnance better than we were wont, because our nether over-loops[1] are raised commonly from the water, to wit, between the lower port and the sea.

In King Henry the Eighth's time, and in his presence, at Portsmouth, the *Mary Rose,* by a little sway of the ship in tacking about, her ports being within sixteen inches of the water, was overset and lost. . . .

We have also raised our second decks, and given more vent thereby to our ordnance lying on our nether-loop. We have added cross pillars in our royal ships to strengthen them, which be fastened from the keelson to the beam of the second deck to keep them from setting or from giving way in all distresses.

We have given longer floors to our ships than in elder times, and better bearing under water, whereby they never fall into the sea after the head and shake the whole body, nor sink stern, nor stoop upon a wind, by which the breaking loose of our ordnance, or of the not use of them, with many other discommodities are avoided.

And, to say the truth, a miserable shame and dishonour it were for our shipwrights if they did not exceed all others in the setting up our Royal ships, the errors of other nations being far more excusable than ours. For the Kings of England have for many years been at the charge to build and furnish a navy of powerful ships for their own defence, and for the wars only. Whereas the French, the Spaniards, the Portuguese, and the Hollanders (till of late) have had no proper fleet belonging to their Princes or States. Only the Venetians for a long time have maintained their arsenal of gallies. And the Kings of Denmark and Sweden have had good ships for these last fifty years.

I say that the aforenamed kings, especially the Spaniards and Portugals, have ships of great bulk, but fitter for the merchant than for

---

1. Meaning the lower gun-deck. The term "over-loop" (German, *überlauf*) became lost in the term *orlop,* as applied to the deck below the lower gun-deck.

49

the man-of-war, for burthen than for battel. But as Popelimire well observeth, the forces of Princes by sea are marques de grandeux d'estate—marks of the greatness of an estate—for whosoever commands the sea, commands the trade; whosoever commands the trade of the world, commands the riches of the world, and consequently the world itself. Yet can I not deny but that the Spaniards, being afraid of their Indian fleets, have built some few very good ships; but he hath no ships in garrison, as his Majesty hath; and to say the truth, no sure place to keep them in, but in all invasions he is driven to take up of all nations which come into his ports for trade.

The Venetians, while they attended their fleets and imployed themselves in their Eastern conquest, were great and powerful Princes, and commanded the maritime ports of Croatia, Dalmatia, Albania, and Epirus; were lords of Peloponnessus and the islands adjoyning; of Cyprus, Candia, and many other places. But after they sought to greaten themselves in Italy itself, using strangers for the commanders of their armies, the Turks by degrees beat them out of all their goodly countries, and have now confined them (Candia excepted) to a few small Grecian islands, which, with great charge and difficulty they enjoy.

The first honour they obtained was by making war upon the Istrii by sea; and had they been true to their spouse, to meet the sea, which once a year they marry, the Turk had never prevailed against them nor never been able to besiege any place of theirs, to which he must have transported his armies by his gallies.

The Genoeses were also exceeding powerful by sea, and held many places in the East, and contended often with the Venetians for superiority, destroying each other in a long-continued sea war. Yea, the Genoeses were the most famous mercenaries of all Europe, both by sea and land for many years.

The French assisted themselves by land with the cross-bowers of Genoa against the English; namely, at the battel of Cressy the French had 12,000 cross-bowers. By sea also with their great ships, called the carrecks of Genoa, they always strengthened their fleets against the English. But after Mahomet the Second had taken Constantinople, they lost Caffa, and all Taurica Chersonesus, and the whole trade of the Euxine Sea. And although they sent many supplies by the Hellespont, yet having often felt the smart of the Turk's cannon, they began to slack their succours, and were soon after supplanted. Yet do the Venetians to this day well maintain their estate by their sea forces; and a great loss it is to the Christian commonwealth in general that they are less than they were; and a precipitate counsel it was of those Christian kings, their neighbours, when they joyned in league against them; seeing they then were, and they yet are, the strongest rampiers of Europe against the Turks.

But the Genoeses have now but a few gallies, being altogether de-
generate, and become merchants of money, and the Spanish king's
backers.

But all the states and kingdoms of the world have changed form
and policy.

The Empire itself, which gave light to all principalities like a
Pharoa, or high tower to all sea-men, is now sunk down to the level
of the soil . . . insomuch as it is now become the most confused estate
in the world, consisting of an Empire in title without territory, who
can ordain nothing of importance but by a Dyet, or Assembly of the
Estates of many free princes, ecclesiastical and temporal, in effect of
equal force, diverse in religion and faction; and of Free Cities and
Hanse towns, whom the princes do not more desire to command,
than they scorn to obey. Notwithstanding, being far less than they
were in number, and less in force and reputation; as they are not
greatly able to offend others, so they have enough to do (being seated
far asunder) to defend themselves. . . .

The Castilians in the meanwhile are grown great, and (by mistaking) esteemed the greatest; having by marriage, conquest, practice,
and purchase, devoured all the kingdoms within Spain, with Naples,
Sicily, Millain, and the Netherlands; and many places belonging to
the Empire, and the princes thereof, besides the Indies, East and
West, the islands of the West Ocean, and many places in Barbary,
Guinea, Congo, and elsewhere.

France hath also enlarged itself by the one-half, and reduced Normandy, Britany, Aquitaine, with all that the English had on that side
the sea, together with Langue dock, Foix, Arminach, Bierne, and
Dauphinie. For this kingdom of Great Britain, it hath had of His
Majesty a strong addition. The postern by which we were so often
heretofore entered and surprized is now made up; and we shall not
hereafter need the double face of Janus, to look north and south
at once.

But there's no estate grown in haste but that of the United Provinces, and especially in their sea forces, and by a contrary way to that
of France and Spain; the latter by invasion, the former by oppression.
For I myself may remember when one ship of Her Majesty's would
have made forty Hollanders strike sail and come to an anchor. They
did not then dispute *de Mari Libero,* but readily acknowledged the
English to be *Domini Maris Britannici.* That we are less powerful
than we were, I do hardly believe it; for, although we have not at this
time 135 ships belonging to the subject of 500 tons each ship, as it is
said we had in the twenty-fourth year of Queen Elizabeth; at which
time also, upon a general view and muster, there were found in England of able men fit to bear arms, 1,172,000, yet are our merchant
ships now far more warlike and better appointed than they were, and

51

the navy royal double as strong as it then was. For these were the ships of Her Majesty's navy at that time:

| | |
|---|---|
| 1. The *Triumph*. | 8. The *Revenge*. |
| 2. The *Elizabeth Jonas*. | 9. The *Hope*. |
| 3. The *White Bear*. | 10. The *Mary Rose*. |
| 4. The *Philip and Mary*. | 11. The *Dreadnought*. |
| 5. The *Bonadventure*. | 12. The *Minion*. |
| 6. The *Golden Lyon*. | 13. The *Swiftsure*. |
| 7. The *Victory*. | |

To which there have been added:—

| | |
|---|---|
| 14. The *Antilope*. | 20. The *Ayde*. |
| 15. The *Foresight*. | 21. The *Achates*. |
| 16. The *Swallow*. | 22. The *Falcon*. |
| 17. The *Handmaid*. | 23. The *Tyger*. |
| 18. The *Jennett*. | 24. The *Bull*. |
| 19. The *Bark of Bullein*. | |

We have not, therefore, less force than we had, the fashion, and furnishing of our ships considered, for there are in England at this time 400 sail of merchants, and fit for the wars, which the Spaniards would call gallions; to which we may add 200 sail of crumsters, or hoys, of Newcastle, which, each of them, will bear six Demi-culverins[2] and four Sakers,[3] needing no other addition of building than a slight spar deck fore and aft, as the seamen call it, which is a slight deck throughout. The 200 which may be chosen out of 400, by reason of their ready staying and turning, by reason of their windwardness, and by reason of their drawing of little water, they are of extream advantage near the shoar, and in all bays and rivers, to turn in and out. These, I say, alone, and well manned and well conducted, would trouble the greatest Prince in Europe to encounter them in our seas; for they stay and turn so readily, as ordering them into small squadrons, that three of them at once may give their broadside upon any one great ship, or upon any angle or side of an enemy's fleet, they shall be able to continue a perpetual volley of Demi-culverins without intermission, and either sink and slaughter the men, or utterly disorder any fleet of cross-sails with which they encounter.[4]

I say, then, if a vanguard be ordained of those hoyes, who will easily recover the wind of any other sort of ships, with a battle of 400 other warlike ships, and a Rear of thirty of His Majesty's ships to sustain, relieve, and countenance the rest (if God beat them not) I

2. A 9½-pounder of 30 cwt.
3. A 5½-pounder of 12½ cwt.
4. Presumably the vessels Raleigh speaks of were fore-and-aft rigged; and the "cross-sails" were square-rigged ships.

know not what strength can be gathered in all Europe to beat them. And if it be objected that the States can furnish a far greater number, I answer that His Majesty's 40 ships, added to 600 before named, are of incomparable greater force than all that Holland and Zealand can furnish for the wars. As also, that a greater number would breed the same confusion that was found in Xerxes' land army of seventeen hundred thousand soldiers; for there is a certain proportion, both by sea and land, beyond which the excess brings nothing but disorder and amazement.

Of these hoyes, carvils, or crumsters, (call them what you will) there was a notable experience made in the year 1574, in the river of Antwerp near Rumerswael, where the Admiral Boysott with his crumsters overthrew the Spanish fleet of great ships conducted by Julian Romero; so contrary to the expectation of Don Lewis, the great Commander and Lieutenant of the Netherlands for the King of Spain, as he came to the banks of Bergen to behold the slaughter of the Zealanders; but contrary to his expectation he beheld his comrades, some of them sunk, some of them thrust on the shoar, and most of the rest mastered and possessed by his enemies; insomuch as his great Captain, Romero, with great difficulty, some say in a skiff, some say by swimming, saved himself.

The like success had Captain Wrest of Zealand against the fleet which transported the Duke of Medina Celi, who was sent out of Spain by sea to govern the Netherlands, in place of the Duke of Alva, for with twelve crumsters or hoyes, of the first troop of 21 sail, he took all but three, and forced the second, being twelve great ships filled with 2,000 soldiers, to run under the Rammekins, being then in the Spaniard's possession.

But whence comes this dispute? Not from the increase of numbers, not because our neighbours breed more mariners than we do; nor from the greatness of their trade in all parts of the world. For the French creep into all corners of America and Africa as they do, and the Spaniards and Portugals employ more ships by many, (the fishing trade excepted) than the Netherlands do; but it comes from the detestable covetousness of such particular persons as have gotten licenses, and given way to the transportation of our English ordnance.

Here Raleigh goes on to complain of the manufacture and export from this country for foreign nations, declaring that unless Spain had had large quantities of our iron guns she could not have removed the brass pieces from her ports to arm the ships of 1588 with, and then goes on:—

Certainly the advantage which the English had by their bows and arrows in former times was never so great as we might now have had by our iron ordnance, if we had either kept it within the land, kept it from our enemies, or imparted it to our friends moderately. For as by the former we obtained many notable victories, and made ourselves masters of many parts of France, so by the latter we might have commanded the seas, and thereby the trade of the world itself. But we have now to our future prejudice, and how far to our prejudice I know not, forged hammers, and delivered them out of our hands, to break our own bones withal.

For the conclusion of this dispute there are five manifest causes of the upgrowing of the Hollanders and Zealanders.

The first is, the favour and assistance of Queen Elizabeth, and the King's Majesty, which the late worthy and famous Prince of Orange did always acknowledge, and in the year 1582, when I took my leave of him at Antwerp, after the return of the Earl of Leicester into England, and Monsieur's arrival there, when he delivered me his letters to Her Majesty, he prayed me to say to the Queen from him, *sub umbra alarum tuarum protegimur;* for certainly they had withered in the bud, and sunk in the beginning of their navigation, had not Her Majesty assisted them.

The second cause was the employing of their own people in their trades and fishing, and the entertainment of strangers to serve them in their armies by land.

The third, the fidelity of the House of Nassau, and their services done them, especially of their renowned Prince Maurice, now living.

The fourth, the withdrawing of the Duke of Parma twice into France, while in his absence he recovered those strong places of Friezland, Deventer, Zutphen, &c.

And the fifth, the embarguing and confiscation of their ships in Spain, which constrained them and gave them courage to trade by force with the East and West India, and in Africa, in which they employ 180 ships and 8,700 mariners.

The success of a counsel so contrary to their wisdom that gave it, as all the wit and all the force the Spaniards have, will hardly (if ever) recover the damage thereby received.

For to repair that ruin of the Hollander's trade into both Indies, the Spaniards did not only labour the truce; but the King was content to quit the sovereignty of the United Provinces, and to acknowledge them for free States, neither holding nor depending on the crown of Spain.

But be their estate what it will, let them not deceive themselves, in believing that they can make themselves masters of the sea. For certainly the shipping of England, with the great squadron of His Majesty's Navy Royal, are able, in despight of any Prince or State in Europe, to command the great and large fields of the ocean. But as I shall never think him a lover of this land, or of the King, that shall persuade His Majesty from embracing the amity of the States of the United Provinces (for His Majesty is no less safe by them than they invincible by him). So I would wish them (because after my duty to mine own soveraign, and the love of my country, I honour them most) that they remember and consider it, that seeing their passage and re-passage lies through the British seas; that there is no port in France, from Calais to Vlushing, that can receive their ships, that many times outward, by westerly winds, and ordinarily homeward, not only from the East Indies, but from the Streights and from Spain, all southerly winds (the breezes of our climate) thrust them of necessity into the King's ports, how much His Majesty's favour doth concern them: for if (as themselves confess in their last treaty of truce with the Spaniards) they subsist by their trade, the disturbance of their trade (which England only can disturb) will also disturb their subsistence. The rest I will omit, because I can never doubt either their gratitudes or their wisdoms.

For our Newcastle trade, from which I have digressed, I refer the reader to the author of the *Trades Increase,* a gentleman to me unknown, but so far as I can judge, he hath many things very considerable in that short treatise of his; yea, both considerable and praiseworthy; and, among the rest, the advice which he hath given for the maintenance of our hoyes and carvils of Newcastle, which may serve us (besides the breeding of mariners) for good ships of war, and of exceeding advantage. And certainly I cannot but admire why the imposition of 5s. should any way dishearten them, seeing there is not one company in England upon whose trade any new payments are laid but they on whom it is laid raise profit by it.

The silk-men, if they pay His Majesty 12d. upon a yard of sattin, they not only raise that 12d., but they impose 12d. or 2s. more, upon the subject. So they do upon all they sell, of what kind soever, as all other retailers do, of what quality or profession soever. And seeing all the maritime provinces of France and Flanders, all Holland, and Zealand, Embden, Breame, &c. cannot want[5] our Newcastle or our Welsh coals, the imposition cannot impoverish the transporter, but that the buyer must make payment accordingly. And if the imposition laid on those things whereof the kingdom hath no necessary use, as upon silks, velvets, gold and silver lace, cloath of gold and silver, cut works, cambricks and a world of other trumpery, doth in nothing hinder their vent here, but that they are more used than ever they were, to the utter impoverishing of the land in general, and of those popinjays that value themselves by their outsides, and by their player's coats. Certainly imposing upon coals, which other nations cannot want, can be no hindrance at all to the Newcastle men, but that they must raise it again upon the French and other nations, as those nations themselves do which fetch them from us with their own shipping.

For conclusion of this chapter, I say that it is exceeding lament-

5. i.e., "Cannot do without."

able, that for any respect in the world, seeing the preservation of the State and Monarchy doth surmount all other respects, strangers should be permitted to eat us out, by exporting and importing, both of our own commodities and those of foreign nations; for it is no wonder that we are overtopped in all the trades we have abroad and far off, seeing we have the grass cut under our feet, in our own fields and pastures at home.[6]

This general statement of the condition of shipping, both of war and commerce, and of the world's trade by sea, was written between 1609 and 1617, that is between forty-three and thirty-five years before the naval war between England and the United Provinces, which Raleigh foresaw but did not fear, broke out. We can see that even at the earlier date all the materials for naval war were present, and judging from what happened at the later date, we can but suppose that development in all directions ultimately conducive to naval war went on. The disputes relative to the sovereignty of the British seas, which spent themselves in the blasts and counter-blasts of literary champions in Charles the First's unfortunate reign, wanted not the sanction of preparation on the sovereign's part for the war to come. Little has been done towards elucidating the share which Charles' understanding of the naval conditions of the kingdom, and the want of understanding on the part of his opposing subjects, may have had in producing the civil war, but it seems to be certain that the chief part of the money question was a naval one, and that the superior classes of ships which Charles prepared and built had a most material effect on the course of the Dutch wars. In the first war the complaints of the Dutch admirals were unceasing as to the inferiority of the Dutch ships to those of the English.

But in any case it is certain that when the first Dutch war broke out in 1652, those two elements—a great sea-borne commerce, and sea-keeping war-ships—which I have spoken of as fundamental in naval war, were abundantly present on both sides. And so far as the sea-keeping element in the war-ships went, not only had it made great advances, but owing to the neighbourhood of the two states at war, and the confined theatre upon the stage of which the drama was played out, this sea-keeping quality was of less importance.

The struggle was for the mastery at sea, whether territorial conquest was or was not to follow success in this respect. As both sides had a large commerce, each was necessitated to protect its own in the first instance. What was its strength in peace was its weakness in

6. *An Abridgment of Sir Walter Raleigh's History of the World, &c.* 1702.

war, and naval force was necessary to prevent the enemy from taking advantage of such weakness. On the other hand, it would be a principal object for each state, after securing the safety of her own sea-borne commerce, to fall upon, to interrupt, and destroy that of her enemy, as being the part of the nation most readily got at, and as counting double advantage in all cases of capture. The mere destruction of a merchant ship was a loss to her owning state, but no gain to the capturing state. The capture of a merchant ship was equally a loss to the owning state, but it was a similar and direct gain to the capturing state.

This great double object of preserving your own sea-borne commerce and destroying that of the enemy might be aimed at directly or indirectly. The naval force might be divided, one half to guard the State's commerce and protect it from the attacks of the enemy, the other half to break through the commerce-guard of the enemy and attack that which had been guarded. In this case there would be battles between the forces which were guarding and the forces which were attacking. There would be two wars going on side by side. The English, to put the case into a concrete and practical form, would be found attacking the Dutch force which was guarding Dutch commerce, and the Dutch would be found attacking the English force which was guarding English commerce.

But the two separate plans of war might be brought together in this way:—that the whole English force might be employed to see its commerce into what were assumed to be safe waters, free from the incursions of the enemy, and might then turn upon the whole Dutch force which had been endeavouring to do the same for its own commerce. Or the plan might be carried out *vice versâ*.

Otherwise, the objects of preserving our own commerce and destroying that of the enemy might be attained indirectly. If one power could beat the other power off the sea and into his ports—that is, considering war-ships only—it is obvious that the commerce of the conquering state would proceed and flourish, and that that of the conquered state would disappear. There might then be simply a series of great battles at sea, in which the element of merchant ships was absent, one fleet attacking the other in the hope of mastering it merely as a means to an end; the end being a free sea for the commerce of the winner, and the power of capturing, destroying, or simply hindering the flow of the commerce of the loser.

There may be all these varieties in the struggle for the command of the sea. That struggle is a phase or condition of naval warfare, and when the command of the sea is achieved by one of the combatants a new phase sets in, as then one side will try to regain a position which it has lost, and the other side will be bent on holding the position it has gained.

We are now, however, only concerned with the previous phase, the struggle for the command of the sea; and it is nowhere so well offered for investigation and study as in the three great naval wars between the English and the Dutch, beginning in 1652, 1665, and 1672. We have seen that descents on the coast of the enemy, which formed the staple of that war by water which, I think, cannot be classed as naval war, became less and less the staple up to dates when the military seamen quoted were able to lay it down that such descents were preventible by sea, but not in any other way. We must not lose sight of this fact on entering upon the principles and practice which governed the three wars mentioned above.

A principal source of Dutch wealth was her fisheries, chiefly carried on off the north-eastern coasts of Scotland. Charles I. had successfully enforced British rights over these waters, and the non-payment of the £30,000 annually, which had been fixed by Charles as license dues, was, in fact, one of the causes of the war. In order to avoid the troubles of search and other interruptions at the hands of the English, a great part of the Dutch commerce, both outward and homeward, passed up north by the Shetland Islands. Other parts came up the Channel towards the Straits of Dover. When the negociations in London finally fell through early in July 1652, the points of attack on the Dutch at once open to England, were the great herring fleet in the Moray Firth; the homeward-bound ships passing Shetland; and the commerce up Channel. Accordingly the very first move on the part of the English was the dispatch of Blake at the head of sixty-six or sixty-eight sail to the North for the purpose of capturing or destroying the Dutch herring fleet, understood to be somewhere off the Moray Firth under convoy and guard of Dutch war-ships. The next open action was the despatch of Sir George Ayscue to Plymouth; there to complete a fleet and to block the Channel against the homeward-bound Dutch merchant ships, and to guard our own trade.

Ayscue had not long returned from the reduction of the Island of Barbadoes, one of the many acts of reprisal which had been going on between the two nations—and which were to all intents and purposes acts of war—for a long time previous to its formal declaration. On the declaration of war, Ayscue was lying with twenty-one sail in the Downs, and the Dutch Ambassadors quitting the Thames on the final failure of the negotiations, fell in, off the Schelde, with Tromp, at the head of seventy-nine sail, and informing him of the general naval condition of England, particularly recommended to his notice the twenty-one sail that were then lying in the Downs.[7] Tromp (Martin, the father of Cornelius) proceeded immediately to act on the hints given, but owing to the occurrence of calms was unable to reach the Downs in time to effect a surprise, and thereupon bore away North after Blake.

Blake on his side sighted the Dutch fleet of herring busses off Buchan Ness (where the figure 1 is placed on the chart), under the guard of twelve or thirteen war-ships, carrying from twenty to thirty guns each. He detached twenty ships of his van to attack them, and after a fight, lasting three hours, about 100 of the busses were taken, two sunk, and twelve war-ships made prizes of. The remainder of the Dutch fled to their own ports. Blake kept some of the busses with him, sent three with the wounded to Inverness, but after unloading them, sent the greater part of the captured busses to Holland with the released prisoners. He then proceeded North to the neighbourhood of Foula and Fair Islands, between the Orkneys and Shetland Islands, for the purpose of carrying out the second part of his orders, the interception of the Dutch merchant ships homeward-bound from the West Indies.

There (see 2 on the chart), on the 26th of July, Tromp sighted him, and both sides prepared for battle, when a gale of wind springing up from the southward and ending at N.N.W., shattered and dispersed Tromp's fleet during the night, while Blake's ships, getting to leeward of the Shetland Islands, remained comparatively unharmed. Tromp with part of his fleet fell back to the Meuse, again followed, but hardly pursued, by Blake. The remainder of Tromp's ships, except two war-ships that were wrecked on the rocks of Shetland, and three fire-ships that appear to have foundered, got safely into the Vlie and the Texel in the beginning of September.

In the meantime, a second Dutch fleet had been fitting out in the Texel under the command of De Ruiter. By August 1st, it had grown to 15 sail and 2 fire-ships; and then later, with a force made up to 22 sail and 4 fire-ships, De Ruiter put to sea and sailed towards the Straits of Dover. The object was to pass to the southward, gathering

7. The authorities on which I chiefly rely for this chapter are *The Life of Cornelius Van Tromp,* published in 1697, in London; and *Columna Rostrata,* by Samuel Colliber, the second edition published in London in 1739. The second work constantly refers to the first, and both are works largely used by subsequent historians whose accounts I have referred to for clearing up discrepancies, of which there are a good many, especially as to dates. The dates I give are O. S.

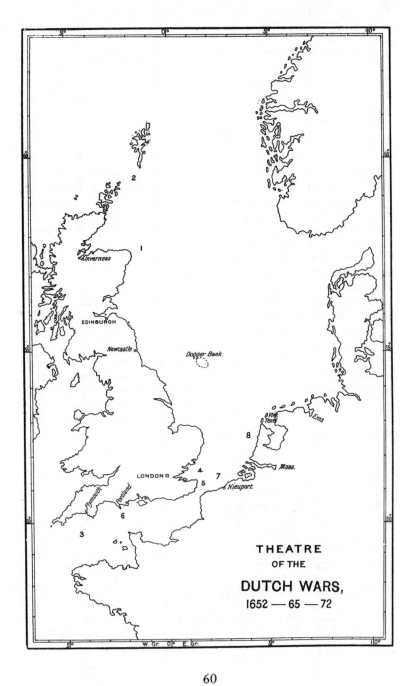

THEATRE
OF THE

**DUTCH WARS,**
1652 — 65 — 72

the outward-bound trade together eastward of the Straits of Dover, and then to convoy them down Channel, and so far to the westward as to place them presumably beyond danger of attack from the British ships. De Ruiter, accordingly, got as far as Gravelines by the 10th of August, where he was joined by the convoy of 50 merchant ships and a reinforcement of 8 war-ships. He proceeded with great caution and with abundant scouts and look-outs, no doubt supposing that he might at any moment be met by the fleet of Ayscue, whom Tromp had failed to get hold of in the Downs.

On the 16th of August the Dutch had got as far as the longitude of Plymouth, but well to the southward towards the French coast; and there, sure enough, was the expected British fleet of 40 sail, 12 of them of great size, 2 being of 60, and 8 of from 36 to 40 guns, with 5 fire-ships. It is claimed for De Ruiter that he had but 30 ships of war, of which only two carried as many as 40 guns, and the rest not more than 30 each. He, too, was hampered with the convoy, now grown to 60 merchant ships.[8]

There was a heavy engagement, which was only put an end to by the approach of night, and it was disputed as to the side on which the victory lay. But the results remained clear enough. The fight took place somewhere about the position marked by the figure 3 on the chart. Ayscue after it, fell back to Plymouth, while De Ruiter next day, the 17th of August, was able to send his merchant ships away on their voyage under convoy of two men-of-war only, and he also followed up the English with some intention of attacking them in Plymouth Sound itself; but, having got within a couple of miles of the Start, a gale drove him off, and caused the abandonment of the idea.

De Ruiter kept well to the westward for a week or two, having information of Blake's return to the south and of his appearance in great strength to the eastward in the Channel. He and Penn were, in fact, preying heavily on the Dutch homeward-bound merchant ships, of which the one brought in eleven and the other six, all ships of great value, and which De Ruiter had obviously proved powerless to protect. He presently made his way in safety to the Straits of Dover, and between Dunkirk and Nieuport came under the command of De Witt, who joined him with the refitted and repaired fleet of Tromp, now forty-five sail strong.

---

8. *Columna Rostrata* admits the heavier British ships, but makes the forces more numerically equal, and claims that twenty merchant ships were capable of fighting, and did fight.

When we review the operations to this point, we can easily separate their distinguishing features. At the first moment of the war the English assumed the attacking, and the Dutch the defending, position. It may perhaps be said that this came about chiefly because, if the idea of cross-raiding upon territory had now passed away as one impracticable in this more advanced stage of naval war, the Dutch had more to defend in the way of sea-borne commerce than the English had. But something may also be said on the side of a belief that the rules of naval war, the boundaries of the probable and improbable, or even of the possible and impossible, were not traced, but were only in process of being traced.

When Blake passed north with a great fleet to do that which did not of itself require a great fleet, he left, as we have seen, Ayscue in the Downs with quite a small force—only seven war-ships—exposed to annihilation by the whole naval power of Holland. It would have been a bad beginning for the war on the English side had there been the destruction of Ayscue, and even an indecisive action afterwards between Tromp and Blake; so that it seems probable that the English took up the attitude of attack, more from a sort of eagerness to damage the Dutch, than to conduct the war to a speedy conclusion. For supposing that England had, at the outset, concentrated her whole strength and thrown it upon Tromp, she would, if then successful, have had everything else in her own hands.

But we see her only solicitous to injure the commerce and the property of Holland at sea. Ayscue, equally with Blake, left all exposed when he passed to Plymouth, leaving the Dutch fleet behind him; and all that remains pretty certain is that the idea of a Dutch raid on the Thames or on any of the numerous ports and harbours left exposed by the departure of Blake north, and of Ayscue west, could have had hardly any place in the minds of the statesmen or commanders of the time.

The Dutch took up, just at the first moment, the rôle of an attacking force; but when the operation against the Downs squadron was abandoned, the Dutch attitude became wholly defensive. Tromp's voyage to the North was only secondarily the attack on Blake's fleet; primarily it was an attempt to protect the herring fleet and then the north-about homeward commerce. If, in process of carrying out these objects, Blake's fleet was attacked, it did not follow that it would have been so dealt with had there been no fishery and no commerce to defend. The action of De Ruiter's fleet was more obviously defensive. It centred wholly round the necessity for protecting and convoying outwards the sixty merchant ships, and for drawing together and protecting homewards the up-channel trade. Ayscue's attitude may perhaps have been in some respects defensive, as guarding a possible homeward-bound trade, but the main object was clearly the attack on the Dutch trade, which was foiled by the strength of the defending force under De Ruiter.

The conclusion of this first phase of the war left De Witt with the Dutch force concentrated near Gravelines, but reduced in numbers, owing to so many ships having required repair and refit after the battle with Ayscue. The English, at the same time, were concentrated about the Thames, and expecting still greater concentration by the junction of Ayscue from the west. De Witt determined, against the advice of his Council, to attack with his sixty-four sail, Blake with sixty-eight; that is to say, the Dutch intended to reverse the former case, and not only to resume the offensive, but to make the attack directly on the war force of the enemy, with the view of the ulterior advantages which a victory would give them.

The battle took place near the Kentish Knock, where the figure 4 appears on the chart, on September 28th, and the Dutch, fighting till night, were worsted and began to think of retreat. Blake's reinforcement then, by sixteen sail under Ayscue, confirmed the intention, and the Dutch retired to Helvoetsluys, but only pursued for a part of the way by the English.

Here we may say that the whole naval power of each nation was brought to bear on the one spot, in order to decide by one supreme effort, which was to remain in command of the sea, and which was henceforth to accept the defensive attitude that was alone available. The result of the battle produced a result which might be anticipated. The Dutch fell back on defensively protecting their commerce, and Martin Tromp in November put to sea with 73 sail guarding a convoy of 300 outward-bound merchant ships.

The English were no longer concentrated. Blake had, for the most part, separated his fleet; 20 of his ships he had detached to convoy a fleet of colliers to Newcastle; 12 others had gone to Plymouth—the historian does not say why, but probably for the double purpose of attacking the enemy's passing commerce at the entrance of the channel, and defending our own—12 more had gone up the Thames to repair and refit. When Tromp put to sea, Blake was in the Downs with only thirty-seven sail besides tenders, and he was therefore open to the destruction which Tromp, hearing of his situation, proposed to inflict on him.

The battle took place on November 20th, near where the figure 5 is placed on the chart, and the English, as might have been expected, were worsted. The fight raged with a fury which only these Anglo-Dutch battles can parallel, from one in the afternoon till night, after which Blake retired up the Thames and left Tromp for the moment master of the sea. He thereupon made some captures of merchant ships, and landed some men in Kent on a cattle-raiding expedition. The party had, however, to leave behind them the greater part of the cattle they had seized, and to fly to their boats with the loss of 100 prisoners.

But as a matter of course Tromp had been successful in his defensive business, and the whole of his immense convoy passed down and out of the channel in safety. He himself followed as far as Ile de Rhé, where, such had been the action of the English upon the Dutch trade, 250 merchant ships had congregated, waiting till a naval force strong enough to protect them up Channel should arrive and release them. Tromp stayed there seven days and then sailed with his convoy for the Channel.[9]

But the command of the sea, and the consequent freedom of the sea to the victorious power, is not gained by a single battle in which strategical failure has been the cause of defeat. On the 18th of February 1653 (old style) Tromp found Blake watching for him off Portland at the head of a fleet of 66 sail. The Dutch admit that they had 70 sail of war-ships; the English aver that they had 80; but they were necessarily much hampered by the presence of the 250 sail of merchant ships. There followed a violent and bloody fight which lasted three days, passing gradually up Channel from the spot marked with the figure 6 on the chart. There were heavy losses on both sides; ships were taken and retaken, and numbers of the merchant ships fell victims in their endeavours to get away. The Dutch confessed to a loss of 24 of these ships; the English claimed to have captured 40. The Dutch further admitted that 4 war-ships were captured and carried to Plymouth and Dover; that 3 more were sunk, and 1 blown up. The Dutch on their side claimed to have taken or sunk six or seven men-of-war, but the English only confessed to one, which, being disabled, they sank themselves. But they allowed that one ship was actually taken, though afterwards recovered.

On the evening of the third day Blake retired to the English coast, leaving Tromp to gather together his scattered forces off Dunkirk, whence they separated into their ports.

9. Burchett says that it was on the voyage to the Ile de Rhé that he hoisted the traditional broom.

Negociations for peace were now set up, but neither side was yet ready for it, and the struggle for the command of the sea went on. The result of the war had not been such as to alter the original attitudes of the combatants. It was indeed otherwise; for whereas the attitude of attack taken up by the English had, as I have already observed, been displayed indirectly upon the enemy's commerce, and not directly on his war ships, so that the battles came about in English waters as a consequence of the Dutch offering protection to their passing convoys, it was now proposed to make a direct attack on the enemy on his own coasts.

Tromp, renewing the bitter complaints as to the inferiority of the Dutch ships, was directed notwithstanding, to convoy 200 merchant ships, bound for France and Spain, to the north of Scotland, and to convoy back the homeward trade assembled in those waters.

Dean and Monk, with Penn and Lawson, being at the head of a fleet which, according to the Dutch, numbered 105 sail, including 26 new frigates, and carrying 2,840 guns, manned by 16,269 men, heard of these orders, and proposed to attack Tromp, or at least, to prevent his getting away from the Texel without a battle. But he was beforehand with them. He got clear away; took his convoy safe, and though he missed the homeward trade, those ships, to the number of 300, arrived safely in their ports without seeing an enemy. This was towards the end of May 1653.

But Tromp had run great risks. While he was in the Texel with the major part of his fleet, a portion was also in Zealand, in the Maas or the Schelde. Dean and Monk's design was to prevent the junction, but though they were late for that purpose they were, on May 15th, actually within five miles of Tromp and his convoy without seeing them. The English captured or destroyed a good many fishing and other vessels on the coast, and even went so far as to land a few men, but with no result. They claimed, chiefly, to have kept the whole coast in a state of alarm.

When Tromp returned, he was reinforced by seventeen sail and a fire-ship, and hearing that a squadron of eight sail and eight merchant ships was in the Downs (it was the squadron of Commodore Bodley from the Mediterranean), it was determined to surround and attack them there, Tromp approaching from the northward and De Witt from the southward. Monk and Dean were at this time in Yarmouth Roads, at the head of the bulk of the English fleet. Bodley's squadron had news of the Dutch approach, and got way into the Thames; Monk had also news, and put to sea after Tromp. The Dutch failing in their primary object, captured a few merchant ships which had got in shore under cover of the forts of Dover and Deal; but though fire was exchanged between the forts and the ships, that was more by way of bravado and insult than of systematic attack, for ships which got close under Dover Castle escaped capture.

Monk and Dean, at the head of some ninety-five sail and five fire-ships, came up with Tromp, now commanding some ninety-eight sail and six fire-ships, in the neighbourhood of Nieuport, and a general action ensued, beginning about 11 A.M. on June 3rd, and lasting till night. Dean was killed during the first day's battle. The fight was renewed next day, June 4th, and the Dutch, thoroughly beaten in the end, retired behind the shoals between Ostend and Sluis, then called the Wielings. The whereabouts of the action is shown by the figure 7 on the chart.

It was after this battle that Vice-Admiral De Witt made his celebrated declaration before the Assembly of the States General:— "Why should I keep any longer silence? I am here before my sovereigns, and am free to speak; and I can say that the English are at present masters both of us and of the seas."

These operations, first the appearance of the Dutch on the English coasts, and now the appearance of the English on the Dutch coasts, were clearly parts of a direct contest for the command of the sea, resulting in its being left, at least for a time, in the hands of the English. The effect of such command was, in the words of the Dutch historian, that the English "held the coasts of Holland as 'twere besieged, after they had stopt up (by blockade) the mouth of the Texel, which obliged the States, to prevent any descent from them, to post some troops on the isles and on the coasts. During which distress, three ships returning from the East Indies richly laden, unfortunately fell into the hands of the English, as did likewise two others coming from Portugal, and three more from Swedeland, whereof two were burnt and the rest taken. And towards the Straits of Callis Captain Wight likewise was taken, with four ships laden with salt." [10]

But the Dutch, though conquered, were not subdued, and were not yet prepared to wholly abandon the struggle for the command of the sea. They moved heaven and earth to re-fit and re-complete their fleet; but the trouble was that, as the 80 or 90 sail under

---

10. *Life of Cornelius Tromp*, p. 131. *Columna Rostrata* says the English took twenty rich ships at the mouth of the Texel, and then the Baltic and the East India ships dared not sail.

Tromp were in the Southern Zealand ports, and the 27 sail un- der De Witt were in the Texel to the northward, while the great, and so far victorious, English fleet lay between and ready to fall on that part of the Dutch force which first put to sea, there was much doubt whether the Dutch could ever draw together in sufficient force at the same time and place to face the enemy.

Nevertheless Tromp put to sea on July 27th with his 80 odd ships, with the intention of bringing on a very partial action with the 106 sail under Monk, Penn, and Lawson. The hostile fleets sighted each other off Egmond, twenty miles south of the Texel, on the 29th July, and Tromp stood away to W.S.W. to draw the English after him and to free De Witt. The engagement was more general than Tromp intended, but when night put a pause to the fighting, he wrote not altogether hopelessly of the ultimate result, if only the squadron under De Witt could get out and join him.

The engagement was very partially renewed on the morning of the 30th of July, on account of the heavy weather; but Tromp's strategy had succeeded so well that De Witt had crawled out of the Texel about midnight on the night before, and Tromp began to see his ships approaching about noon, and by 5 in the afternoon the two fleets had formed a junction and turned to seek the enemy once more.

There was a tremendous encounter on the 1st August near about where the figure 8 is placed on the chart, which lasted all day, and the veteran leader, Tromp, being killed, fortune turned finally and decidedly against the Dutch, and they made for the shelter of their ports. They acknowledged to a loss of 9 ships, taken or burnt, of 500 men killed and 700 wounded. But the English claimed that the Dutch loss was between 20 and 30 men-of-war, burnt or sunk, and between 5,000 and 6,000 men; while admitting their own loss to be two ships burnt, 400 men killed or drowned, and 700 wounded; no less than 8 captains being amongst the former, and 5 amongst the latter. But the English made no captures, and were themselves not in a condition to keep the sea.

As a consequence of the undoubted fact that it became necessary for the English to return to their own ports, the Dutch claimed the accomplishment of their design to free their ports from blockade, and next month De Witt, now in supreme command, proved his case by escorting a considerable convoy towards the Sound, and conducting back a similarly large fleet of merchant ships into the Texel towards the end of October. But the Dutch carried bravado rather too far; for, determining to keep outside their ports, their fleet was met at anchor off the coast by a furious three days' gale, which shattered the Dutch and forced the English into their harbours, so that all thought of a further struggle was abandoned.

Then too, political necessities caused Cromwell to listen more favourably to the Dutch proposals for peace; and a final treaty was signed in April 1654. The Dutch got easier terms than had before been entertained. They were not now called on to admit the right of search; to open free trade in the Schelde, to limit the number of their war-ships, or to renew the license dues for their fishery; but they agreed to admit the English dominion of the seas, that is, of the British seas, by striking to the English flag; to accept the Parliament's Navigation Act, and to promise other reparations and acts which had not to do with the naval aspect of the question.

The English claimed, as the result of this war, which had lasted just one year and eleven months, that they had been victorious in five general actions, and had made 1,700 prizes valued at £6,000,000 sterling; while they did not allow that Holland had made one quarter of their captures, either in number or value.

But what concerns us here is not so much the facts of the war as the principles which underlay the action taken, and the practical issues which such principles bring to light.

In the first place, the war was wholly naval, wholly on the water, and yet brought Holland to her knees almost as effectually as an invasion could have done; and yet at nothing like the cost to the English, either in blood or treasure, which an invasion would have entailed. This is strikingly brought to mind by recalling that the value of the captures made in two years or so (for they had begun before war was formally declared) came to about twice the whole revenue of the country for the same period.

Then we see that it was probably commerce which kept it as a naval war, and that in the early stages, commerce, its protection over defined trade routes, and its attack at suitable points, governed almost absolutely the movements of the fleets of both nations. But as the war went on, and doubtless, we may say, became more understood, we have greater concentrations of force and more direct attempts to master the force. Because the Dutch trade must be mainly conducted past the British coasts, the English fleets are found there, and the battles take place there. But as the struggle develops and, I believe we may say, is better comprehended, the attack by the power which has slowly been gaining, is made indirectly on commerce by successful direct attacks upon the enemy's fleet near his own coasts.

The vast concentrations of naval force merely for naval operations were not to be found in previous wars. They were a feature of all the Dutch wars, but in later wars were more the exception than the rule. The broad reasons for such concentrations have been shown with sufficient clearness by the course of the narrative, but there are some inner causes which will require future treatment. For the present we shall probably do well to consider them as arising directly from the necessities of a struggle for the command of the sea, and to observe how very small a share the attack upon territory occupies while this great struggle is going on.

# CHAPTER THREE

I N THE FIRST Dutch war, the leading events of which were sketched in my last chapter, we had an excellent example of the struggle for the command of the sea, carried on between two maritime powers of not very unequal naval force, but one of which, Holland, appeared to be much weaker on the sea because of her great dependence on sea-borne commerce, and the necessity she was under of protecting it.

This defensive attitude, which she must latterly have known to be a weak one, was forced upon her in a war carried on at sea, by the necessities of her national life, unless she were possessed of sufficient naval force to have defended her commerce by one part of it, and to have directly attacked the forces of her enemy with the other part of it. But not having such a sufficiency of naval force, or at any rate acting as though she had not, she suffered heavily in the loss of ships and cargoes, and disproportionately with the English loss in that way. I have not had means of comparing the actual amount of the sea-borne commerce of Holland and of Great Britain during the period of the war, but I think we may infer from its transactions, that Great Britain had not nearly so much property on the water as Holland had, and was consequently not nearly so much hampered by the necessity of protecting it as Holland was, and that we may fairly argue that the greater success on our side was as much due to the weakness of Holland's naval position, on account of her greater commerce, as it was to our greater naval force.

At least we may say of the first Dutch war, that it was, on a very extended scale, that sort of "bare action at sea," of which we have seen Sir William Monson speak somewhat slightingly at an earlier date. Yet the Dutch themselves admitted that they were brought to greater straits by this twenty-three months of sea war than by the

70

eighty years of land war which they carried on against the Crown of Spain.[1] But we shall see presently that just as the Spanish contest taught us what the nature of naval war really was, and started us, as it were, on the new footing when we came to take up a new war, so this first Dutch war confirmed the belief, hinted at by Monson and Raleigh, that a great struggle may begin and end on the sea; and went a step further in establishing rules of naval warfare.

I am not concerned in this treatise to go much into the causes of the wars I use for illustrations, and I shall pass over those which led to the second Dutch war. It was the practice in those days to begin early in the way of what men were pleased to call reprisals; and long before the formal declaration of war by the Dutch in January, and by the English in March 1665,[2] there had been covert attacks going on between the two nations, both on territory and shipping. In the matter of shipping, the most notable "reprisal" was the attack by Sir T. Allen, with eight or nine men-of-war on some forty Dutch merchant ships off Cadiz, which were under convoy of four war-ships commanded by Commodore Brackel; several merchant ships were taken or sunk, and the Dutch commodore was killed. This was on the 29th December 1664, consequently before the actual declaration of war. A great seizure was also made of 130 merchant ships from Bordeaux, but many of them were reclaimed by France and released as not being good prize.

But this indication of how the war would run was sufficient, with other causes, to determine the Dutch in making a great change in their method of carrying it on. They had laid to heart the lesson of the former war, and now saw the impossibility of continuing the struggle for the command of the sea, which was to be done by means of attack, and attempting to protect a great commerce, which was a defensive operation, at the same time. The case was this with them. If they could muster strength enough to make a direct attack on the British fleet, then that fleet could not afford to separate heavy detachments from it for the purpose of attacking commerce, or in fact for any other purpose, the danger of such detachments having been clearly shown by the battle of November 20th, 1652, between Blake and Tromp. They had no hopes of producing a force consid-erable enough to make this attack, if part of it was to be dissipated in defensive duties which would not be required to any extent if the

1. *Columna Rostrata*, p. 139.
2. *Columna Rostrata* says February, but the *Life of Cornelius Tromp* says March 14/4.

71

general naval forces of the British could be overcome, and the command of the sea in the hands of the Dutch thereby established. There was another thing to be said. The men who were employed in carrying on a commerce certain to disappear if it could not be protected, would be uselessly employed in the Mercantile Marine if the War Marine lacked power to maintain its superiority at sea. They were at the same time much wanted to complete the complement of the numbers of ships which must be fitted out if the war was to be conducted with any hopes of success. The cessation of commerce and trade for a time might be a heavy blow to the United Provinces, but at least the enemy was not directly benefited as he would be if, as in the last war, he made such very numerous and rich captures at sea. If the States began the war by accepting and facing a loss, it at least left their hands more free to engage in the direct struggle for victory.

This reasoning determined the action of the States General. An ordinance was issued absolutely "prohibiting all subjects of the United Provinces to stir out of their ports upon pain of confiscation of their ships and merchandises." They likewise ordered that the fisheries of all kinds should be put a stop to, and the more certainly to secure obedience, they forbade the importation of herrings and other salt fish.[3]

This act was no doubt an admission of inferiority, but not a submission to the superior force.

In my first chapter I drew attention to the prohibition of the West Indian commerce for one year by the King of Spain. Anticipating, as I shall constantly do for the sake of illustrating principles, I here note how Prussia, in 1870, prohibited her merchant ships all over the world from putting to sea, lest they should fall into the hands of France. In these two cases, the nations giving up their sea commerce for the time were simply doing what they could not help. Neither Spain nor Prussia had the power to protect their commerce, and they had the choice of two evils when the choice was plain. It was better that their commerce should suffer a pause than that it should simply fall into the hands of the enemy and enrich him.

The case was different with Holland. She dropped her commerce for a time, not because she could not hope to protect it, but because she could not make a struggle for the command of the sea, and protect her commerce at the same time. She was like a tigress pausing

3. *Life of Cornelius Tromp*, p. 261. *Columna Rostrata*, p. 213.

in her spring and gathering all her forces together to make it with effect.

But though commerce was thus strictly prohibited, there were a large number of Dutch ships on their way home when the order was given, and I think, too, that it is not impossible that the order was not completely obeyed. The Government having, by the ordinance, shaken themselves clear, as it were, from all responsibility in the protection of merchant ships, was the less likely to have interfered with the more venturous of the merchants. Thus, though in this war the protection of commerce ceases to occupy the prominent place it took up in the first war, and the Dutch fleets no longer hamper themselves with great strings of vessels neither very able nor very willing to offer defence, yet commerce still remains to some extent an object of attack to the English, and is, in cases, defended by the Dutch war-ships.

But that the English were somewhat of the same mind as the Dutch may be inferred from Pepys' note of January 15th, 1664–5. He records Sir G. Ayscue declaring in Council, that "the war and trade could not be supported together."[4]

The English, in consequence of false information respecting the Dutch movements, hurried their fleet to sea while still short of stores, provisions, and men. James, Duke of York, having Sir William Penn on board him as his Captain of the Fleet, with Prince Rupert and the Earl of Sandwich as his vice and rear-admirals, appeared off the Texel on the 24th April. His fleet consisted of 109 "men-of-war and frigates," and 28 fire-ships and ketches, manned by 21,000 men. Immediate captures followed of several merchant ships, which the Dutch made no effort to prevent. Even had the Dutch been ready for sea, which they were not, they were really paralysed by the position of the English fleet. It was understood in England that James had "used all possible means to provoke the Dutch to a battle,"[5] but this was impossible, because of the divided state of the Dutch fleet, and the concentrated state of the English fleet. Thirty-one of the Dutch were in Zealand in the Maas and the Schelde, the remainder were in Holland and Friesland, in the Texel and the Vlie. The English fleet off the Texel was lying across them all, and threatening any that put to sea with destruction.

But what the strategy of the English prevented, the conditions of

4. Quoted in G. Penn's *Life of Penn*, vol. ii., p. 312.
5. Ibid., p. 325.

weather and the incomplete state of the ships allowed. A heavy gale drove the whole of the English forces off the coast, and the damages received, as well as the necessity of completing the fleet compelled a return to an anchorage off Harwich, where the store-ships and victuallers made their appearance.

Thus left free, the Zealand part of the fleet put to sea and formed a junction with the Holland and Friesland parts from the Vlie and the Texel, on May 12th. The fleet so assembled, consisted of 103 "men-of-war," 7 yachts, 11 fire-ships, and 12 galliots, carrying 4,869 guns, and manned with 21,631 men.[6] The whole were under the command of Admiral Opdam, and were gathered into seven squadrons, each under its admiral. They made sail across the North Sea to seek the English fleet in its own waters.

The Dutch made a great prize as they neared our shores, capturing nine rich Hamburgh ships, valued at between £200,000 and £300,000, which were under convoy of but one frigate of forty-four guns.[7]

James, in his anchorage off Harwich, still half manned and busy with his victuallers and store-ships, heard of the sailing of the Dutch and of their capture of the Hamburgh ships. Fearing to be caught amongst the shoals about Harwich, and to be thereby powerless to avert the mischief which might ensue, James proceeded, with his victuallers and store-ships, to the more open anchorage of Sole, or Southwold, Bay. Here he brought up on June 1st in the early morning, about five miles off shore. The storing and victualling went on, and also by perhaps a happy fortune, the supply of men arrived in the nick of time.[8] The same afternoon the Dutch were seen eighteen miles E.S.E. The victuallers were sent to Harwich, and the fleet shifted further out, want of wind compelling a second anchorage, which was finally quitted at 10 o'clock at night. All next day, June 2nd,[9] the fleets manœuvred in sight of each other, but it was not till about half-past three on the morning of June 3rd that fire was opened.

The fleets met off Lowestoft, and the battle lasted the whole day, turning, as night approached, into a retreat by the Dutch and a pur-

6. *Life of Cornelius Tromp*, p. 268.
7. The *Good Hope. Life of Penn*, vol. ii., p. 326.
8. *Life of Penn*, vol. ii., p. 323.
9. There is often the difficulty of one day in the dates, the civil day beginning at midnight and the nautical day at noon; so that one writer may call the forenoon of a day June 2nd and another June 3rd, according as he used civil or nautical time.

suit by the English. During the chase many prizes were taken by the English, but the pursuit was slackened in the night by the mysterious interference of one of the Duke's suite while he slept; and though the chase was continued during daylight of the 4th, the Dutch were able to anchor amongst the shoals off the Texel, where the English dared not follow for want of knowledge of the locality, without further molestation. James saw the Hollanders pass into the Texel, and then returned to England to repair and refit.

The English in this battle claimed to have captured eighteen sail of the Dutch—though some were recovered by them—to have sunk fourteen, and to have burnt others. The Dutch allowed that nine ships were taken, one blown up,[10] seven or eight burnt. The English lost the Earl of Marlborough and Admiral Sampson killed, and Lawson mortally wounded; and 250 others killed, with 340 wounded; and the Dutch carried off a 46-gun ship, the *Charity*.

In this first phase of the war we have the complete abandonment of every other idea but a direct and equal struggle for the command of the sea. The English, by their promptitude in getting to sea, were able to repeat the strategy of the close of the former war, and by placing themselves in force off the Texel, they lay between the Zealand and Holland branches of the fleet, and prevented their junction. We know not how things might have progressed had the weather permitted the Duke of York to maintain the position; nor can we say what might have taken place had the Dutch been able to put to sea earlier, and to have followed up the English with greater speed than they did, so as to have attacked them in their disordered state. As it was, we simply see complete concentration of the naval power of each nation, with a clear conviction on both sides that until one or other fleet has proved victorious, the war can fall into no other phases.

Master of the sea for the time, but apparently not so wholly recovered, or ready, as to be able to transfer the war to the Dutch coast and keep it there, the Earl of Sandwich, now at the head of the English fleet, proceeded to undertake two enterprizes which the victory had left him free to do. In the matter of the reprisals before the war actually began, Sir Robert Holms had attacked and reduced several settlements of the Dutch on the West African coast, had then passed over to New Netherlands (now New York), and had brought

---

10. Admiral Opdam's ship, with the admiral in her. The locality of the battle is shown by the figure 1 in the chart on p. 84.

that province into subjection. But De Ruiter had followed on his heels, re-capturing to a great extent after him, and making many captures of English merchant ships in the West Indies.

From this expedition De Ruiter was now returning round the North of Scotland, and Sandwich, hearing of it, made a push towards the Dutch coast to intercept him, but failed; for De Ruiter, by keeping far to the northward, and touching at Bergen, in Norway, got safe into the Ems. This was the first attempt which Sandwich was free to make in overwhelming force, so that had he succeeded in meeting De Ruiter's small squadron,[11] he would have made short work of it; for he had with him some seventy sail.[12] The second attempt was what the Dutch became open to so soon as they had been forced into their own harbours.

Sandwich got news that some seventy sail of Dutch merchant ships, including the Turkey fleet and ten East India ships, had taken refuge at Bergen. Still being free from fear of molestation by a superior fleet, he detached Sir John Tiddiman with twelve or fourteen men-of-war and three fire-ships to attack them. But the Dutch had made good use of the time at their disposal to prepare a defence, and partly by mooring the heaviest ships so as to keep their guns bearing, and partly by landing guns and erecting temporary works, they had made their position a very strong one. So that Tiddiman's attack, much hindered as it was by the wind, which kept him from advancing and blinded him with smoke, was a complete failure.

Sandwich does not appear to have made any attempt to keep permanently at sea on the Dutch coast. The idea of a strict and continued blockade of the Dutch ports must either have been absent from the minds of the commanders, or else the ships in their interior economies and arrangements were still unable to keep the sea for any continuance.[13] Perhaps both causes operated. At a later date the "great ships" were still of a tender sort, not fit to be trusted at sea in the winter months, both from their tendency to labour and leak in a sea-way, and also from their unhandiness and the consequent dangers they ran of lee shores and other dangers of navigation. But

---

11. De Ruiter had originally twelve sail with him. *Life of Cornelius Tromp*, p. 253.

12. *Life of Penn*, vol. ii., p. 361.

13. Pepys records Sir Wm. Coventry as "disliking our staying with the fleet on the Dutch coast, believing that the Dutch will come out in fourteen days, and then we with our unready fleet, by reason of some of the ships being maimed, shall be in a bad condition to fight them on their own coast." (July 30, 1666). *Life of Penn*, vol. ii., p. 412.

again, it seems certain that commercial blockade was not understood. If the Dutch ports could be watched closely it was certain there were no better positions for making sure of the homeward trade. Yet it seems that when Sandwich detached Tiddiman to operate against the ships in Bergen, he himself took the rest of the fleet to the Shetland Islands, and was there watching for the returning Dutch ships on the 8th of August.[14]

The Dutch ports were in this way left open, and their fleets left free to reassemble and combine. This was done, and on information of the divided state of the English, the Hollanders sailed towards Bergen in hopes of falling on Tiddiman's squadron. Seeing no signs of him, they took the Bergen merchant fleet under convoy about the end of August, hoping to bring the 70 ships safe into their ports. But here the great enemy of naval operations, the wind, put itself *en évidence,* and scattered both merchant fleet and war ships. Sandwich was back again now, in the middle of the North Sea, and on the 5th September was 90 miles NNW from the Texel, having been for the two previous days picking up largely amongst the scattered Dutch war, and merchant, ships. He had then taken four men-of-war of 40 to 54 guns each, three East Indiamen, and seven other merchant ships. Several other great prizes fell into the hands of the English at the same time, but both fleets appear to have been a good deal broken up and detached, the Dutch not having recovered their dispersion, and the English devoting themselves to prize-making, so that no general action took place.

Sandwich, with but 18 sail about him, and his prizes, got back to Sole Bay on the 11th of September, while most part of the Dutch sought refuge in Goree a few days later, and the scattered squadrons of the English soon found their way home also.

In England everything was now disorganised, as the plague was at its worst all through the months of August and September. The war ships returned into port, and there was no heart to refit them for fresh operations. It was otherwise with the Dutch. Notwithstanding further damages from wind, they managed to get a fleet of 90 sail to sea on the 1st of October, with the intention of falling in great force on the detached squadrons which they hoped to find at anchor in Sole Bay, off Harwich, in the Downs, or at the mouth of

14. It is difficult to say now, how much the contention between the soldier and the sailor element in our fleets at this time had to do with the apparent want of system. Penn's influence was very great, but the military fleet commanders, such as Monk and Sandwich, were bitterly jealous of him and may—as Monk certainly did—have scorned the sailor's advice.

the Thames. On the 5th, the Dutch appeared off Yarmouth and Lowestoft, but neither there nor at Sole Bay were there any war ships to be seen. In fact, no traffic of any kind appears to have been stirring, for they seem to have captured only one small vessel. While they were thus to the northward, however, and now working to the southward with light winds, 16 men-of-war lying off Harwich got news of their presence, and instantly weighed and ran up the Thames, where they were seen by the Dutch on the 7th, but too far off to be got at. At the mouth of the Thames the Dutch anchored for the night, and next morning made for the Downs, in hopes of surprising some vessels said to be there. But calms and light winds frustrated their intentions, and gave the ships time to escape. From their anchorage at the mouth of the Thames, they reconnoitred and sounded higher up, and might possibly have concerted some other design in the apparent total absence of anything to oppose them. But their crews became terribly and unaccountably sickly, and the sickness showed every tendency of increase. The position was also that there was nothing to be done. All possible prizes were in the harbours and up the rivers; there was nothing going in and nothing coming, or likely to come, out. A determination was arrived at to break up the fleet and send it home. But a small group of six light frigates and four galliots were left to watch the mouth of the Thames for three days, simply to notify to any Dutch war ships arriving, that the fleet had retired. A squadron of 18 of the healthiest ships under Admiral Sweers was also told off to keep the sea for three weeks longer, and to cruise off the Dogger Bank, as well to offer convoy to any homeward-bound Dutch merchant ships coming north about, as to lie across the English trade to Hamburgh and the Baltic, and to attack it. But nothing noticeable came of the proceeding, and the war ceased for the winter months.

The only point of principle which it here seems necessary to take note of, is the small result to either side of a mere temporary command of the sea. The greatest successes of the English against merchant ships were when the war fleets were all but in sight of one another; the greatest successes of the Dutch in the same way were just before the battle of Lowestoft. When the English by their promptitude obliged the Dutch to remain in port, little or nothing came of it. When the English, broken up and disheartened by the Plague, left the sea free to the Dutch, they themselves sum up the result as follows: "The Dutch fleet then did nothing that expedition but cause some alarms upon the coast of England, and all the honour they gained by it was only that of having offered battle to the

STRUGGLE FOR COMMAND OF THE SEA

English fleet whilst they kept themselves within their harbours, as being debarred by a raging and pestilent distemper from accepting it, and having interrupted the commerce of the English merchants, by keeping the mouth of the Thames blocked up for about sixteen days together." [15] It would appear, so far, as if something more than mere temporary command of the sea is required before full advantage can be taken of it.

Early in 1666, a new element was introduced into the war by the alliance of France with Holland, the French declaration of war against England, and her threatened junction of a fleet of thirty men-of-war with the Dutch. [16] Further difficulties for England developed in the declaration of war against her by Denmark and Brandenberg. This French fleet put to sea from Toulon on the 9th January 1666, and was under the command of the Duke of Beaufort, but it did not get as far as Rochelle till near the end of August; it was at Dieppe on the 14th of September, but made no further effort to join the Dutch, and not finding them there, it returned to Brest and nothing more was heard by sea of the French alliance with Holland.

But when the English fleet was ready for sea, towards the end of May, the French fleet, which had been joined by six Hollanders with fire-ships and ketches, was still a threat, and to meet it Prince Rupert was detached to the Isle of Wight, probably to St. Helens, to bar the passage and prevent the junction with the Dutch.

The English fleet put to sea towards the end of May, and before Prince Rupert was detached, it consisted of 81 men-of-war, mounting 4,460 guns, and manned by 21,085 men. Prince Rupert's detachment left it about 61 sail in strength.

The Dutch having put to sea about the 21st of May with a fleet of 96 sail, carrying 4,716 guns and 20,642 men, had anchored before the 1st of June between Dunkirk and the North Foreland, and there Monk, now Duke of Albemarle, proposed to attack them with only two out of the three divisions of his fleet.

It was blowing hard when the English sighted the Dutch, and the naval officers were strongly against an attack, not only because of the inferiority of force, but because in such a stormy wind, they being to windward, they were unable to use the lower deck guns— the heaviest tier. But Monk overbore all opposition to his will, and

15. *Life of Cornelius Tromp,* p. 324.
16. O. Troude, *Battailles Navales de France,* vol. i., p. 107, makes the force 13 ships of from 56 to 84 guns; 16 of from 36 to 42 guns; 3 of 26 and 28 guns, and a small vessel. This was a very heavy force for the time.

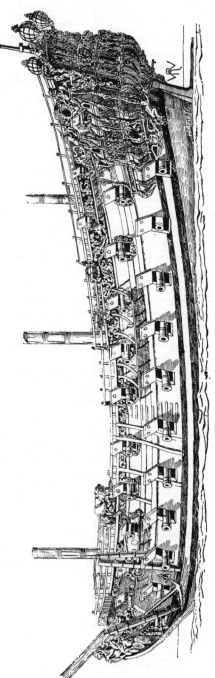

The *Royal Prince*

ran down upon the Dutch without preserving that order which was becoming recognized as a necessity in a sea-fight. The result was a four days' combat of the severest and bloodiest character. The English were throughout the attacking force, but a large balance of victory remained in the enemy's hands.[17] The first day's battle ended at 10 o'clock at night, when the English claimed to have burnt two Dutch ships, but to have lost three by capture, and to have had Vice-Admiral Sir William Berkeley killed. The night was spent in preparing for the next day's battle, when the Dutch lost one or two ships burnt, and Vice-Admiral Van der Hulst killed. Nevertheless, the Dutch having received a reinforcement,[18] Albemarle began to fall back to have the support of Prince Rupert, who was coming to his assistance. The retreat was made in good order, but Monk was obliged to burn certain disabled ships, to prevent them from falling into the enemy's hands. The Dutch followed, but not closely.

On the third day, June 3rd, the *Royal Prince,* bearing the flag of Sir George Ayscue, the largest and heaviest ship in the English fleet, ran on the Galloper shoal, and being threatened by fire-ships, surrendered.[19] The ship was burnt, and the crew, including the admiral, made prisoners.

Prince Rupert had been warned to quit St. Helens and rejoin the main fleet, and it was known that he had sailed on the afternoon of the 1st. He appeared on the evening of the 3rd, and joining Albemarle, the battle was renewed till night. Next morning, the fourth day of the fight, the Dutch were seen a long way off, and the English making sail for them, the battle was renewed at 8 A.M. and lasted till 7 P.M., when a fog put a stop, and as it turned out a final stop, to the combat.

Each fleet returned to its own harbours; ours was in a terrible plight. "The sad spectacle," says Evelyn; "more than half that gallant bulwark of the kingdom miserably shattered; hardly a vessel entire, but appearing so many wrecks and hulls, so cruelly had the Dutch mangled us."[20] We lost nine or ten ships, beside the *Royal*

17. The site of the first day's battle is shown by the figure 2 on the chart.

18. "Sixteen great ships." *Life of Penn,* vol. ii., p. 389.

19. The *Royal Prince* was the work of Phineas Pett. She was launched at Woolwich in 1610 in the presence of King James, the Queen, Prince of Wales, Duke of York and other royal and noble personages. She was 114 feet long, 44 feet broad, and was pierced for 64 guns, though carrying but 55. She was estimated to measure 1,200 tons. The actual armament was, two 30-prs., six 24-prs., twelve 18-prs., eighteen 9-prs., thirteen 6-prs., and four "port-pieces." See Charnock's *History of Marine Architecture,* vol. ii., *passim.* The cut is taken from his plate.

20. *Life of Penn,* vol. ii., p. 395.

*Prince;* had nearly 600 men killed, 1,100 wounded, and 2,000 prisoners. The Dutch admitted that they had lost from four to six men-of-war.

The Dutch had so far gained a victory, but they were under the impression not only that the victory was more complete, but that its effects were more permanent and far reaching than they really were. In their mistaken view they not only hurried their fleet of sixty sail out of the Texel on the 25th of June, but prepared with it a fleet of transports carrying troops, in order to make a descent on our coasts, having by their victory, as they supposed, secured themselves from interruption at sea. With this fleet, considerably reinforced from other ports, they appeared at the mouth of the Thames. But at the Nore, to their disappointed astonishment, lay a new English fleet computed at eighty-eight sail, with fire-ships and ketches. These ships were the repaired and refitted remains of the beaten fleet, with additions, all collected and approaching completion, by the great exertions of Sir William Penn, now one of the Commissioners of the navy.

The Dutch hopes were entirely frustrated by this unexpected sight, and they found themselves reduced to carrying out the simple operation of blocking the Thames, which they did till the 19th or 20th of July, when the English fleet put to sea after them.[21] This latter was now composed of eighty-nine men-of-war, with eighteen to twenty fire-ships; and the Dutch fleet was of the same force.

The English came up with the Dutch at a point N.E. by E. of the North Foreland on the 25th of July, and a desperate battle of the usual type ensued.[22] Prince Rupert and Albemarle held a joint command (in one ship) of the Red Squadron, while Sir Thomas Allen, commanded the White, and Sir Jeremiah Smith the Blue. The Dutch were under the command of De Ruiter. The fight began about noon and continued all day, the Dutch retreating towards their own coast, and the English following. The pursuit was maintained all night and through the next day, with very light winds. The Dutch

21. The reasons given by the Dutch author for making no attack are rather confused and obscure. "The English fleet, who had advice of the setting out of the Holland fleet, knew so well how to secure themselves of all the posts where any descent could be made, by placing there both horse and foot, that they quite broke all the designs of the Hollanders, who saw themselves thereby disabled to attempt anything for want of good sounders." *Life of Cornelius Tromp,* p. 374.

22. The locality is marked by the figure 3 on the chart. It was often the case that the sound of the guns in these great battles were heard in London, and it was so on this occasion. See *Life of Penn,* vol. ii., p. 409.

ultimately found shelter behind the shoals which lie off Ostend, then called the Wielings; while the English, fearing the dangers of shoal water, anchored to the northward, in the Schoonevelde, watching them. The Dutch necessarily admitted the English victory; the usual counter-claims made the English lose either one ship or four ships, and the English claimed that the Dutch had lost twenty ships, sunk or burnt, and 7,000 men killed and wounded.

The Dutch, unable to renew the battle, betook themselves to repairing their losses and refitting. The English, thus free, "passed along the whole coast of Holland, taking ships at the very mouths of the harbours, and causing a hot alarm wherever they appeared." [23] On arriving near the Vlie, they heard that a great fleet of merchant ships was lying in an exposed position in that river, and also that there were certain unprotected magazines of stores on the Islands of Vlie and Schelling. It was determined to make an attack, and Sir Robert Holms, at the head of nine frigates, five fire-ships, and seven ketches was despatched for the purpose. He anchored at the mouth of the Vlie on the 8th of August, and sending in a ketch to reconnoitre, received from her the intelligence that there were about 200 merchant ships thus open to him. He proposed to attack the ships first, and sent the *Pembroke*—the frigate which drew least water of any in his squadron—with five fire-ships, to burn the merchant fleet. Several ships were destroyed in this way, and the rest cut their cables and ran into shoal water. Thereupon Holms sent in twenty pinnaces, which followed up the unfortunate merchant vessels and burnt all of them except three or four privateers, one trader to Guinea, and a few of the Baltic traders.

Having thus finished with the ships, Sir Robert despatched two frigates and some ketches to make a descent on the Island of Vlie. But this proved a failure in consequence of the rain rendering the fire-arms useless.

There was better success on the island of Schelling, where the men, divided into eleven companies, landed and laid the town of Brandaries, containing 600 or 700 houses, in ashes. Sir Robert had thoughts of repeating the operation on other towns, but having to wait twenty-four hours for tide to suit the time, and fearing a change of wind, he rejoined the main fleet, which, after capturing twelve or fourteen more Dutch merchantmen, returned home. It was supposed that the value of the ships and cargoes destroyed in the Vlie came to more than £1,100,000, without counting the dam-

23. *Columna Rostrata,* p. 182.

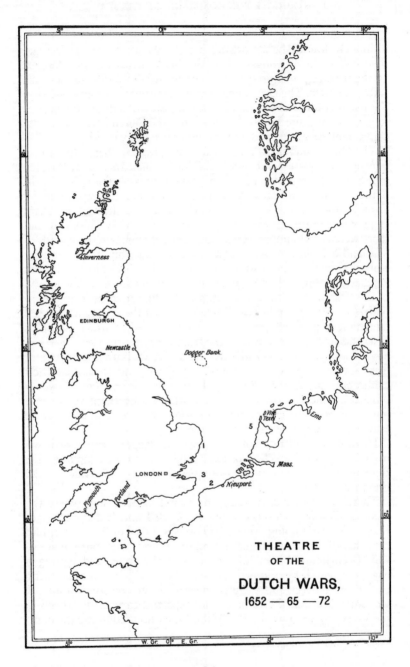

age done on shore. If we are at all justified in drawing conclusions as to what this sum meant in that age, by comparing it with the public revenue then, and assuming a proportionate sum now, the result is rather startling. The British revenue then was a million and a half; it is now ninety millions. If we can suppose £66,000,000 worth of our shipping property being now destroyed at one *coup*, we may perhaps realize what the loss meant to the Dutch in 1666.

But it is important to recall the conditions under which such attack and destruction became possible. The Dutch fleets had been beaten into their ports in such condition that for the time they dared not present themselves at sea. The English fleet was in full control, for the time, of the Dutch waters off the coast. It was in a position to entirely prevent Sir Robert Holms' operations from being interfered with by any force arriving over sea. The English force detached from the main fleet was a very small one, and only a single ship, and that the lightest of the nine frigates, was actually engaged. Quite conceivably, the presence of only a couple of Dutch frigates in the Vlie would have sufficed to preserve this vast property in safety.[24]

As some sort of reply to this, four or five Dutch men-of-war fell upon some seventeen English ships in the Elbe, near Glückstadt, and drove them, with loss, up to Hamburgh. But this was obviously, not a legitimate operation of war.

The French alliance had been as yet of no manner of use to the Hollanders. Contemporary historians say that the terms of the alliance were such as could only issue in making France strong by sea, both in providing her with ships built in Holland and by Dutch skill, and by giving her the benefit of Dutch nautical experience. But negociations were now (August 1666) in progress to bring the Duke of Beaufort up from Portugal in order to form a junction with the Dutch somewhere between Boulogne and Dieppe.

To effect the object, De Ruiter got to sea with a replenished and refitted fleet of 71 men-of-war and 27 fire-ships, having as his second and third in command, Admirals de Gent and Bankert. On the 29th of August the fleet anchored between Dunkirk and Nieuport, and then, hearing that the Duke of Beaufort had got so far on his way to join him as to have arrived at and left Rochelle, De Ruiter

---

24. "I had an opportunity of much talk with Sir W. Penn to-day (he being newly come from the fleet)," writes Pepys, on August 22nd, 1666, "and he do much undervalue the honour that is given to the conduct of the late business of Holms in burning the ships and town, saying, it was a great thing indeed, and of great profit to us in being of great loss to the enemy; but that it was wholly a business of chance." *Life of Penn*, vol. ii., p. 415.

weighed on the 1st September, and made sail through the Straits of Dover.

From remarks in Pepys' diary it seems certain that our fleet was at this moment not at all complete. It was particularly deficient in fire-ships. "But, Lord!" cries Pepys, "to see how my Lord Brouncker undertakes the despatch of the fire-ships when he is no more fit for it than a porter!"[25] This and other deficiencies may account for what followed, and may tend to reconcile the otherwise irreconcilable stories of the Dutch and English recorders. The Dutch story, which presents a good deal of perplexity, even by itself, is that near Boulogne the English fleet came in sight, advanced on the Dutch, then fled, pursued by the Hollanders, who were unable to bring them to action. The English story is that they made every effort to bring the Dutch to action, but that the latter hauled into shoal water where they could not be got at, and then a gale of wind sprang up and drove the English off the coast. All that seems certain is that nothing was done; that the Duke of Beaufort never advanced beyond Dieppe.

The Dutch, however, captured an English ship, the *Royal Charles*, of 56 guns and 200 men.[26] But on the other hand Sir Thomas Allen, who commanded the White squadron of the English fleet, met a part of the French fleet, captured the *Ruby*, of 70 guns and 500 men, drove ashore and burnt some others, and forced the rest up the Seine. It seems probable, on the whole, that the threat of the English fleet was sufficient to prevent the junction, and that very possibly Rupert and Albemarle felt that if that end could be secured by the threat, it was a safer plan than attacking the Dutch in the immediate vicinity of so large and powerful a division as the French fleet composed.

There is at this point an indication of a change in the conduct of naval war which subsequently became a permanent characteristic, the features of which must be dealt with later on. Practically, up to this time, we have heard little or nothing of detached cruisers. But now we hear that while the main fleets of both nations were in the Channel to the southward, there was an action between a squadron of five Dutch cruisers, and another of English cruisers under Com-

25. Ibid.
26. I suppose this was a merchant ship. There was a *Royal Charles*, carrying the flag of Admiral Hubbard in the English fleet, but she carried 82 guns and 700 men. See Charnock's *History of Marine Architecture*, vol. ii., p. 398.

modore Robertson near the Texel. Three of the Dutch were captured or destroyed.

We come now near the most curious episode, and also the best known of all that occurred in the three Dutch wars—the Dutch raid on the Medway and Thames.

Negociations for peace had been set up as early as July in 1666, and they continued with increasing hopes of result through September, October, and November. Then Breda was agreed on as the place where the plenipotentiaries should meet to settle terms finally.

Apparently, at first, the possible approach of peace had no influence on the naval preparation, as on the 2nd October 1666, the Duke of York gave directions for arranging the winter service: an immediate convoy to Gottenberg to bring home our merchant ships, another to guard the merchant fleet to the Mediterranean, and to bring home the ships at Leghorn; winter guards for the narrow seas to secure the trade between Newcastle and London, a few ships in the Downs, and "the chief station at Portsmouth, which may require a good strength, since no man knows what either Dutch or French may attempt for passing the Channel for a conjunction," a guard "for securing the trade at the Land's End and soundings, which, if the French lie about Brest (whither they are gone), may require good ships."[27] But in a few days there was a great question of money, with heat and strong language in the Council between Prince Rupert and Mr. Pepys. The former declared no fleet was ever brought home in so good a state as the last; the latter averred that Sir William Penn, who was making the inquiry at Sheerness, had written that he dreaded the reports he was to receive from the surveyors of the defects of the fleet.[28] And then Pepys and the Court and everyone else seemed to forget all the grave issues surrounding them, and to be concerned only in attiring themselves "solemnly in the Persian manner,"[29] and were ready to listen to the artfully arranged suggestions of the Dutch, that the war was over, that peace was virtually certain, and that they were disbanding and dismantling their fleet.

Pepys' diary is so curiously illustrative of the circumstances out of which the raid arose, that I cannot do better than quote, as I find it quoted, in the *Life of Penn*.

27. Sir W. Coventry to Sir W. Penn. See *Life of Penn,* vol. ii., p. 422.
28. Ibid., p. 424.
29. Evelyn on the 18th October, quoted in ibid., p. 425.

*March 6th,* 1667.—To Whitehall; and here the Duke of York did aquaint us (and the King did the like also afterwards, coming in) with his resolution of altering the manner of the war this year; that is, we shall keep what fleet we have abroad, in several squadrons. So that now all is come out; but we are to keep it as close as we can, without hindering the work that is to be done in preparation to this. Great preparations there are to fortify Sheerness and the yard at Portsmouth, and forces are drawing down to both those places, and elsewhere by the sea-side; so that we have some fear of an invasion; and the Duke of York did himself declare his expectation of the enemy's blocking us up here in the river, and therefore directed that we should send away all the ships that we have to fit out hence.

What had happened is told by the Duke of York himself. "The Parliament," he says, "giving but weak supplies for the war, the King, to save charges, is persuaded by the Lord Chancellor (Clarendon), the Lord Treasurer (Southampton), the Duke of Albemarle, and the other Ministers, to lay up the first and second-rate ships, and make only a defensive war in the next campaign. The Duke of York opposed this, but was over-ruled." [30]

Pepys goes on:—

*March 23rd.*—At the office, where Sir W. Penn came, being returned from Chatham, from considering the means of fortifying the river Medway, by a chain at the Stakes and ships laid there with guns, to keep the enemy from coming up to burn our ships; all our care being now to fortify ourselves against their invading us.

*March 24th.*—To the Duke of York, where we all met, and there was the King also; and all our discourse was about fortifying of the Medway, and Harwich (which is to be entrenched quite round) and Portsmouth. And here they advised with Sir Godfrey Lloyd and Sir Bernard de Gunn, the two great engineers, and had the plates drawn before them; and, indeed, all their care they now take is to fortify themselves, and are not ashamed of it; for when, by and by, my Lord Arlington came in with letters, and seeing the King and D. of York give us, and the officers of the Ordnance, directions in this matter, he did move, that we might do it as privately as we could, that it might not come into the Dutch Gazette presently: as the King's and D. of York's going down the other day to Sheerness was, the week after, in the Harlem Gazette. The King and D. of York both laughed at it, and made no matter, but said, "Let us be safe, and let them talk; for there is nothing will trouble them more than to hear that we are fortifying ourselves." And the D. of York said, "What said Marshal Tourenne,

---

30. *Life of King James II.,* vol. i., p. 425, quoted in ibid., p. 451.

when some in vanity said that the enemies were afraid, for they entrenched themselves? 'Well,' says he, 'I would they were not afraid, for then they would not entrench themselves, and so we could deal with them the better.'"

What appears remarkable in all this is the clear forecast of what would happen, two months before it did happen. It cannot be said that there was any surprise in the Dutch action, nor does it appear that there was much deception on their part. Every one seems to have known perfectly well that if the fleet was not kept up, the enemy would take advantage of it, and sail up the Thames to do what mischief might be done.

The Dutch fell in completely with the expectation. With a fleet of 60 sail and a body of troops, De Ruiter put to sea on the 1st of June and made straight for the Thames, designing not only to copy the example set by the English in the Vlie the year before, but being supplied with troops, to make a much heavier descent upon the country. They anchored at the mouth of the Thames on the 7th, and hearing that 10 or 12 English frigates, with a convoy of 20 merchant ships bound to Barbadoes, were in the Hope,[31] a detachment of 17 light frigates, with fire-ships and small vessels, was prepared and despatched up the river under the command of Admiral de Gent, on the 9th of June.

It is worthy of remark at this point, how precisely, so far, the practice followed that pursued in the Vlie. The main fleet lies outside keeping guard; the shipping is made the first object of attack, and a detachment of light ships is sent to conduct it. The descent upon the land comes afterwards in both cases, even though in the latter there was military force which there was not in the former.[32] In the case of the Vlie, the attack is planned and made after the sea has been cleared of fleets capable of interfering; in the case of the Thames, it is undertaken with the knowledge that no naval force exists which is capable of interfering.

De Gent met with foul and light winds, and was never able to reach a higher point than a mile and a half below the Lower Hope (that would be somewhere off Thames Haven), and meanwhile the ships there all escaped to the upper reaches of the river. This part of the expedition having miscarried, attention was turned to Sheerness and its newly arranged and apparently incomplete defences.

31. The Lower Hope, above Thames Haven and below Tilbury Fort.
32. The whole of the troops, however, were not immediately available. See below.

However to-day [observes young Cornelius De Witt, the son of the Pensioner, who was attached to the fleet in a civil capacity], about noon [33] (the 10th June), as the tide began to come in, we advanced as far as the mouth of the river of Chattam. We presently gave orders to the land troops and marine soldiers to make a descent, and to attack the fort of Sheerness. In the meanwhile we advanced with our men-of-war, and anchored before the same fort. At our approach, one of the King's frigates with some other vessels, and some fire-ships that were there, betook themselves to flight, and the men in the fort ran away likewise before our troops got thither; so that after the fort had been cannonaded about an hour and a half, our seamen scaled it to pull down from thence the English banner. We found there fifteen pieces of cannon, which we carried off to our ships; and a great magazine of masts, yards, and in general of all necessaries for the rigging of ships, valued at near 400,000 livers. We gave order to all our captains to carry, each of them, on board a good quantity, and to set fire to the rest. Because the most part of the troops were separated from us by foul weather, the general officers thought not fit to engage themselves too far up the country with so few people, or else they might have done a great deal of mischief. We are, however, of opinion to keep the river of London blocked up, and to hinder the passage of ships there, as much as 'tis possible for us. And to that effect Lieutenant Admiral De Ruiter is to come up and joyn us with the main body of the fleet.[34]

Since my last letter of the 10th [he again writes to the States-General] by which I informed your High and Mightyneses of the taking of Sheerness, we have received fresh marks of God's protection by several glorious advantages we have newly obtained. After we had detached away some advice-yachts, and several boats armed, to go and sound the passage from hence to Chattam, we resolved to send up thither to-day Lieutenant-Admiral de Gent's squadron; and accordingly by the favour of a good N.E. wind, we unmoored from Sheerness at six in the morning (of June 12th). About noon we arrived near some English men-of-war, having on board them very large guns, and being very well manned, who made a show at first as if they would make a brisk defence; but as soon as we had burnt four or five of them, some of the others were deserted, so that we took them. I cannot at present give you a particular account of what ships perished in the flames; but I know very well the *Royal Charles,* carrying ninety brass guns, and another carrying a like number, fell into our hands. There are still four or five more a little above us, against which we sent some of ours, and because there is a very great

33. "Up;" says Pepys, "and news brought us that the Dutch are come as high as the Nore, and more pressing orders for fire-ships." *Life of Penn,* vol. ii., p. 441.
34. *Life of Cornelius Tromp,* p. 425.

consternation among the English, we doubt not but to take them. According to the advices we have had of the enemy, they have sunk sixteen or eighteen ships, the most part fire-ships, to block the passage of the river against us. But, in spite of all these precautions, our ships are passed up, and we flatter ourselves with the hopes to bring along with us those which we shall have taken.[35]

Albermarle was in command at Chatham, and was an eye-witness of all the destruction wrought, which, no doubt, was minimized as much as possible in his official report, which was presented to Parliament in February 1668. He complained bitterly of everything. Nothing was complete. Batteries ordered were incomplete; the *Royal Charles,* which had been ordered up the river three months before, was left below to be captured. The ships sunk were not sunk in the right place, and ships ordered to be sunk were not sunk. He "could not get a carpenter but two that were running away." He "had no assistance from Commissioner Pett, nor no gunners nor men to draw on the guns, except the two masters of attendance." And so on, with the usual string of excuses made by those who have failed. But he had seen the guard-ships burnt, and the *Royal Charles* (82) carried off on the 12th, and the *Great James* (82)—otherwise the *Royal James*—the *Royal Oak* (76), and the *Loyal London* (90) burnt on the 13th, while he looked helplessly on, which was enough to set a man throwing the blame on somebody else, and particularly so to him as one of the advisers of this "defensive war." For the ships were all flag-ships, the very finest in the navy, and had carried admirals' flags at sea under his command only a very few months before.

This act of destruction completed the work in the Medway. The Dutch fell back to the mouth of the river again, blocking it and putting a stop to all commerce by their presence. But troops were landed in Sheppy, and foraged indiscriminately for the use of the fleet. De Gent was also detached on the 15th of June to the Shetland Islands to pick up and convoy home the Dutch East India ships. Attempts were also made to send a light squadron up to Gravesend, but between newly-sunken ships and newly-erected batteries the defences were sufficient to frustrate the plan.

The Dutch being reinforced by fresh troops, it was determined to make an attack on Landguard Fort, Harwich, and the plan settled was as follows:—1,600 soldiers and 400 seamen were landed—I think it must have been on the beach towards Felixtowe—out of fire

35. Ibid., p. 426.

from the fort. Vice-Admiral Evertz was, with fourteen men-of-war, to attack the fort on the sea-side, while Rear-Admiral Van Nes was to enter the harbour and attack from that side. Then, when the fire was subdued, the land force was to advance and complete the capture. But they had reckoned without their host; for the shoal water prevented either squadron from operating; only a distant and useless fire being opened by Evertz. The troops made some attempts to advance on the fort in the open, but seeing that without the supporting fire of the ships it would be impossible to succeed, they re-embarked.

The Dutch now set about more regularly blockading the Thames by smaller force higher up, while detachments watched off Harwich and the North Foreland to guard against surprise either from north or south.

The news of the conclusion of peace reached the Dutch on the 4th of July, but such was the elation of the States at their success, that, on the plea that the treaty was not fully ratified, De Ruiter was ordered into the Channel to prey upon the English commerce and to alarm the southern ports; while Van Nes was directed to push up the Thames again to do what mischief he might. De Ruiter, very possibly because of his knowledge of the situation, did little but to create alarm. But there was a sharp encounter between Van Nes and Sir Edward Spragge, who had got together some naval force and a good provision of fire-ships. The Dutch failed to make any impression, and in the end resumed the blockade of the Thames until the ratification of the treaty of peace relieved them from that duty.

# CHAPTER FOUR

T HE DUTCH, throughout the whole of their second war with England, had carried it out on the princple of a simple and direct struggle for the command of the sea. They had nerved themselves for it by the abandonment of their commerce for the time, in order that neither their attention nor their forces should be diverted for a moment from the attainment of the main object in view. The result was that the protection of commerce dropped out of the regular programme, and great battles no longer hinged on the necessity of protecting convoy.

The completeness of the change of system between the first and second Dutch wars is easily lost sight of from the confused, un-dramatic, and pointless way in which the stories have generally been told. But we note it when we observe that out of the seven battles which marked the progress of the first Dutch war, four arose directly out of the necessity of protecting commerce, and that three times, if not four, it was chance which prevented the occurrence of battles under similar circumstances; and in the second war, though there were captures of merchant ships on both sides, no battle came about in consequence of an endeavour to protect them. Thus, in the first war, we see it begin in July 1652 with an attack on the large squadron protecting the Dutch herring busses. Immediately after-wards, the accident of a gale of wind prevents Tromp from bringing Blake to action near the Shetland Islands, as a means of securing the return of the homeward-bound West India ships. In August, De Ruiter fights Ayscue off Plymouth, in defence of his convoy of 60 ships. In November, Tromp attacks Blake near the Straits of Dover, in order to leave the Channel free for the passage of 300 outward-bound Dutch ships. In February 1653, Blake in the Channel endeav-ours to intercept Tromp's convoy of 250 homeward-bound ships. In

May, Dean and Monk all but bring Tromp to action off the Dutch coast, in order to make themselves masters of the 200 ships he was convoying outward; and in June, Evertz was only prevented by the accident of wind from attacking Bodley in the Downs, when he was in charge of eight merchant-ships.

In the second war, all this had passed away. Not a single battle arose out of commerce protection, and no outward-bound convoy left the ports of Holland. There were attacks, and very heavy ones, upon merchant shipping, but the heaviest were made upon ships at anchor in port; as at Bergen, and in the Vlie, on the English side, and as at Glückstadt, and the attempt on the ships in the Lower Hope on the Dutch side. It was more by chance than of set purpose that the Dutch captured nine English merchant ships on their way to fight the battle of Sole Bay; and that the English possessed themselves at sea of some of the scattered merchant ships, which they had failed to master at Bergen.

On both sides, again, we may observe a tendency to push the advantages even of a temporary command of the sea. This is shown principally in the successful and unsuccessful attacks on shipping in harbour; but more strongly in the descents upon the land, as at the islands of Vlie and Schelling, where the English appeared to land with their ordinary crews only; and at Sheerness and Harwich, where the Dutch employed regular troops. Still we have to note that these descents, as they were called, were only made when temporary command of the sea had been gained, and then only by detachments, the main body of the fleet being in all cases, as it were, securing the rear of the attacking parties.

Naval war had, in fact, found its limits and settled down into its bearings. The things which could and the things which could not be done with reasonable hopes of success were making themselves manifest, and it was being seen in what direction the ultimate appeal to naval force lay.

In both wars the English had had, on the whole, the best of it, and the Dutch, on the whole, the worst of it; and things at the end of the second war remained so much as they had been at the beginning of it—the raid on the Medway and Thames being quite understood on both sides to have been deliberately courted by the English—that the third Dutch war was laid out on the same principles as the second.

There were the usual reprisals before war was declared, and England, taking advantage of her position as lying across the stream of Dutch commerce, fell upon it in March 1672 at the back of the Isle

94

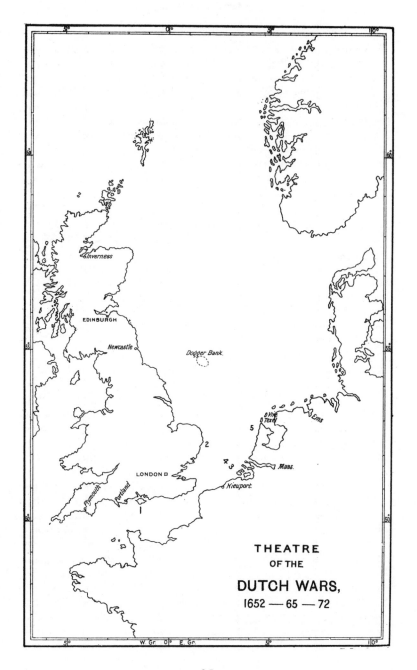

THEATRE
OF THE
DUTCH WARS,
1652 — 65 — 72

of Wight (no. 1 on the chart), and the small force that could be got together under Sir Robert Holms was sufficient to levy a heavy contribution upon the unfortunate and unprepared Dutchmen.

France, which had failed to make herself of any use to Holland as an ally in the second war, was very much of the same mind towards England in the third war. But not quite; for she now brought a contingent of 36 men-of-war and 22 fire-ships under Count D'Estreés, and formed a junction with the Duke of York at the back of the Isle of Wight on the 14th of May, the united fleets sailing immediately to the favourite open anchorage of Southwold, or Sole Bay, on the coast of Suffolk. But it may be usefully pointed out that the French alliance was employed, not to produce an overwhelming force at sea, but merely to relieve England from some part of the expense of the war. The Dutch generally sent to sea a fleet as large as that of the Allies.

On the outbreak of the war, the Hollanders prohibited sea-borne commerce in much the same terms as in 1665 and 1666. They were eager to contest directly the great point at issue, and during the hours of darkness before day broke on May 28th, the cannon of the look-out ships announced to the allied fleet then at anchor, the approach of the enemy (no. 2 on the chart).

The Allies were 65 sail of English and 36 sail of French, with 22 fire-ships, besides small vessels. The Duke of York commanded in chief, under the red flag; the white squadron was wholly French, under D'Estrées; and the blue was commanded by the Earl of Sandwich. The Dutch were 91 sail of men-of-war, and 44 fire-ships, besides 23 yachts and small vessels. Their fleet was also in three squadrons, De Ruiter commanding in chief with the red flag; Admiral Bankert commanding the white squadron; and Admiral De Gent the blue.

The Allies were practically surprised. Many ships had to cut their cables to get into action, and the battle began between 7 and 8 A.M. De Ruiter said of it that he had never been in so continuous and obstinate a fight. The whole French squadron held back, and took as little part as they possibly could in the action. They retired out of the way to the southward, but were followed up to some extent, and lost two of their ships. Sandwich in the *Royal James* was determinedly attacked by fire-ships. The ship was fired and burnt, and Sandwich was drowned in attempting to escape from her. But notwithstanding this loss, and notwithstanding the defection of the French squadron, the Dutch were worsted, and fell back towards their own coasts, followed up by the English and by the French, who rejoined next day. The Dutch claimed to have burnt the *Royal James,* to have sunk two first-rates, and to have destroyed two other ships. They admitted that one of their ships was taken and another sunk.

The Allies now appeared off the Dutch coast with some intention of making a descent somewhere in Zealand, but in the near presence of the Dutch fleet found it would not be feasible. They then made some preparation for a descent on the island of Texel, but circumstances of tide caused the abandonment of the idea, and the squadrons were employed in the simple blockade of the Maas and the Texel.

The Dutch at this time were terribly pressed by the advance of the French armies by land, and the alarmed state of the sea-coasts. They sued for peace without success, but did not feel themselves strong enough to attempt another sea-fight with the Allies. But their privateers were in operation, and one of them carried an English East India ship as a prize into Bergen. The English also made prizes, and hearing at length that fourteen East India ships were on their way home north of Scotland, they cruized by the Dogger Bank in hopes of intercepting them. The merchant-ships, however, got safely into Bergen without having been seen, and as winter approached, all the war forces returned into their respective ports.

At the beginning of 1673 the Dutch were full of a novel device, the idea of which has more than once since proved attractive, though I believe it has never been put in practice. They thought it might be feasible to block up the Thames by sinking vessels there, and for this purpose prepared eight ships with stones at Amsterdam, which were afterwards taken into the Texel. I assume that the early appearance of the English fleet at sea prevented any attempts to carry this design into execution. I can find no reason stated, only that the attempt was not made.

In the early part of May, the Dutch fleet began to assemble in the Schooneveld, the anchorage off the mouth of the Schelde. De Ruiter is said to have failed in a design to intercept the English Canary, Bordeaux, and Newcastle merchant fleets in their passage into the Thames, and had then returned to the Schooneveld,[1] but it is not mentioned by my earlier and fuller authority. However this may be, there they were on the 22nd of May.

The allies had joined their forces off Rye, and they, too, had new

---

1. Burchett, p. 403. Lediard, vol. ii., p. 600, who also seems to speak as if De Ruiter, with 42 sail and his stone vessels, was off the Thames on the 2nd May, and frightened off by news of a fleet in the river.

ideas as to what was before them, for they took on board a body of troops with the intention of effecting a landing somewhere in Zealand. They had 84 men-of-war, and 26 fire-ships and small vessels. In order to prevent the tendency to hang back which had been displayed at Sole Bay the year before, the French were now distributed in the fleet, and not drawn together in a separate squadron as had before been the case. Rupert commanded the Red Squadron, D'Estrées the White, and Spragge, who had distinguished himself in the Thames in 1667, commanded the Blue.

The Dutch were 70 men-of-war besides fire-ships, under De Ruiter, Tromp, and Bankert; but their fleet was not complete, and was being gradually augmented. The Allies came in sight of the Dutch fleet thus anchored, on the 22nd May; but the weather was foggy, and the lie of the shoals thereabouts was not known to the former fleet. Soundings gained could not be fixed in consequence of the fog, and the advance on the Dutch was delayed, the allied fleet anchoring in the neighbourhood. Bad weather followed for two or three days, and still further postponed action; but on the 28th of May, the anniversary of the Battle of Sole Bay, both fleets were under way and came to action (no. 3 on the chart).

The battle began about 2 o'clock in the afternoon, and it lasted in the usual confused form[2] until 10 o'clock at night, when the Dutch claimed a victory, but anchored under cover of their shoals.

Great slaughter had been done on the English ships in consequence of their being crowded with troops; and it must be added that it could only have been by entire miscalculation that these troops were on board, as taking ships crowded with useless men into a fleet action must have been well understood to be a needless sacrifice of life. It seems clear that the Allies must have assumed that the Dutch fleet would not appear at sea, and that they could have made their contemplated descent without interruption. They were now in this position, that while they had lost but two men-of-war, both French, and the Dutch had lost one, which was disabled, and sank during the night with great loss of life, they claimed a victory without being able to follow it up, and so disprove the Dutch claim in the same direction; for crowded with wounded, and embarrassed with the troops, they were not at all desirous to renew the action, however much it might be necessary to keep a watch on the movements of the Dutch fleet.

2. "The two Royal Fleets made a motion, and having cast their squadrons into the form of a crescent made up directly towards the Dutch."—*Life of Cornelius Tromp,* p. 464.

As a consequence of this inaction the Dutch recovered their spirits and hopes, and on the 4th of June they made good their claims by putting to sea to assume the offensive directly. They were near the Allies by noon, but these drew off so persistently to the northwestward, that it was not till 5 o'clock in the evening that the battle began (no. 4 on the chart). The various historians are in direct contradiction over the chief events of the battle, which were, whether the Dutch, as Cornelius Tromp distinctly says they did, chased the Allies to within five miles of Sole Bay, and were only prevented by darkness from continuing the battle,[3] or whether the English turned and drove the Dutch back to Schooneveld, which is the English statement.[4] It may be noted as something in dispute which cannot be settled here. What is material to note is that there was a second battle nine days after the first, in which the Dutch assumed the offensive, and that after it each fleet retired to its own shores.

Perhaps it may here be usefully remarked that one of the historians[5] not only admits the unwillingness of the Allies to come to action on account of their being hampered with their wounded, but claims that the Dutch, after their stay on their own coast, were reinforced and refitted in a way which was impracticable for the Allies at sea. This is, no doubt, possible, though it is denied by the Dutch so far as any reinforcement goes; but it illustrates the position taken up by a competent authority, not from his knowledge as a seaman, for he was not one, but from his experience as a naval statesman. This was the Duke of York's secretary, Sir William Coventry, and Pepys records his opinion in the following words:—"30th (July 1666).—To Sir W. Coventry, at St. James'. I find him speaking very slightly of the late victory (the victory off the North Foreland, which was followed by the cruise upon the Dutch coast); dislikes their staying with their fleet up their coast, believing that the Dutch will come out in fourteen days, and then we, with our unready fleet, by reason of some of the ships being maimed, shall be in bad condition to fight them upon their own coast."[6] Not precisely contemplating the same circumstances, but still with a tendency to the same line of thought, Lord Howe wrote in a similar strain a hundred and thirty years later. Doubtless these views operated on both sides of the North Sea, and militated against any attempt at that persistent

3. Ibid., p. 476.
4. Berkley, p. 514. Burchett, p. 403. Lediard explains it, vol. ii, p. 602, by saying the Dutch being to windward were able to hold off, and did so.
5. Lediard, vol. ii., p. 601.
6. Quoted in *Life of Penn*, vol. ii., p. 412, already quoted in chap. 3.

watching of Dutch or English ports which was so much enforced in later wars, and so notably on this very Dutch coast by Duncan. Both in liability to damage by weather, and in defective victualling, it must probably be admitted that the ships of the middle of the seventeenth century and those of the end of the eighteenth differed largely, and with disadvantage in the former period. The practice after this battle, and after so many others, of both sides retiring into port and leaving the sea open, must to some extent be assigned to these causes, though possibly more to mere custom existing till another custom supervened.

No ships were lost on either side in the encounter of the 4th of June; but the Dutch authority states that the Allies admitted a loss of over 3,000 men, and this, if true, confirms the account of the crowded state of the ships, and supplies further proof of the reasons why they were not keen about close action. But, notwithstanding the lessons to the contrary which they would seem to have received, as to the great difficulty of making a descent on the enemy's shore until his fleet had been fully and finally dealt with, the Allies were still full of the project; and having landed their wounded, they took on board 7,000 fresh troops, and put to sea again on the 17th of June.

But the Dutch meanwhile showed an advance in the art of naval war by detaching a small squadron of observation to the Thames, under Rear-Admiral de Haan, who, on his return, was able to report having seen some 70 men-of-war at anchor off Sheerness, and of having heard that 30,000 troops were to be embarked at Tilbury Hope in preparation for a descent on Zealand. The Dutch found themselves unable to bring together sufficient naval force to make sure of fighting on something of an equality with the 60 English and 30 French ships of war which appeared before the Maas and Schevelling[7] on the 23rd and 24th of June. In proximity to the 70 Dutch ships ready in the waters of Zealand, no descent was attempted, and the Allies passed to the northward off the Texel, along the coasts of Holland and Friesland to Vlie, Ameland and the Western Ems, and then back to the Texel again.

The only claim made by the English historians to success in this demonstration is that it harassed the enemy's troops on the coast, and kept them continually alert; that it blocked up his ports, and endangered his returning East India merchant fleet, of which, however, but one was taken. On the other hand, a fleet crowded up with

7. Scheveningen, the port of the Hague.

troops, which were made no use of whatever, was in almost a critical condition in case even the inferior Dutch fleet should come upon it.

The Dutch stood these insults and threatenings to their coast for a fortnight, and then, about the 3rd of August, about the time that the Allies got back off the Texel, they put to sea, and stood alongshore to the northward. Foul winds, and possibly great caution, hindered their progress, so that it was not till the 10th of August that the fleets sighted each other, and about eight o'clock in the morning joined in a furious and final battle for that command of the sea which had never yet fallen, and was not now to fall, fully into the hands of either power.

The Allies were, as before observed, 90 strong under the former commanders—Rupert, D'Estrées, and Spragge. But a trust was once more placed in the French, which were once more and finally to betray. D'Estrées commanded the white squadron, which was composed entirely of his own ships. The Dutch were 70 strong, under De Ruiter, Cornelius Tromp, and Bankert. The fight that ensued is said by the author of *Columna Rostrata* to have been "like a general war of the elements," and it lasted till after sunset (no. 5 on the chart). This could not have been, considering the great numerical inferiority of the Dutch, had not D'Estrées from the very first held aloof and left the English and Dutch to fight it out while he looked on. Tromp was in the *Golden Lion,* and Spragge in the *Prince.*[8] These two fell upon one another, until both ships were so disabled that they shifted their flags to the *Comet* and *St. George,* and fell upon one another again. The *St. George* became a second ship disabled under the feet of the English admiral, and he then passed into a boat to go on board the *Royal Charles*; but on his way a shot cut his boat in two, and he was drowned. In other parts of the fleet equally stubborn contests were carried out, but in the end it does not seem to have been contested that the Dutch were victors. There was very slight loss of ships on either side; the English admitted a yacht sunk, and the Dutch only allow a loss of a few fireships, either sunk or "uselessly spent"; but there was great loss of men and officers. The English, besides Spragge, lost four captains, and the Dutch lost two vice-admirals, de Liefde, and Sweers, with two captains, and many superior officers wounded. The destruction of men in the English fleet was said to be very heavy, no doubt from their crowded condition. The Dutch claim to have kept the sea till

8. The historians say the *Royal Prince,* but it was probably the *Prince,* 90, built at Chatham in 1670. See Charnock, vol. ii., p. 426.

the 12th September, without sign of any attempt by the English to contest their substantial victory.

This was the last act of the war. The English nation was sick of a Catholic alliance against a Protestant State, and the navy was heartily sick of consorts in battle whose policy it was to induce them to enter into action with inferior forces of their own, and then to leave them to do the best they could. Peace was concluded in February 1664, and the next time destiny brought English and Dutch into hostile naval operations, she brought them in side by side in the third possible change of alliance between the three great European nations. It had been first Dutch and French against the English, out of which very little had come. It was next French and English against the Dutch, out of which only a little more had come. It was next to be English and Dutch against the French, out of which a great deal was to come.

I have, perhaps, sufficiently remarked upon the leading characteristics of the first and second Dutch wars, and how the first was carried on with the idea that the command of the sea was not a primary necessity; that an extensive commerce, which was in a sense the life-food of the State, might be protected by forces which were only large enough to contend on a fair equality with the enemy's war-ships bent on the capture or destruction of the very thing which the Dutch forces were assembled to protect; how the enemy, the English, with a smaller commerce, and consequently less distractions, were able to devote themselves almost completely to assuming the offensive; how, after pursuing this policy throughout the first war, the Dutch, learning their lesson, wholly changed it on the outbreak of the second war, and practically held their own, though with marked signs of inferiority, in a direct contention for the command of the sea, throughout it; and then, having reached firm ground in the wanderings of experience, held to it on the outbreak of the third war, and maintained it with really improved success throughout its course.

These are broad principles which lie, as it were, in prominent boulders on the plain landscape, as we survey, in the brief and not keenly critical or too closely investigating way we have done in these chapters, the further formation of the rules of naval war. As to what may specially come from a comparison of the general conduct of the third war with that which characterized the second, I think we may almost say that impatience with the method adopted in the second war was manifested on both sides in the third. There had been a descent on the shipping in the Vlie, which had been extraordinarily successful to the English and extraordinarily damaging to the Dutch. There had been a desecent by the Dutch on the dismantled war-ships of the English at Chatham, which, though quite as successful to the Dutch, could only have been made up by the counters representing insult, to the damage they had suffered in the Vlie. Then, again, there had been Tiddiman's unsuccessful attempt on the merchant fleet at Bergen, and men must have considered that probably a heavier force would have succeeded.

Altogether, when the third war broke out, there must have been a good deal of floating feeling about in favour of something more dramatic and telling than a continuation of the long string of pitched battles, which wound its way back through twenty years of remembrance; and so there is soon on the side of the Dutch the idea of snatching an advantage, not by necessary exertion and sacrifice, but by something with a preponderating element of chance in it. So the stone ships to block the Thames are prepared, and so, if some of the historians are right, does the scheme come to nothing, because the presence of superior English force eliminates chance. So do the English take on board troops for a descent on the Dutch shores, as it seems, on the chance that the Dutch fleet would not interfere; and then, after it is found how much the Dutch fleet does interfere, and has to be fought off the Schooneveld twice; and how heavy the loss of life has been in consequence, so far as we may gather, of too great reliance upon chance, even then this desire of a descent favoured by chance is not weakened. Fresh troops are embarked, who appear to have been useful as targets for the Dutch chiefly in the one operation—a general action of the old type—in which it was found feasible to engage.

It may be difficult to say with the materials before me—there may be none, in fact, which would give us the exact truth—but yet there is ground for believing that men did not lay sufficient stress on the circumstances surrounding the successes of the Vlie and the Medway, and hoped for the successes without the presence of like conditions.

Sandwich need have had no apprehensions in detaching Tiddiman early in August, for he was there himself with a full and victorious fleet, the Dutch having been, not two months before, frightfully beaten back into their ports, and full of the confusions, bickerings, and divided counsels, that the beaten side is prone to.

When Rupert and Albemarle detached Sir Robert Holms on the peculiarly successful enterprise in the Vlie, it was but a fortnight after the Dutch, thoroughly beaten in the battle off the North Foreland, had been driven behind the shelter of their shoals, leaving the victorious English entirely unopposed at sea; and when the Dutch made their appearance in the Medway, and carried off and burnt some of our finest war-ships, it was because the English had deliberately disarmed and unmanned those ships, clearly anticipating, and recording their anticipation three months before, that they would be attacked in the way they were. And on such grounds, the Dutch would have shown greater wisdom and prescience had they postponed all idea of blocking up the Thames in 1673 until they were assured of being able to protect the detachment employed in the duty; and the Allies would have shown a clearer apprehension of the situation had they been fully prepared to guarantee a landing without interruption from the Dutch fleet, without loss of communication with their own ships after landing, and with security for their re-embarkation. The histories do not tell us why these troops were so uselessly and so slaughterously carried about for two weeks on the Dutch coast, but reading between the lines, we seem to see that it was the want of these guarantees that enforced it.

One of the earlier historians considers that the advance of the Dutch to fight the battle of the 4th of June was an unusual proceeding on their part, "for, from the first action against the English in these seas, anno 1652, till this time, they had seldom voluntarily engaged out of sight of their own coast; nor had they ever been the aggressors in any one considerable fight, except twice, when they had the fortune to surprise the English, first in the Downs, in the time of Blake, and then in Souldbay, the former year (1672)." [9] I hardly think we can say that this was so, unless we injudiciously mingle the question of strategy which would determine the locality of the battle, and the question of tactics which would determine its conduct. At present I hardly touch at all upon the tactics pursued in these wars, and may dismiss Colliber's observation with the remark that inasmuch as it generally happened that the Dutch were to leeward, not by their choice, but by the accident of wind, it was hardly in their power in those days to become tactically the aggressors. Strategically, I think, we must rather accept the opposite view, and say that the Dutch in the three wars showed latterly a greater and not a less tendency to fight near home. In the first war, the last battle off the Texel was the only one which could properly be said to have been fought on the Dutch coast, and in the second war, the capture of the cruisers by Robertson off the Texel was the

9. *Columna Rostrata*, p. 238.

only fight on that side of the water. In the third war, on the other hand, three out of the four great battles were fought on the Dutch side of the North Sea; and I hardly think it was choice on the part of the Hollanders. I should say rather that a review of all the circumstances would show that they felt a decreasing power as each war went on, so that if the English had of themselves been as determined to beat the Dutch off the sea in 1672–73 as they had been in 1652–54, the war might have taken a different form, and the Dutch might have been pressed closer home than they were; but the third war was distasteful to the prevailing opinion in England, and the alliance with France served as an economy, not as an increase of force.

Without going more thoroughly into statistics than is conformable to the scope of this work, I cannot say how the question of the protection and loss of commerce may have affected exactly the conduct of the war and its popularity. My principal authority tells me that in the third war the loss of merchant ships by capture on both sides was considerable, but that it was greater on the side of the English than on that of the Dutch, simply because the Dutch prohibition left only the homeward-bound ships open to the English attack.[10] The immense destruction at the Vlie, and the considerable captures of the ships from Bergen, had in the second war probably far over-balanced the scale as against the Dutch; while in the first Dutch war we might almost say that the main effort had been immediately directed upon their enemy's commerce by the English. But if, while the battles of the war fleets, in consequence of the defections of the French, were fought without adequate result, and if English commerce had been suffering to a greater extent than that of the Dutch, there was some business objection to join to the moral one, and demand a cessation of the third war. English merchant shipping was immensely on the increase, as in 1688 it was estimated to have doubled since 1666, and if the Dutch by the prohibition of their own commerce were able to make the English losses proportionately the greater, the gain in so acting could be demonstrated.

All these wars were begun and ended on the sea. Even the successful raids that were made into territory extended hardly beyond the water territory, and the prizes drawn were water prizes. We may say it was the near equality of the combatants in every way which kept the battles off the land. When it was found difficult to get through with arrangements for even mere rushes at the land, the

10. Ibid., p. 250.

organizing of great expeditions such as Spain had set her heart on was out of the question. The wars adhered to the more unstable element simply, perhaps, because neither side could get off it.

While all that was really important in the drama was played in European waters, the byplot circulated in more distant parts of the world, wherever there were English or Dutch interests to attack or defend. In the first war, Van Galen on the one side and Commodore Bodley on the other fought in the Mediterranean over the right to carry on their own commerce unmolested, and to prevent the other from carrying on any at all, and did it with varying fortunes.

And then the old system of cross-raiding, begun in an irregular war of reprisals, was ushered in and continued amongst the distant possessions of both States in Africa and in the West Indies. Sir Robert Holms, entirely unopposed because no attempt or preparation to oppose him was or could have been made, ravaged down the West Coast of Africa, as already mentioned, to Cape Verd, Goree, Elmina, which withstood him, and Cape Coast Castle. Then he passed over to New Netherland, as New York was then called, and reduced it, because there was nothing to prevent him doing so. And then came the other side; for news reaching Holland of the mischief that had been quietly done, the Dutch Government proceeded to undo it again, or to do it over again equally secretly. De Ruiter, then at Cadiz, slipped away quietly in Sir Robert Holms' footsteps, to retake, if possible, all that had been taken. He was, in some cases, successful, and he took the original English post of Fort Cormantin, though Cape Coast Castle and Chama held out against him. Then passing over to Barbados, he found himself not strong enough for more than the capture of merchant ships which were there, and at Monserrat, Nevis, and Newfoundland, after which he returned home to be placed in command of the home fleet as we have seen.

But later on, in 1666–67, we had that transfer and re-transfer of islands in the West Indies from State to State which, from beginning to end, seems to have been characteristic of war in those latitudes. The English began by taking St. Eustace, Tobago, and other places from the Dutch. Then the Dutch, under Commodore Quiryns, made themselves masters of Surinam. Next the French and Dutch together all but possessed themselves of half the Island of St. Christopher's. A naval expedition from Barbados, to restore things at the former island, failed on account of dispersal by wind. The Dutch still gaining strength, Evertson recovered Tobago, and made many prizes on the coast of Virginia. But then Sir John Harman arrived from England at St. Christopher's with twelve frigates, in March

1667. This made a concentration of the French and Dutch necessary, and stopped the raiding till it was decided which nation was to
have the control in these waters. There was a general action in May
off St. Christopher's, as to which the immediate results are disputed; but the ultimate result was the separation of the French and
Dutch, leaving the English in command of the sea, and enabling
them to retake Surinam.

An early operation of the third war was the recapture of Tobago
by five or six ships and a regiment of foot from Barbados, under Sir
Thomas Bridger. On the other side, the Dutch population possessed
themselves of the Island of St. Helena, and drove the English Gover-
nor and people into the ships at anchor. But Commodore Mondy
with four ships-of-war, on his way to offer convoy to the East India
fleet, wanting fresh water and perceiving he must retake the Island
to get it, proceeded to that business and concluded it.

These special features of naval war will probably have to be re-
considered in some detail before we have done with them, in order
to get more closely at their principles. We may say that in all the
wars where the command of the sea was incomplete, and where territories which might be captured were tenable after capture, this
kind of thing went on. I believe, so far as I can see, that at the moment all that is before us is to note how closely conquest follows the
naval steps, and how all other power is, as it were, swallowed up by
naval power. It is not, of course, that even in this very early stage,
we do not see how naval force may be rendered unable to effect its
purpose; but the general result seems to give great preponderance to
him who has the power over the water, and each possessor of this
power seems to sweep all up as it progresses, leaving it to be again
swept up by the next naval possessor of the broom.

# CHAPTER FIVE

I N THE PREVIOUS chapters I have endeavoured to trace the rise of
true naval war and its nature; and then to show how, owing to
the position which sea-borne commerce takes as the major part of
the wealth and stability of nations, there may be, and have been,
wars wholly naval—wars where the operations on the land, or
against the land, have been insignificant, or else wholly absent, in
comparison with the operations on the water.

But as naval war arose and developed without premeditation,
and even without knowledge at first of what it really meant, it followed that it was only by degrees that men came to understand
what kinds of naval force were required in the economies of naval
war, and how these kinds of force could be most effectively distributed. If the first Anglo-Dutch war exhibited itself on a wholly
new plan, a plan which had never been seen in the world before, it
was quite possible to regard it as something exceptional, and to
suppose that earlier types of war might revive. It did not follow at
once that maritime nations should prepare for that kind of war, and
no other; it was not certain that this struggle for the command of
the sea was for ever after to be the one aim of naval nations, in the
first instance; and that unless there was at the outbreak of the war
excess of power on one side sufficient to assert and maintain it, the
Anglo-Dutch type of war was permanent.

But when a second and a third war succeeded, of which the lines
were, if anything, marked out in deeper cuts than ever, it could not
but follow that all who had control over naval services should endeavour to prepare them for that kind of war and no other.

And what, so far, was this kind of war? It was, doubtless, chiefly
a series of general actions between the most powerful forces that
each side could bring to bear against the other. Secondarily, it was

the defence and attack of commerce at sea. Thirdly, it was the attack and defence of commerce in port, supplemented here and there by attempts to damage the sources of naval strength, and to a very small extent by attempts to damage property on land. It had been made clear that the defence and attack of commerce could, and sometimes must, go on side by side with the direct struggle for the command of the sea; but equally clear that the power against which the balance turned by ever so little in the great primary contest, was terribly handicapped as to the defence of its commerce. It had also been fully demonstrated that it was entirely hopeless to think of making attacks on shipping in port, on sources of war supply, or on property on land, unless there were at least an assured local command of the sea surrounding the point attacked. This was possibly the lesson least easy to learn, seeing that until the advent of the Dutch wars the system of cross-raiding had not been abandoned.

Almost obviously some differentiation of naval force should have followed the determination of the Dutch in the second and third wars to abandon all attempts to defend their commerce, and by consequence to suppress it for the time. On the Dutch side, their whole power would be thrown into the form which was considered most suitable for the great fleet action, but they might also have looked to a small expenditure on vessels most suitable for attacking the commerce of the enemy at sea. On the English side, the knowledge that the Dutch were determined to throw their whole energies into the general fleet action, as a direct endeavour to get such a command of the sea as would enable them to restore their commerce, would compel special attention to the preparation of the fleet for general action. The absence of Dutch commerce would equally divert attention from the provision of means for commerce attack, and there would remain commerce defence. But even here the attitude of the Dutch would have been such as not to arouse great apprehension, and, therefore, even commerce defence might have held in general estimation a subordinate place.

Strategically, the effect was on both sides towards a differentiation of force into that which was considered most suitable for the general fleet action, and that supposed most efficient for the attack and defence of commerce, apart from those great efforts which had characterized the first Dutch war, but which were eliminated from the second and third by reason of the Dutch withdrawal of their merchant ships from sea. Further, the strategical effect of the time was to minimise the force set apart for the secondary object.

The practice of privateering may be supposed to have tended still more to minimise the provision of public force for the attack on commerce. We have seen already [1] that, in the reign of Elizabeth, the practice of allowing subjects to fit out war-ships for preying on the enemy's commerce was in full force. The historians speak less of it in the Dutch wars, but still say enough to assure us that it was in effective force. To some extent, it relieved the states on both sides from the provision of a large force of vessels for the attack on commerce.

But if the strategical conditions of naval war thus tended to a differentiation, the tactical conditions tended even more strongly that way. When the general action—the purely naval action of ships under sail—took, in the first Dutch war, its place as a revival of the military battle of the ancients and of the middle ages on the water, it was a novelty, and there was little sense either that it would ultimately require particular classes of ships or assume any particular form. Preparations for a sea-fight had not, before this time, assumed either characteristic. There was no differentiation of force, and hardly any adoption of form.

We have seen that on the part of Spain, in 1588, the idea of a regular sea-fight appears to have been altogether absent. There was in the Spanish Armada, in fact, no differentiation of force, and no established order of fight.

But neither was there on our own side. We collected an immense force, but in the lists handed down to us there is no sign of any classification, of any gathering together of classes of ships for the purpose of concerted action. There were several lists or groupings of the ships, but all of them without classification. There were 34 ships serving with the Lord High Admiral, all apparently Queen's ships, and their gradations went steadily down from the *Triumph,* of 1,100 tons and 500 men, to the *Signet,* of 30 tons and 20 men. Of 10 ships "serving by tonnage with the Lord Admiral," the gradation of class descended pretty evenly, from the *Edward of Maldon,* of 180 tons and 30 men, to the *Peppin,* of 20 tons and 8 men. With Sir Francis Drake were 32 ships, from the *galleon Leicester,* of 400 tons and 160 men, to the *Carvel,* of 30 tons and 24 men; and so on through several other divisions consisting of smaller ships, but each list offering a gradual fall in the force of the ships from the highest to the lowest. [2]

1. Page 27.
2. See Charnock's *History of Marine Architecture,* vol. ii., p. 59.

An analysis of the lists gives us 197 ships in all, manned by 15,785 men. The tonnage of some are omitted, but that of 175 of them came to 29,744 tons, and their sizes were thus distributed:—

| Ships. | Tons. | Ships. | Tons. |
|---|---|---|---|
| 1 | 1,100 | 5 | 300 |
| 1 | 1,000 | 7 | 250 |
| 2 | 800 | 26 | about 200 |
| 3 | 600 | 33 | 150 |
| 6 | 500 | 19 | 100 |
| 5 | 400 | 66 | under 100 |
| 1 | 360 | | |

There are thus no gaps, no points at which we can say, here are a group of ships suited to one purpose, and here a group suited to another. All the traces of classification fall into one fact that as the ships grow smaller so they grow more numerous.

A list of the navy at the Queen's death in 1603, handed down to us by Sir William Monson, supplies the following analysis:—

| Ships. | Tons. | Ships. | Tons. |
|---|---|---|---|
| 2 | 1,000 | 2 | 400 |
| 3 | 900 | 3 | about 300 |
| 3 | 800 | 7 | 200 |
| 2 | 700 | 3 | 100 |
| 4 | 600 | 8 | under 100 |
| 4 | 500 | | |

In this list we have the same steady gradation downwards, from the most to the least powerful ships, but with the difference that the smaller ships are not so numerous, there being 20 ships of 400 tons and upwards and only 21 below that size. This is probably explained by the practice, which then obtained so largely, of mingling private enterprise with that of the State; so that dependence was placed on the merchants to supply the smaller vessels required.

Take, again, the list of the Queen's ships in the expedition of Essex to Cadiz,[3] and we find 17 ships which, as the fighting force, did not carry soldiers. There were 3 ships with crews of 340 men, 6 with 200 to 300 men, 2 with from 100 to 200 men, and 6 carrying under 100. Here still is the regular gradation from large to small,

3. See ibid., p. 151.

111

without any sign of classification or grouping such as would lead us to infer adaptation to particular purposes.

But in the early part of the seventeenth century there was a tendency to group the ships, which afterwards developed into the well-known system of rating which has only fallen out of use in our own day. But the proposal of Sir Robert Dudley (Duke of Northumberland), referred to, and the subsequent systems of classification and rating, were not prompted by considerations either strategical or tactical, having to do apparently only with convenient nomenclature, account, and finance.

Dudley's classification was as follows:—(1) The *galleon*, of 80 guns; (2) the *rambargo*, a light frigate or pinnace; (3) the *galizabra*, a galleas; (4) the *frigata*; (5) the *galeron*, a galley; (6) the *galerata*, a small galley; (7) the *passa-volante*, a dispatch vessel.

From the nature of this grouping, it is plain that the attempted classification was no more than a desire to put into order that which had no order, and to group several diverse classes into one or two which fairly represented the mean of them. This plan of grouping was not adopted, though it may have hastened the adoption of another one. This was the one adopted by His Majesty's Commissioners originally appointed to report on the state of the navy on the 12th February 1618. They reported on the numbers and tonnage of the ships they found, but it was not till they came to propose what the navy should be that they used any classification, or found any necessary. Then that which they used, and which remained the official classification for many years, had nothing to do with strategy or tactics, but was solely an administrative device. The navy proposed to be maintained and classed was:—

|  |  |  |
|---|---|---|
| 4 "Ships Royall," | 800 to 1,200 tons. | |
| 14 "Great Ships," | 600 to 800 | „ |
| 6 "Middling Ships," | 450 | „ |
| 2 "Small Ships," | 350 | „ |
| 4 "Pinnaces," | 80 to 250 tons.[4] | |

Not only do we detect no strategical or tactical idea in the names, but the descending dimensions are regular, and all that we can certainly assure ourselves of is that there was, for some reason or another, a preference for ships of nearly, but not quite, the largest class.

In a list of the navy at the close of James I.'s reign, 33 ships are

4. Ibid., p. 247.

given; but except for the increase in the numbers of ships of from 600 to 900 tons, the descent is steady from 1,200 tons and 55 guns to 80 tons, as if there were an equal use for all sorts of ships, except for those carrying 32 to 44 guns, and of from 600 to 900 tons.[5]

The system of dividing the larger ships of the British Navy into six rates appears to have been introduced during the Commonwealth. It was certainly fully adopted as early as 1660. About this time it was recognized that first rates carried over 70 guns; second rates, 60 to 70; third rates, 50 to 60; fourth rates, 38 to 50; fifth rates, 22 to 30; and sixth rates, 10 to 20. What we have to observe is that the divisions and classes are all administrative and financial. Nearly every man's pay, from the captain downwards, was regulated by the rate of the ship he happened to be serving in. But apart from this, there was the convenience—largely used—of speaking of the rate instead of the ship; and for years the master shipwrights at the yards received orders to build such and such a rate, and they were not expected to ask for any directions after receiving this simple order.

But if we reflect for a moment over this early constitution of the "rates," we can see that it not only omits to notice what strategy and tactics might demand, but it is the negation of it, supposing strategy and tactics should demand anything but a regular gradation of force. On the face of it, if we have such a classification as is just described, the inference is that we are going to build an equal number of each class. The last thing we should think of is that, for the purposes of war, some of these classes will require to be immensely swelled, and some reduced to a minimum, if not eliminated altogether. So the establishment of a series of rates or ranks, which lasted all through our wars, and which existed, in theory at least, till some seven years ago, may have been a direct hindrance to naval progress, which experience, indeed, perceived and threw off, but which was, nevertheless, a hindrance as long as it lasted.

The system of rating in a regular gradation downwards seems to have been common to several nations during the latter part of the seventeenth century. My chief authority, Charnock, is sometimes not quite satisfactory as to accuracy in minor matters, and I think he would be guilty of interpolating into original documents, by way of explaining them, without giving full notice that he has done so. Therefore, when he gives us, without quoting his authority, a table of the strength of the French Navy in 1681, under the head of five

5. Ibid., p. 274.

"rates" and four smaller groups, we are not altogether certain whether or no the rates are an interpolation. However, as given, the first rates average 90 guns, the second 72 guns, the third 53 guns, the fourth 42 guns, the fifth 30 guns; and then there are "small frigates," fire-ships, barca-longas, and pinks.[6]

But it may be said that navies and fleets about the time of the outbreak of the first Dutch war—that is, about the middle of the seventeenth century—pretty fairly conformed to the ideal put forward in the system of rating, and ships were built less with the view of definite duties corresponding to their size and strength, than with the view of completing the tale of each particular rate in some approach to numerical symmetry.

The British Navy stood thus on the 27th December 1653:—

1st Rates: 3 of 891 to 1,556 tons, 64 to 104 guns, and 350 to 700 men.

2nd Rates: 11 of 721 to 875 tons, 54 to 66 guns, and 260 to 400 men.

3rd Rates: 11 of 532 to 800 tons, 44 to 60 guns, and 200 to 300 men.

4th Rates: 63 of 301 to 700 tons, 28 to 50 guns, and 100 to 220 men.

5th Rates: 35 of 105 to 500 tons, 12 to 36 guns, and 30 to 200 men.

6th Rates: 9 of 55 to 255 tons, 6 to 36 guns, and 25 to 130 men.

4 fire-ships of 10 guns and 30 men.

8 victuallers of 10 to 12 guns, and 30 to 40 men.

In this list, though the mass of the ships are absorbed in the fourth and fifth rates, these rates themselves cover a very wide field, being as high as 50-gun ships, and as low as 12, pointing still more clearly towards the administrative rather than the tactical or strategical origin of the system of rating.

But this date, 1653, was one where already the experience of war had had its effect. Two years and a half before, there had been the same number of first and second rates, but only 7 third rates, and 20 fourth rates, and only 4 fifth rates. The result of the experience of war had been, therefore, to increase the numbers of the middle-class ships. We must remember what we have seen the nature of this war to be—namely, one where the attack and defence of a commerce which was collected in great masses formed the moving principle. It does not seem impossible to connect the increase of middle-sized ships directly with such a method of carrying on the war; but,

6. Ibid., p. 310.

then, I think we must allow that the fleet action, pure and simple, fell into the second place. And there was as yet little in the fleet action to cause the clear differentiation which it afterwards did.

I am not now going into the tactical question more than to trace its bearing on the differentiation of force; but it is essential that we should keep in mind that up to the end of the first Dutch war the tactics employed were of a kind that allowed all classes of ships, without distinction, to take part in a general action. We have already seen that this was so, and it is made clear to us, from the numbers of ships employed, that the whole navy on each side, ships large and small, fought together.

Sir William Monson, writing between 1635 and 1640 probably, give us a very fair view of the tactical ideas in his earlier days, and the point at which they had arrived when he wrote; and we can see all through that there was nothing to lead the men of that day to set apart particular classes of ships for the general action. Indiscriminate numbers rather than selected types would probably have represented the idea of force in the naval mind under the circumstances.

> The strict ordering of battles by ships [says Sir William Monson] was before the invention of the bowline, for then there was no sailing but before the wind, nor no fighting but by boarding; whereas, now, a ship will sail within six points of thirty-two, and by the advantage of wind may rout any fleet that is placed in that (the half-moon) form of battle.
>
> The weather at sea is never certain, the winds variable, ships unequal in sailing; and when they strictly seek to keep their order, commonly they fall foul one of another; and in such cases they are more careful to observe their directions than to offend the enemy, whereby they will be brought into disorder amongst themselves.
>
> Suppose a fleet to be placed in the form of a half moon, or other proportion to fight, if an enemy charge them home in any of the corners of the half-moon, they will be forced to bear up room into their main battle; and there will ensue dangers and disorders of boarding one another, insomuch that it will not be possible for a general to give new directions, but every ship must fight at its will, not by command.
>
> For the avoiding of such confusion, the instructions of a general ought not to consist of many words, for the greatest advantage in a sea-fight is to get the wind of one another; for he that has the wind is out of danger of being boarded, and has the advantage where to board, and how to attempt the enemy. . . .
>
> The wind being thus gotten, a general need give no other directions than to every admiral of a squadron to draw together their squadrons, and everyone to undertake his opposite squadron, or

115

where he shall do it for his greatest advantage but to be sure to take a good distance from one another, and to relieve that squadron that shall be over-charged or distressed.

Let them give warning to their ships not to venture so far as to bring themselves to leeward of the enemy; for so shall they either dishonour themselves, to see such a ship taken in their view, or in seeking to relieve her they shall bring themselves to leeward, and lose the advantage they had formerly gotten; for it will be in the power of the enemy to board them, and they not to avoid it which was the only thing coveted by the Spaniards in our time of war by reason of the advantage of their ships, as I have before expressed.[7]

Confirmatory of these views as to the methods of fighting which were in vogue when the first Dutch war broke out, we have the orders of the Earl of Lindsey to the captains of his fleet which he fitted out in 1635.

If we happen [he says] to descry any fleet at sea, which we may probably know or conjecture designs to oppose, encounter, or affront us, I will first strive to get the wind (if I be to leeward), and so shall the whole fleet in due order do the like, and when we come to join battle, no ship shall presume to assault the admiral, vice-admiral, or rear-admiral, but only myself, my vice-admiral, or rear-admiral, if we be able to reach them; and the other ships are to match themselves accordingly as they can, and to secure one another as cause shall require, not wasting their powder at small vessels or victuallers, nor firing till they come side to side.[8]

This promiscuous sort of fighting, which is fairly well exhibited in the plate on page 118, might take in ships of every class, and did not tend to set up any one class over any other. But the opening of the Dutch wars brought the fire-ship into prominence, and in the early battles it was a terrible weapon. But, this being so, it was only natural that some measures should be taken to reduce its power. One great source of this power was the way in which the ships during a fight were distributed in masses, for a fire-ship drifting down from to windward upon such a mass was certain to grapple some ship. Again, it was soon discovered that a promiscuous attack and defence was a very uncertain and a very unsatisfactory one. We have seen how much all the great actions in the Dutch wars partook of the character of pitched battles, and the fact must have appealed

7. Monson in *Churchill's Voyages,* vol. iii., p. 320.
8. Ibid., p. 297.

with double force to those who had the conduct of naval affairs in charge at the time.

The Dutch seem to have been earliest in devising means both to weaken the power of the fire-ships, and to bring the fleet not only under better control, but into such form as would insure the exertion of its collective power. This was the establishment of the Line as the fighting formation, and we get it in the English navy as early as March 31st, 1655. Probably no doubt exists to prevent us giving to Sir William Penn the full credit of commencing the great tactical revolution. We have it in the "Instructions for the better ordering of the fleet in fighting," issued at that date by Blake, Monk, Disbrowe, and Penn; but it will be seen that, though we have the Line introduced, it is done, as it were, tentatively, and without any of that conviction which gave it in after years so rigid a position in naval tactics. Article 2 says:—

> At sight of the said fleet (an enemy's fleet), the vice-admiral, or he that commands in chief in the second place, and his squadron, as also the rear-admiral, or he that commands in chief in the third place, and his squadron, are to make what sail they can to come up to the admiral on each wing, the vice-admiral on the right, and the rear-admiral on the left; giving a competent distance for the admiral's squadron, if the wind will permit, and there be sea-room enough.[9]

Here we have the old idea of promiscuous fighting in squadrons prevailing, an idea which would admit of all classes of ships taking their share in the fight, the notion—traceable in previous quotations, and in this, so far—being that ships would seek out their matches and fight the battle out in a series of duels. But in Article 3 we have, faintly and tentatively, the new idea.

> As soon as they shall see the general engage, or make a signal by firing two guns, and putting out a red flag on the fore-topmast head, that then each squadron shall take the best advantage they can to engage the enemy next to them; and, in order hereunto, all the ships of every squadron shall endeavour to keep in a line with the chief, unless the chief of their squadron be either lamed, or otherwise disabled (which God forbid), whereby the said ship which wears the flag shall not come in to do the service which is requisite. Then every ship of the said squadron shall endeavour to get in a line with the admiral, or the commander-in-chief next to him and nearest the enemy.[10]

9. *Life of Sir William Penn*, vol. ii., p. 77.
10. Ibid.

Naval Action between the Dutch, English, and French, on the 21st August, 1673

These instructions formed the basis of those issued by James Duke of York when he took command of the fleet, and dated 27th April 1665.[11] These latter show the greater precision in the order of fighting, which had been at least theoretically arrived at. The second instruction changes its form, and runs:—

> At sight of the said fleet, the vice-admiral (or he who commands in chief in the second place), with his squadron; and the rear-admiral (or he who commands in chief in the third squadron), with his squadron; are to make what sail they can to come up, and to put themselves into that order of battle which shall be given them; for which the signal shall be the Union flag put on the mizen peak of the admiral's ship; at sight whereof, as well the vice and rear-admirals of the red squadron, as the admirals, vice-admirals, and rear-admirals of the other squadrons, are to answer it by doing the like.

Here is, in some sort, the abandonment of promiscuous fighting. A precise order of battle is in the background, and to be put in force by signal. The third instruction runs thus:—

> In case the enemy have the wind of the admiral and fleet, and they have sea-room enough, then they are to keep the wind as close as they can lie, until such time as they see an opportunity, by gaining their wakes, to divide the enemy's fleet; and if the van of His Majesty's fleet find that they have the wake of any considerable part of them, they are to tack and stand in, and strive to divide the enemy's body; and that squadron that shall pass first, being got to windward, is to bear down on those ships to leeward of them; and the middle squadron is to keep her wind, and to observe the motion of the enemy's van, which the last squadron is to second; and both of these squadrons are to do their utmost to assist or relieve the first squadron that divided the enemy's fleet.[12]

The other instructions which, for our present purpose, it is important to note are numbers IV., VII., and VIII. Number IV., stands thus:—

> If the enemy have the wind of His Majesty's fleet, and come to fight them, the commanders of His Majesty's ships shall endeavour to put themselves in one line, close upon a wind, according to the order of battle.

---

11. I quote from ibid., app. L. There is an undoubted copy of the Duke of York's instructions in the library of the Royal U.S. Institution.

12. It is strange that, with these words in existence, there should have been thought to be novelty in Clerk of Eldin's plan of "breaking the line." The author of the *Life of Penn* justly remarks upon the case.

Instruction VII. runs thus:—

In case His Majesty's fleet have the wind of the enemy, and that the enemy stand towards them, and they towards the enemy, then the van of His Majesty's fleet shall keep the wind; and when they are come within a convenient distance from the enemy's rear they shall stay, until their own whole line is come up within the same distance from the enemy's van; and then their whole line is to tack (every ship in his own place), and to bear down upon them so nigh as they can (without endangering their loss of wind); and to stand along with them, the same tacks aboard, still keeping the enemy to leeward, and not suffering them to tack in their van; and in case the enemy tack in the rear first, he who is in the rear of His Majesty's fleet, is to tack first, with as many ships, divisions, or squadrons, as are those of the enemy's; and if all the enemy's ships tack, their whole line is to follow, standing along with the same tacks aboard as the enemy doth.

Instruction VIII. runs:—

If the enemy stay to fight (His Majesty's fleet having the wind), the headmost squadron of His Majesty's fleet shall steer for the headmost of the enemy's ships.

It may be said of these instructions, that their spirit, if not their letter, governed the conduct of sea fights as long as they were carried out under sail. But we must not suppose that because the Line was thus set out on paper as the fighting formation, not *par excellence,* but alone, that it at once assumed its full position in fact. It was slow in accomplishing its destiny. According to Père Hoste, it was the formation taken up by both English and Dutch in the battle of the 29th of July 1653; and according to the same authority it was fully employed by the Duke of York in the battle off the Texel, in June 1665. But it was dropped again by Albemarle in the battle of June 1666; and by the way Sir William Penn speaks of it, it seems clear that there was still controversy as to whether a line was, or was not, the best form in which to throw a fleet for fighting purposes. Pepys reports what Penn said of the fight, a few days after its unfortunate results were made known:—"He says three things must be remedied, or else we shall be undone by this fleet. That we must fight in a line, whereas we fought promiscuously, to our utter and demonstrable ruin; the Dutch fight otherwise, and we whenever we beat them.[13]

So that though the line was established on paper as the fighting

13. See *Life of Penn*, vol. ii., p. 399. Two other things were mentioned.

formation soon after the outbreak of the first Dutch war, and though it was very precisely spoken of in authoritative instructions at the beginning of the second Dutch war, it had probably not got an absolutely firm hold in the third Dutch war. The term "line of battle" does not occur in the Duke of York's instructions. It is not used by Lord Torrington in 1690, who, when he writes describing the French fleet then in sight, does not speak of "line-of-battle ships," but of ships "fit to lie in a line." [14]

The advantages of the line were, however, certain to give it permanence. It was, in the first place, the great defence against fire-ships; for when the fleet to leeward was drawn out in one thin line, it was comparatively easy to open out so as to let the fire-ships drift harmlessly through. I suppose that it was this fact that ultimately abolished the fire-ship as a weapon. It was at the height of its value when fleets fought in masses, as I have said; but the more certain it became that both fleets would draw out into line, the less was the hope of an effective use of the fire-ship. As I am now on the differentiation of naval force, I may as well finish with the fire-ship at once, its reign really coinciding with the date before and during the line of battle. We have seen what a prominent part the fire-ship played all through the Dutch wars, though it is not always easy to say what numbers were employed in each fleet. But in 1678 there were 6 fire-ships to a fleet of 77 rated ships. Ten years later there were 26 fire-ships to 52 rated ships ready for sea. At King William's death there were 87 fire-ships to 123 ships of the line. In 1714 there were about 50 fire-ships to about 123 sail of the line. In 1727 the fire-ship had become less popular, as there were only 3 or 4 to 123 sail of the line. In 1741 there were fire-ships at home, in the West Indies, and in the Mediterranean, but there were only 17 to a total of 180 rated ships, 129 of which were in commission. At the peace of Aix-la-Chapelle (1748) we had but 5 fire-ships against a total of 174 rated ships. At the peace of Paris (1763) there were 8 fire-ships in commission at home to 55 sail of the line. At the peace of 1783 we have further hints of the decadence of the fire-ship, as there were only 7 then serviceable, though there were 273 rated ships afloat. After the outbreak of the revolutionary war we cease to hear of them as parts of an ordinary fleet, and at the peace of Amiens (1802) we only find 9 or 10 ships spoken of at a time when the navy contained nearly 1,000 ships of all classes. The number of fire-ships in

14. Entick, p. 548. The earliest use I find of the term is in the *Life of Cornelius Van Tromp*, printed in 1697.

commission during the revolutionary war was 3 only, from 1794 to 1799. Then it rose to 7 for that year and for 1800, falling again to 3 in 1801, and to 1 only in 1802. In 1804 and 1805 there was 1 fire-ship in commission, but after this they disappear altogether as an effective weapon.

The history of the fire-ship does not lack parallels in naval annals. It springs into favour as a weapon because the method of fighting in masses of ships clustered together offered peculiar facilities for its employment, but almost at once, the defence of drawing the fleets out into a long single line becoming established, the position of the fire-ship was weakened, and it was a less important weapon than it had been. But the impetus it had received originally pushed it on, so that, though it was really weakened, it was held in higher estima-tion, and increased its numbers to a maximum at the end of William III.'s reign. Then experience begins to offer counteracting resistance to the waning impetus, and the weapon becomes gradually dis-credited. Yet it hangs on for years, after all thought of using it as it was originally used has passed away.

Taking the rise, progress, and fall of the fire-ship as an illustration of the differentiation of naval force, and the rules which govern it, we can recur to the line of battle and trace its effects. I have already pointed out how, in promiscuous fighting between two fleets, every class of ship was admitted, because, as there was no special order or rank of the ships, each could generally, and did generally, seek out her match and fight the battle out in a series of duels. But as soon as the single line became established, each ship had her fixed place which she could not quit, and hence, if there were great diversities in the strength of ships forming the line, the weakest was quite likely to find herself opposite the strongest in the ensuing battle. The action of the establishment of the line-of-battle tended, there-fore, in the first place, to the excision of the weaker ships from their place in the line, and to the embodiment of Lord Torrington's idea of having only "ships fit to lie in a line"—that is, of having what afterwards came to be called line-of-battle ships.

But, further, the tendency of the Line must have been to increase the power of the individual line-of-battle ship, so as to reduce the numbers, as a line of great extent would be unmanageable, and, in fact, could not be maintained as a line in view of changes of the wind. But on the other hand, the increase in the force of the individ-ual ship would not have been carried to an extreme. The fear of put-ting too many eggs in one basket might always be expected to oper-ate, and though it might not prevent the occasional building of a

ship which was gigantic by comparison, it would prevent the reduction of the line-of-battle ships to a very small number of very powerful ships. But just the same causes which prolonged the life of the
fire-ship beyond the period when it could be usefully employed,
would tend to prevent its being seen, even through some courses of
years, that the real line-of-battle ship was a medium ship, neither
descending to the lowest nor ascending to the highest rank in the
scale of force. The custom which had obtained in the days of promiscuous fighting of building ships of all classes, with the idea that
all classes could fight side by side in the general action, might be
expected to prevail long after the reason of the thing had demanded
a uniform pattern line-of-battle ship of medium power.

But as the general action to be fought out in two opposing lines of
ships became established, the attack and defence of commerce,
which had existed before this time, called for suitable war-ships to
carry it out. The establishment of the line-of-battle not only differentiated a powerful class of ships for taking part in that fighting formation, but as it excluded the smaller classes of ships from partak-
ing in the general action it met half way the demand for special
ships for looking after commerce, either by way of attack or defence.

It would appear probable that the commerce protectors or at-
tackers would be naturally the smaller class of vessels, because, in
the case of great convoys, what happened in the first Dutch war
would most naturally repeat itself, and that a line-of-battle force
would be employed on both sides. Where the convoy was small, the
economy of war would not permit of weakening the main line of
battle for so inferior a service; and while a lighter force might serve
for the attack, so would a lighter force form a sufficient defence.
The mere fact that a defence by way of convoy was furnished might
put aside all idea of attack. For though it might be possible to furnish inferior force to attack unguarded merchant ships, it might be
difficult to withdraw from the main force enough to make itself distinctly superior to the light force which was guarding a merchant
convoy. Then, too, there must always have been the two words
about convoy. A large concourse of merchant-ships would make a
tempting prize, which it would be worth an effort to secure; a proportionately powerful force might not safely be found to guard it.
The alternative would be to break up the convoy into several sections, each under a light guard. It would be unlikely that all should
be attacked, and those that were attacked, a light guard might be
sufficient to defend. The general tendency on the whole would be to
have a very numerous and very light set of ships, for the especial

123

purpose of protecting their own commerce and attacking that of the enemy.

We thus get a tendency towards such a differentiation of naval force as would set apart as line-of-battle ships those specially designed to fight in a line, and to act in concert, as the main strength of the naval position; the citadel as it were of naval power; that arrangement of naval force before which every other nature of naval force must bow, and which could not be overcome but by a greater quantity of like force. The necessity for this setting apart of a special class of ships to fight in the line of battle was fully admitted in 1744, and Admiral Lestock's anonymously published pamphlet against Mathews contains language forcibly pointing to the position the line of battle had taken, and to the certainty that sooner or later uniformity in the ships composing the line-of-battle would be established as the necessary outcome of sea-fights so conducted.

> A line of battle [says the anonymous pamphleteer] is the basis and foundation of all discipline in sea-fights, and is universally practised by all nations that are masters of any power at sea; it has had the test of a long experience, and stood before the stroke of time, pure and unaltered, handed down by our predecessors as the most prudential and best concerted disposition that can possibly be used at sea. This order consists in a fleet of ships being extended in a straight line either ahead or abreast one ship of another, to keep as close together as the weather will permit, that at all times every ship may be ready to sustain, relieve, or succour one another. It is directed that each ship in the line of battle shall keep within half a cable's length of one another, which is about 50 fathoms; that if His Majesty's fleet should have the wind of the enemy, the van shall steer with the van of the enemy, and there engage them, by which means every ship knows her adversary, and from the foremost in the van to the rear, attacks them successively.[15]

Thus the line-of-battle promised to establish uniformity, and also that the line-of-battle ship would approach this uniformity on the lines not of ships of extreme force, for then there would be too few of them, nor yet of a very low force, for then a fleet to be strong must be too numerous to handle. This was what was before the line-of-battle ship, and yet not of early accomplishment because of the force of custom and the tradition of the promiscuous manner of fighting.

15. *A Narrative of the Proceedings of His Majesty's Fleet in the Mediterranean, and the Combined Fleets of France and Spain, from the Year 1741 to March 1744.* London, 1744.

But as the line-of-battle ship was thus differentiated and parted from every other sort of war-ship, it followed that the fleet would require adjuncts in the shape of lighter ships to serve the purpose of look-outs or scouts. These ships would naturally be of much weaker force than the line-of-battle ship, for they would not take part in the fight; but they would require to be of good size so as to be able to keep company with the fleet, and so as to have a speed greater than the fleet itself in order to out-sail it and return to it in the exercise of the functions of the look-out. These duties pointed to the heavy frigate, but to a ship as far below the line-of-battle ship in force as would allow of her carrying out the special *rôle* of attending on the fleet.

Lastly, there was the much lighter attendant on commerce either by way of attack or defence, and if the practice of large convoys should fall, as it might, into disrepute, the tendency of these lighter and smaller vessels—not of the smallest size, but still low down in the scale of force—would be to grow.

This differentiation of naval force into three classes: (1) the line-of-battle ship, (2) the frigate, and (3) the light cruiser, seems to grow naturally out of the conditions of naval warfare which we have seen established; and yet judging by the progress we have seen, we should expect the differentiation to be of slow growth. It must, I think, be admitted as a fact that the naval mind is unaccustomed to project itself onward. It is so practical that it will not move until it is pushed; and thus, though I think we can clearly trace the progress of differentiation of force, it never was complete; and all we can say is that as years went on it grew nearer and nearer to the ideal, so that at the close of naval war about 1813, we get the remarkable results which will be seen.

I have already shown that in the earlier parts of the Dutch wars the differentiation was not marked. I will take as a later instance, the composition of the fleet of August 1666, commanded by Prince Rupert and the Duke of Albermarle.[16] That fleet stood as follows:—

| Ships. | Guns. | | Ships. | Guns. | | Ships. | Guns. |
|---|---|---|---|---|---|---|---|
| 1 | of 102 | | 4 | of 64 | | 5 | of 42 |
| 1 | „ 90 | | 6 | „ 60 | | 2 | „ 44 |
| 2 | „ 82 | | 12 | „ 58 | | 3 | „ 42 |
| 1 | „ 80 | | 1 | „ 56 | | 5 | „ 40 |
| 2 | „ 76 | | 2 | „ 54 | | 4 | „ 38 |
| 2 | „ 72 | | 6 | „ 52 | | 1 | „ 34 |

16. See Charnock, vol. ii., p. 397.

| Ships. | Guns. | Ships. | Guns. | Ships. | Guns. |
|--------|-------|--------|-------|--------|-------|
| 2 „ | 70 | 9 „ | 50 | 1 „ | 30 |
| 1 „ | 66 | 14 „ | 48 | | |

Perhaps the absence of differentiation is as well marked in this fleet as it could be, but it is also well marked in a list of the whole navy drawn up by a Royal Commission in 1686.[17]

| Ships. | Guns. | Ships. | Guns. | Ships. | Guns. |
|--------|-------|--------|-------|--------|-------|
| 5 of | 100 | 2 of | 64 | 6 of | 42 |
| 3 „ | 96 | 5 „ | 62 | 1 „ | 38 |
| 10 „ | 90 | 3 „ | 60 | 6 „ | 32 |
| 2 „ | 82 | 9 „ | 54 | 6 „ | 30 |
| 1 „ | 80 | 1 „ | 50 | 2 „ | 28 |
| 4 „ | 72 | 19 „ | 48 | 1 „ | 18 |
| 28 „ | 70 | 3 „ | 46 | 5 „ | 16 |
| 1 „ | 66 | 1 „ | 44 | | |

Then, at the death of William III. (1702), the navy stood thus:[18]—

| Ships. | Guns. | Ships. | Guns. | Ships. | Guns. |
|--------|-------|--------|-------|--------|-------|
| 8 of | 96 to 110 | 2 of | 66 | 1 of | 44 |
| 12 „ | 90 | 1 „ | 64 | 1 „ | 40 |
| 16 „ | 80 | 17 „ | 60 | 28 „ | 32 |
| 1 „ | 74 | 3 „ | 54 | 16 „ | 24 |
| 2 „ | 72 | 1 „ | 53 | | |
| 22 „ | 70 | 38 „ | 48 | | |

We hardly trace any definite objects in the changes shown in the second list, the result of sixteen years' experience. There is some simplification and reduction in the number of types, a slight increase in the number of the heaviest line-of-battle ships, an increase in the 60-, 48-, and 32-gun ships, but we can hardly say that the real wants of the navy were being met. It is more as if opinion was swaying about, uncertain of its own aims, and acting in one way at one time and in another at another time. According to Schomberg, all the ships down to and including those of 48 guns were considered as proper to form the line of battle, but if this were so, it is only an evidence how little advance had been made in the true direction, for nothing could exceed the incongruity of so arranging a sea fight that

17. Entick, p. 534.
18. *Schomberg's Naval Chronology*, vol. iv., p. 4.

a 48-gun ship should find herself matched against a 90-gun ship, or a 53-gun ship against a 110.

The navy of 1727 begins, in more than one way, to show the influences on differentiation of the causes enumerated. And there is besides an increased simplification in the matter of reduction in the number of types. The navy stood thus: [19]—

| Ships. | Guns. | Ships. | Guns. | Ships. | Guns. |
|--------|-------|--------|-------|--------|-------|
| 7 | of 100 | 23 | of 70 | 24 | of 40 |
| 13 | „ 90 | 24 | „ 60 | 1 | „ 30 |
| 16 | „ 80 | 40 | „ 50 | 28 | „ 20 |

13 sloops of 4 to 10 guns.

Schomberg now excludes all ships below 50 guns from place in the line of battle, which, if he has contemporary authority to justify the statement, shows the action of causes which would raise the force of the individual line-of-battle ship and make the type uniform. Then, too, we have the exhibition of the gap between the force of the smallest line-of-battle ship, and the largest frigate, in the sudden drop of from 50 guns in the one case, to no more than 40 in the other. The admission of the new class, the Sloop, with no more than 10 guns, is a distinct effect of the causes sketched out, and certain to operate sooner or later.

We may now take the ships in commission in different parts of the world in 1741, through which we can trace still more clearly the tendencies of differentiation. At home the force in commission is stated as follows: [20]—

| Ships. | Guns. | Ships. | Guns. | Ships. | Guns. |
|--------|-------|--------|-------|--------|-------|
| 3 | of 100 | 7 | of 70 | 4 | of 40 |
| 6 | „ 90 | 2 | „ 60 | 15 | „ 20 |
| 10 | „ 80 | 13 | „ 50 | | |

10 sloops 4 to 10 guns.

In the West Indies the force was:—

| Ships. | Guns. | Ships. | Guns. | Ships. | Guns. |
|--------|-------|--------|-------|--------|-------|
| 8 | of 80 | 16 | of 60 | 3 | of 40 |
| 7 | „ 70 | 3 | „ 50 | 6 | „ 20 |

3 sloops of 8 guns.

19. Ibid., p. 10.
20. Ibid., p. 17.

In the Mediterranean we had.—

| Ships. | Guns. | Ships. | Guns. |
|---|---|---|---|
| 2 | of 80 | 3 | of 20 |
| 5 | „ 60 | 1 | „ 8 |
| 2 | „ 50 | | |

In these three fleets we can in some sort discern an increase in line-of-battle ships of what might be called upper middle strength, as—counting the 50-gun ships as of the line of battle, but nothing below that—we have 57 line-of-battle ships of from 60 to 80 guns, and only nine of more than 80, and only 18 of less than 60. And also in the ships below the rank of line-of-battle ship, we only get 7 of 40 guns, that is of the heavy frigate class we have spoken of, but 38 of a much smaller class, not carrying more than 20 guns. Here is distinct approach to that differentiation which reason leads us up to when we are able to look calmly back on the naval warfare of the past and to discuss its principles. But we can note that our ancestors saw through a glass darkly, and in the struggles of constant wars established principles without pausing to identify them, and without knowing, perhaps, how much they were unconsciously guided by them.

A further illustration can be drawn from the navy as it was found in commission at the death of George II., in 1760, with its distribution on the different stations.

### At Home.

| Ships. | Guns. | Ships. | Guns. | Ships. | Guns. |
|---|---|---|---|---|---|
| 7 | of 90 | 10 | of 64 | 6 | of 32 |
| 2 | „ 80 | 2 | „ 60 | 5 | „ 28 |
| 24 | „ 74 | 3 | „ 50 | 3 | „ 18 |
| 2 | „ 70 | 1 | „ 36 | 11 | „ 10 to 14 |

In this home fleet we see quite plainly the growth of the upper middle strength of the line-of-battle ships; the widening of the gap between the weakest line-of-battle ship and the heaviest frigate; and the distinct proportionate increase in the numbers of the lighter cruisers.

### In the East Indies.

| Ships. | Guns. | Ships. | Guns. | Ships. | Guns. |
|---|---|---|---|---|---|
| 1 | of 50 | 1 | of 28 | 1 | of 24 |
| 1 | „ 20 | 2 | „ 14 | | |

In this squadron we have the 50-gun ship passing out of the line of battle as it were, and becoming a heavy cruiser for distant and detached service. She is then accompanied not by ships in a regular descending scale, as she would have been during the period of the Dutch wars, but by a group of very much lighter cruisers, the heaviest of which has not, perhaps, half her force.

### In the West Indies.

| Ships. | Guns. | Ships. | Guns. | Ships. | Guns. |
|---|---|---|---|---|---|
| 2 | of 50 | 1 | of 32 | 2 | of 28 |
| 4 | „ 20 | 1 | „ 14 | | |

Where the characteristics of the squadron—which was divided into two between Jamaica and the Leeward Islands—are similar to those in the East Indies.

### In the Mediterranean.

| Ships. | Guns. | Ships. | Guns. | Ships. | Guns. |
|---|---|---|---|---|---|
| 1 | of 50 | 1 | of 32 | 2 | of 28 |
| 1 | „ 14 | 1 | „ 10 | | |

Where we have still the same thing.

### In North America.

| Ships. | Guns. | Ships. | Guns. | Ships. | Guns. |
|---|---|---|---|---|---|
| 6 | of 64 | 15 | of 32 | 15 | of 14 to 18. |
| 5 | „ 50 | 11 | „ 28 | 9 | „ 8 to 12. |
| 3 | „ 44 | 14 | „ 20 | | |

In this squadron there is less of the marked differentiation we are beginning to see. But if we look at the three 44-gun ships as what I may call "border ships," being almost strong enough for the line of battle and unnecessarily heavy for the duties of a frigate, we still have the three classes of line-of-battle ship, frigate, and light cruiser; the multitude of the latter being entirely in accordance with the forecast which could have been made at the date of the third Dutch war. Nothing was gained by such varieties in force as 64, 50, and 44-gun ships. A stronger line of battle could have been produced of fewer and heavier ships all of one class; and although progress towards this ideal is slow, I think the reader will now see that we are on the high way to its realisation.

### The Newfoundland Squadron.

| Ships. | Guns. | | Ships. | Guns. | |
|---|---|---|---|---|---|
| 1 | of | 64 | 1 | of | 20 |
| 1 | „ | 50 | 5 | „ | 14 to 16 |
| 2 | „ | 28 | 7 | „ | 10 to 12. |

The differentiation of force in this squadron may be seen to conform more to the approaching rule, and to assimilate to that found in the East and West India Squadrons.

We may now pass at once to the Revolutionary and Napoleonic Wars, of which the length and persistence may be supposed to have brought all the rules and principles of naval war to a climax. I have thought that the best way of exhibiting the operation of the causes we have seen at work in differentiating naval force is by using the graphic method, and exhibiting curves which show the proportions of each kind of force, and the quantities during each year from 1793. We have pretty well seen what was coming, and had our forefathers, in 1794, had before them in a clear light all the points we have been discussing, I think we may fairly assume that they would have done at first what they did at last, and so conducted the war with a greater economy.

For what is plain to be seen, I think, is, that for naval warfare not a great many types of ships are required. Whether there be or be not a line of battle, there must be some fighting formation which is under all circumstances better than any other. The fact that a form of battle is established compels a uniformity of type of ship, because form prescribes place and prevents ships seeking their match. Therefore it becomes waste to produce a few excessively powerful ships to fight in a general action, while it is a danger to allow weak ships to take part in it. In the one case the excess of power may be, most probably will be, wasted against an inferior adversary; in the other case, ships of greatly inferior force may be hopelessly beaten by those of medium or average strength.

Then I think we can see that there should be an immense fall in the strength of the strongest cruiser below that of the weakest battle-ship. It should seem also that this strongest cruiser has her place as the eyes of the fleet, even as set forth by James Duke of York in his instructions. Then would come another heavy fall in the strength of the light cruiser, of which the special function is guarding our own commerce and attacking that of the enemy. I do not see

130

that anything is gained by great variety in type. There is always the consideration present that there is no guarantee that even with the infinite variety of type, such as we see composed our navy in 1686, the particular ship most suited to the service will be where time and place requires her. Much more likely is it that the wrong types will be everywhere. In one case the ships available will be too weak, and risks will be run; in another case the ships available will be too strong, and money will be wasted.

These thoughts spring from our study of the nature of naval war as far as we have carried it. I offer circumstantial evidence of their correctness in the growth of differentiation as we have traced it, best seen above all, in the following three figures.

The first figure shows us the nature of the whole navy in commission, year by year, from 1793 till 1813. It impresses on us two points; the gradual elimination of what I call the "border ships," the ships that were and were not line-of-battle ships. There is evidence enough that the navy did not like them; they came steadily down from the Dutch days of promiscuous fighting, and we had continued to produce them because our fathers had done so. Custom went on with them as an essential part of naval force until about 1796, but the practical experience of war eliminated them. They were found in constantly diminishing numbers year by year, when they closed at a minimum in 1813.

This figure also exhibits in a striking manner the way in which the pressure of war experience demanded increase in the number of cruisers. The line-of-battle force once established in superiority required no further increase. But the demand for increase of cruisers, nearly all of which were engaged in the attack of the enemy's commerce and the defence of our own, sprang up immediately, rose to a great height during the Revolutionary war, but sprang to its greatest and almost fabulous height when our line-of-battle strength was unimpeached in any part of the world.

The second figure gives us, with great force and clearness, the interior changes in the line-of-battle force and its differentiation. We have seen it coming, no doubt, through what has before been said, yet the precision of the result has in it the nature of a surprise when plotted out in such a graph.

From the year 1793 to 1796 the tendency would almost seem to belie teaching, and to reverse the processes which had gone on in former wars. Up to 1796 there was an increase of each class of line-of-battle ships, that is to say, a swinging off from the uniformity

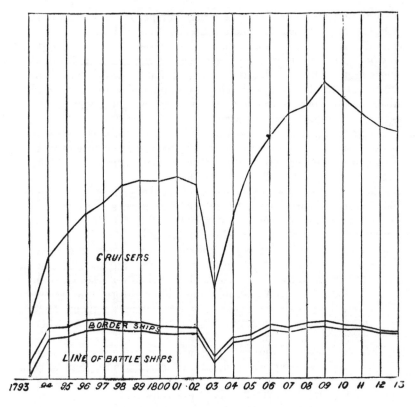

Ships in Commission from 1793 to 1813

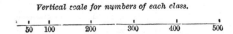

*Vertical scale for numbers of each class.*

which reason would have pronounced for, and in 1796, there were in commission 22 ships of from 90 to 120 guns; 5 of 80 guns, 54 of 74, 24 of 64, and 25 border ships of from 44 to 56 guns on two decks. This was really an approach to the old thing, and an advance in an altogether wrong direction, if the subject were to be reasoned out. But no sooner was this point reached than the reason of the case—still, possibly, without consciousness—began to prevail. By

132

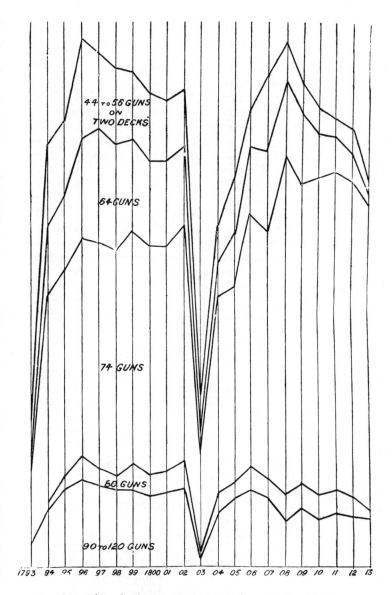

44 TO 56 GUNS
ON
TWO DECKS

64 GUNS

74 GUNS

50 GUNS

90 TO 120 GUNS

1793 94 95 96 97 98 99 1800 01 02 03 04 05 06 07 08 09 10 11 12 13

Line-of-Battle Ships in Commission from 1793 to 1813

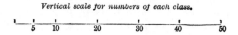

Vertical scale for numbers of each class.

5    10    20    30    40    50

133

1801, the border ships had fallen to 15, the heaviest types of the line-of-battle ships, those from 80 to 120 guns had diminished by 4. The 64's on the otherside had diminished in number by 4, while the 74's had increased by 4. Practically the Napoleonic war was simply a development of right reason, stimulated by the spur of experience. The heavy and the light line-of-battle ships continually diminished in number, while the upper middle rank of that class of ship, the 74, continually increased. When the naval war practically came to an end in 1813, the 74 occupied almost the whole field. The border ships and the 64's had practically disappeared on the one side, there being but 4 of the former, and 2 of the latter. On the other side, the heavy line-of-battle ships of 80 guns and upwards had dwindled to a minimum, there being but 14 of them in commission. Their function was less a question of force than of accommodation, and the chief reason for their existence was the space they afforded to the admiral and his staff. But the 74's were no less than 85 in number, and if we regard the tendency of the curves as drawn, it is not too much to suppose that a continuance of the war would have seen the line of battle reach its ideal, and beheld it composed of a single type of ship, that ship being of the upper middle class.

The third figure does for the cruisers what the second has done for the line-of-battle ships; it shows their growing interior differentiation. And here, in observing that the tables are all prepared from the elaborate "Abstracts" furnished by James in his naval history, we must note that James does not make the clear distinction between ships of the line and cruisers till the year 1803. It is as if the absolute wall which ought to exist between the two classes of ships and their function, had not struck him at an earlier part of his work. This, again, was a portion of the ancient inheritance, the ideal of promiscuous fighting, which these plates show to have been so utterly swept away in the long sea wars with France and Spain.

In this figure we can trace all the general tendencies of differentiation amongst the cruisers with great ease. Just as the weaker line-of-battle ship is seen to disappear gradually, carrying with it the border ship, so does the very heavy frigate of 40 to 44 guns, never very numerous, give place so as to increase and emphasize the impassable gap which separates the battle-ship from the cruiser. But when the gap is marked enough, that class of cruiser which should be specially the attendant on the fleet, and which is nearest to the gap, begins to grow. All through both wars there is a tendency in the 38- and 36-gun frigates to aggrandise and swell in their position. In

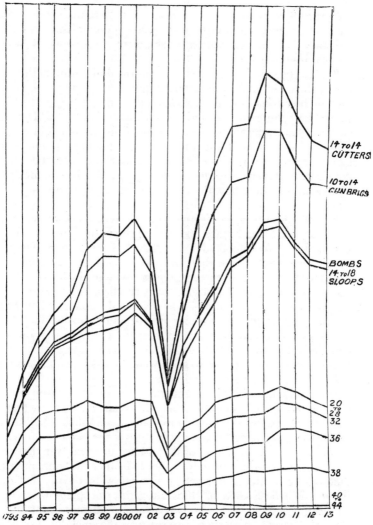

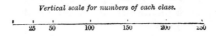

14 ᴛᴏ 14
CUTTERS

10 ᴛᴏ 14
GUN BRIGS

BOMBS
14 ᴛᴏ 18
SLOOP S

20
ᴛᴏ
28
32

36

38

40
ᴛᴏ
44

1793 94 95 96 97 98 99 1800 01 02 03 04 05 06 07 08 09 10 11 12 13

Cruisers in Commission from 1793 to 1813
N.B.—The line which extends part of the way above the bombs
represents fire ships.

*Vertical scale for numbers of each class.*

25    50    100    150    200    250

135

the year 1809, when our navy reached its maximum force, there were 44 38-gun, and 36 36-gun frigates in commission, and next year they reached their highest development, there being 48 38-gun, and 49 36-gun frigates.

But side by side with this growth was the dimunition in the number of ships carrying from 20 to 32 guns. While the proportion of these lighter frigates to the heavier had been in 1798, 74 to 55, in 1810 it had altered to 54 to 97, and in 1813 to 38 to 86. That is to say, that just as the gap between the line-of-battle ship and the frigate had distinctly established itself, so was the natural and proper gap between the frigate and the light cruiser in course of establishing itself. And then, as to these light cruisers, the third figure shows us that it was there that the enormous increase in our navy took place.

In 1809 the cruisers of 20 guns and over in commission numbered 147, but, excluding bombs and special ships, the cruisers carrying less than 20 guns numbered no less than 403. And if we are to judge by the curves exhibited, there was from the first a continued demand for the services of these vessels, a demand which did not cease till the enormous total just given was reached. After 1809–10 we may presume that we had not only secured the command of the sea by the impregnable front of our line of battle, but we had everywhere so overspread the sea with these light cruisers that our own commerce threaded a safe way through them; the enemy's commerce could not show, and so great were the risks, that the attempts upon our own commerce collapsed.

I have now traced the differentiation of naval force through all its changes in England, and I think a case is made out to show that the state of the classes of ships continually developing, and brought nearly to complete perfection at the close of the Napoleonic war, is a permanent one; that it is of the essence of naval war that there should be battle-ships of uniform type, neither the most powerful that can be produced nor yet greatly below that type; that there should then be a class of ships altogether incapable of facing a battle-ship in fight, and in no way armed to attempt it, but of substantial character, with speed in a sea-way, the chief duties of which would be attendance on the fleet. There appears no reason in what has here been discussed why this type also should not be uniform. Then it looks as if the next type might fall to a great inferiority below the class just mentioned, but should make up for its individual weakness by its number.

The Crimean war was hardly a naval one; and if it had been otherwise, the changes from sail to steam, and from the paddle to the screw, both of which it brought to a head, would vitiate the results of any continuation of the statistics for that period; but it is not unworthy of remark that the war followed the example of the graph on page 135 in producing 155 small steamers, gun-boats, a class unknown before.

# CHAPTER SIX

T HERE BEING no example of the attempt to secure the command of the sea as an end so complete as that of the Anglo-Dutch wars, I traced pretty fully their history, and drew special attention to the methods employed on both sides. It is important to remember that in these wars there was no ulterior object in the aims either of Dutch or English. Both nations depended largely on sea-borne commerce for their prosperity, and if one nation should succeed in obtaining such a command of the sea as would enable it to control the commerce of the other, the latter would certainly be brought to her knees. Holland was so well aware of this, that in the second and third wars she felt it necessary to temporarily suspend her commerce, in order the more freely to contend for the direct command of the sea, or at least to prevent England from obtaining such a command as might give her a permanent control over the Dutch commerce. Her policy was so far successful that she did prevent the command of the sea being thoroughly gained against her, and shortened the wars by the firm and resisting front which she was ever able to show.

But we have seen that both nations were desirous of pushing the war off the sea, whenever even temporary command of it promised to permit the attempt. Troops were embarked at different times by both nations, and were actually landed by the Dutch when a mistaken policy on the English part allowed the Dutch sufficient command of the sea to undertake it. It is true that on neither side of the North Sea did the idea of operations on land extend beyond harrying, alarming, and destroying, within the immediate neighbourhood of the coast. But supposing the command of the sea had been absolutely in the hands of one side, and that that did not suffice to obtain the terms demanded, it is conceivable that the side in power might have aimed at more permanent occupation of the enemy's territory, resting on the sea base for supplies. If the population of one nation had been greatly in excess of the other, and its land forces proportionately stronger, the ultimate aim of this nation might have been a military expedition. Conquest of territory might have been the aim of the war, and the command of the sea might have been looked at not as the end, but only as the means to an end. Conceivably, if the military power were immensely greater on one side than on the other, the more powerful nation might hope to end the war by that sort of sudden conquest, which, when undertaken on a large scale, is called invasion, and this without much care as to the permanent command of the sea. The attempt might even go further; the idea might be that the greatness of the force, and the suddenness of its landing, might achieve conquest, and conclude the war with such speed as to render sea communications unnecessary and therefore to leave out of question the command of the sea even for a time, the invasion being conducted by way of surprise or evasion.

There are not wanting examples of this kind of operation, or attempted operation. The Spanish Armada, Hoche's expedition to Bantry, Napoleon's invasion of Egypt, and the Italian attack on the Island of Lissa are all cases in point, though not encouraging in their results, as to that particular method of conducting war. I shall have to treat of these and other operations of like nature in subsequent chapters, but I only advert to them to make clear the distinction which exists between that form of operation and the one of which I am about to treat. This is the case where the naval and the military operations are separate, and where a purely naval war, however short it may be, is carried on simply to clear the way for the military operation which is to follow.

The operation is nearer akin to that which will also require to be investigated, where a power having already the command of the sea, and intending a military expedition for the success of which command of the sea is necessary, sets apart a naval force to mask the naval force of the enemy, and, therefore, to make assurance doubly sure.

There are no more perfect illustrations of the operations I have in view than the several great endeavours of France to secure the command of the sea, in order to pass across the Channel a military force large enough to effect the conquest of the country before sufficient time had elapsed to change again the face of the naval supremacy.

But I think it should be observed that in every case of invasion, either of this kind or of the kind above spoken of, the invading power hoped for assistance in the country invaded. In one case, that of the invasion of the Prince of Orange, the certainty of help in the invaded country was so complete, and the doubt of possible naval opposition so marked, that we must almost leave it out of any class of naval operations possible to be formed. The balance of political opinion, far more than of force, either naval or military, determined the conduct of the design. But it may be taken as the extreme type of invasion, and as differing from other invasions more in degree than in kind. In every one of the French attempts on England, France believed that the landing of her troops would be the signal for insurrections in her favour all over the country, and of a great rallying to her standard of a disaffected population. In her attempts on Ireland, it was the same. In the case of Spain, Philip was confident that a vast body of oppressed Catholics would support him as soon as his troops disembarked, and was only depending on that help coming to him on a large scale which in the landing at Kinsale his troops received on a small scale. Even in Egypt and the East the fanaticism of the French led them to suppose they would be received as friends and deliverers, and would find a home and a base for further operations against the English possessions in the East, even in the very probable contingency of being cut off from France.

Certainly this view, that the French troops, if they succeeded in landing on the English shores, would be sufficiently supported by the people to effect the intended purpose of restoring James to his throne, completely governed the operations which led to the abortive battle of Beachy Head.

A considerable French army had been landed in Ireland, and the ex-king James had gained such power there that large forces had departed from England to make head against him, William himself quitting the country on the 11th June 1690 to take the head of his army in Ireland. England itself was, therefore, left to the government of Mary as Regent, and to a military defence of which the chief strength was a hastily called-out militia. The naval defence was so backward, and so much delayed, that Lord Torrington, that Admiral Herbert who had escorted King William to Torbay, had resigned his office at the Admiralty sooner than be a party to the unpreparedness for events by sea which was then the uppermost policy.[1] Nottingham, the Secretary of State and Torrington's enemy,

1. "Lest any of these matters should be laid to my charge, I think it necessary to acquaint this honourable court that not seeing matters so well in the Admiralty as I thought the service required, and that it was not in my power to prevent it, I humbly begged and obtained the King's leave to be dismissed from that commission and giv-

was able to overrule prudent counsels, and by despising the French as an enemy at sea, really left the country open to grave dangers.

The French were no doubt well informed, through James's partisans, of the opportunity that was opening to them. They had a full belief that, in the absence of William and the English army in Ireland, a success in the Channel which would enable them to carry a small military force across would bring about a general rising and restore the ex-King. Indeed, arrangements had gone so far as to fix the 18th of June as the date for the outbreak of the insurrection.

The French intention was then to appear in the Channel in greatly superior force to any that the English and Dutch were likely to produce. A part of the fleet was to make for the Thames to support the Jacobite rising in the capital; while the other part was to join the galleys, and land 8,000 men in Torbay with arms for a much greater number. After so landing them, this part of the fleet was to sail into the Irish Sea and prevent the return of King William and his troops.[2]

The main body of the French assembled at Brest under the command of Vice-Admiral Comte de Tourville, and the ships at Toulon under the orders of Vice-Admiral Châteaurenault were ordered to join him.

On the English side, the fitting out of a suitable fleet was not only delayed but postponed; but some slight comprehension of the danger was shown in the orders which had been given to Vice-Admiral Killigrew in the early spring. This officer sailed from Torbay with a squadron and convoy for the Mediterranean on the 7th of March, making first for Cadiz. He had with him one second-rate, four third-rates, seven fourth-rates, one fifth-rate, and two fire-ships, besides apparently four Dutch ships, two of which unfortunately foundered on the way out. According to the reckoning of those days, this gave Killigrew, when he sailed, sixteen ships "fit to lie in a line." His orders were to proceed to Cadiz, and to forward the trade to its different destinations up the Mediterranean, and then with the remainder of his squadron, which would be seven ships and the Dutch, to watch the motions of the Toulon fleet, and if it passed the Straits of Gibraltar westward, he was to follow it.

---

ing any further attendance at that Board; that since I could not prevent the mischief, I might have no share in the blame." Torrington's defence, quoted by Entick, p. 548. His quitting of the Board, and being succeeded by the Earl of Pembroke, took place January 20th, 1689, according to Schomberg's *Naval Chronology,* vol. v., p. 191, but this must be a mistake for 1690.

2. Lediard, vol. ii., p. 634.

He was much delayed in every way; took the usual month, which a century later was still the usual month, to reach Cadiz, but there was considerably hampered by the hindrances placed in his way by the Spanish authorities. He was still there with most of his ships on the 9th of May when expresses reached him from several quarters that the Toulon fleet of ten sail, three of them carrying 80 guns each, had been seen off Alicante, Malaga, and Gibraltar successively. Killigrew sailed next morning for Gibraltar, where he not only picked up the rest of his ships, but heard that fourteen ships, presumably the French squadron, had been seen at anchor in the Bay of Tetuan near Ceuta, and just opposite Gibraltar, the night before. He at once made for this point, having with him ten sail of English, "fit to lie in a line," beside two fifth-rates and two fire-ships, as well as five Dutch ships.

None of the French fleet were found at anchor, but in a short time they were all seen to the northward, and sail was made in chase. The French and English historians have squabbled a good deal over whether either side was willing or unwilling for an encounter. Presumably, Châteaurenault would have shown a singular want of sense had he courted a battle, which might have prevented that great concentration of force which he was about to complete at Brest. Anyhow, there was no action. The French passed the Straits, and Killigrew, having apparently little comprehension of the French strategy, or of the possibly momentous results of his delay, proceeded to Cadiz, and busied himself in arranging for convoys and such like matters of inferior import. He had been ordered to follow the French if they passed the Straits; he certainly obeyed his orders, but so leisurely that when he reached Plymouth Sound, after the 30th of June, it was only to learn that Torrington had been beaten, that the French were in command, though not in undisputed command, of the Channel, and that it behoved him to get his very inferior force right up into Hamoaze, and out of harm's way, with as little delay as might be.

Beside the main force of the English and Dutch, slowly—very slowly—assembling at St. Helens, and this force of Killigrew's, which I have traced out and home, the only other English force of importance was that under Sir Cloudesley Shovel, which, however, had only amounted to six men-of-war under his immediate command when De Tourville's preparations were complete.[3]

3. Ships at Plymouth are also mentioned, but I have no account of their number or force.

As to the main fleet, I have already spoken of its delay. Of the fact of this delay, there is but little doubt. As to the causes, they seem to have been a point for bitter argument between the navy and the politicians. Torrington's defence makes it quite clear that he had been urging all through the winter the necessity of hastening and increasing the preparations, and had been as steadily withstood by the Earl of Nottingham. "I appeal to him," said the prisoner on his trial, "whether I did not tell him, when I had urged many reasons for strengthening our fleet, which he only answered with, 'You will be strong enough for the French,' 'My Lord, I know my business, and will do my best with what I have; but pray remember it is not my fault that the fleet is no stronger. I own I am afraid now, in winter, whilst the danger may be remedied; and you will be afraid in summer, when it is past remedy."[4] Burnett accuses Torrington of being "a man of pleasure," and that he delayed joining the fleet. It seems impossible that this can be true, for Torrington in his defence expressly charges some of the wrongdoings on the fact that he did not join the fleet till the 30th May.[5] As the court-martial honourably acquitted Lord Torrington, and as the King made it extremely hard for all who had defended him, it seems pretty clear what the navy of the day thought about it all, and what view the politicians took.

However, the result of all was that on the 23rd June 1690 Torrington found himself at St. Helen's at the head of no more than 50 men-of-war and 20 fire-ships in the face of a sudden announcement that the French, 120 strong, were at the back of the Isle of Wight.

The Comte de Tourville at Brest, being joined by the Toulon fleet which Killigrew had failed to follow, found himself at the head of 70 ships fit for the line, 5 frigates, 16 fire-ships, and 15 galleys. He was totally unwatched, as one of the clever things the Regency had done, and for which it blamed its subordinate, the Commander-in-Chief, was absolutely and entirely to omit the making of any attempt to gain intelligence. Not a cruiser watched the port of Brest, not a cutter even guarded the approaches to the Channel.

"All very well," said Torrington, "to blame me for this."

> Some think that in some measure I am chargeable with it. Surely they do not mean before I came to the fleet, which was not till the

4. Entick, p. 548.
5. Burnett, however, had but a hazy notion of anything that took place. He evidently thinks our ships assembled at Plymouth, whereas they assembled in the Downs, and Torrington found them there. See *Memoirs of Lord Torrington* (then Captain Byng, in command of the *Hope*, 70), p. 43. Torrington in his defence states that his orders were not signed till the 26th May, ibid., p. 550.

30th of May! And from that time forward we had always ships at sea, not only as scouts, but some ever upon the coast of France. It is said, we had no scouts out when the French appeared, and it is very true; nor is it my fault. For all our ships' boats being employed to fetch the Earl of Pembroke's regiment, I desired the Dutch, who had the outguard, to take that care upon them; and it seems those that Vice-Admiral Callemberg had appointed for that service delayed it, to take in some necessaries at the Isle of Wight. And it is certain that the first notice I had of the French was by the appearance of five of their scouts.

I thought, and still think, that the material intelligence is the strength of an enemy's preparation and how that is to be employed. If we had any such intelligence it has been concealed from me; for the first notice I had of Monsieur de Chatteau Renaut's joining the French fleet, was the sight of his flag flying off the Isle of Wight.[6]

Châteaurenault, as we have seen, had been able to evade Killigrew, who had not followed him up as he should have done, and he had consequently been able to form his junction with de Tourville unnoticed and unmolested.[7] The Comte de Tourville consequently was able to sail from Brest on the 13th June at the head of the force mentioned,[8] and he proceeded at once for the Isle of Wight.

However startling it may have been for an admiral lying at St. Helen's to learn, after hardly any warning, that an enemy's fleet of 120 sail, twice his strength at least, was quietly at anchor in Freshwater Bay, Lord Torrington does not seem to have lost his head for a moment. A profound strategist as well as a most experienced seaman, he saw exactly how the land lay, and at once proposed to make the best of the very bad job which the neglect of his advice

6. Ibid., p. 548.

7. One of the reasons given why Killigrew was unable to bring him to action was the foulness of his ships' bottoms. They had been seventeen months "off the ground," whereas the Frenchmen were just out of Toulon "clean."

8. In reference to the last chapter, it may be useful to give the exact force of the ships in the line:

| | | | | | |
|---|---|---|---|---|---|
| 110 guns ......... 1 | 74 guns .......... 2 | 58 guns .......... 6 |
| 104 „ ........... 1 | 72 „ ........... 1 | 56 „ ........... 1 |
| 90 „ ........... 2 | 70 „ ........... 1 | 54 „ ........... 3 |
| 86 „ ........... 2 | 68 „ ........... 5 | 52 „ ........... 3 |
| 84 „ ........... 2 | 66 „ ........... 1 | 50 „ ........... 2 |
| 80 „ ........... 7 | 64 „ ........... 1 | 44 „ ........... 1 |
| 76 „ ........... 2 | 62 „ ........... 9 | 40 „ ............. „ |
| | 60 „ .......... 11 | |

Showing that though the necessary differentiation of force was approaching, the French idea was yet a long way from understanding what a "line-of-battle" ship really meant.—*See* O. Troude, vol. i., p. 198.

and warnings had led up to. He had had on the 22nd of June his earliest intimation that the French had put to sea for the eastward; and now, at 8 o'clock in the morning on this 23rd, he received the astounding intelligence above noted. He at once weighed, but the wind was so light as to leave his fleet chiefly at the mercy of the tides, and being no further than off Dunose he wrote to Lord Nottingham:—

> We sailed this morning, but the wind taking us short we are not far from Donose. If the French have continued their station, we are not above five leagues asunder. Our fleet consists of 50 men-of-war, and 20 fire-ships; the odds are great, and you know it is not my fault. To-morrow will probably be the deciding day. Let them tremble at the consequence whose fault it was the fleet is no stronger; for my part, I will, with God Almighty's help, do my duty, and I hope everybody here will do so too. If we are to expect any more Dutch, I hope they will be hastened to us; it is not impossible they may come time enough for a share, because the sea is subject to accidents. We have as yet but 18 Dutch with us, after all De Witt's great promises.

The lightness of the wind compelled the Admiral to anchor for the night off Dunose, and next day was reinforced by three Dutch and two English men-of-war. At daylight on the 25th Torrington weighed with his 55 sail to a light N.E. wind, and with the intention of bringing the French to battle if possible, but it became so thick that he had to anchor again; but presently, the wind shifting to the S.W., it cleared, and then he saw the French about twelve miles to the S.W., in a line on the port tack, standing, that is, to the W.N.W. Torrington weighed, and forming his line stood to the S.S.E. on the starboard tack, the French thus growing more and more on their starboard beam as they advanced; being also to windward, and having therefore full opportunity of bringing on a general action, which their undoubtedly great superiority of force justified, nay urged, them in doing. I need not particularize in this place the movements of the respective fleets, beyond establishing the point, distinctly stated by Lord Torrington, that the French might have brought him to action on this 25th of June, and did not.[9] But on this

9. Sometimes there is nothing more puzzling than to make out, from the accounts of historians, what fleets actually did. In this case Lediard and Entick have followed Burchett, not perceiving that Torrington's statements do not agree with their own vague ones. Berkeley gives a mere paragraph to the whole thing. The author of the MS. Memoirs of Lord Torrington (Byng), now printed by the Camden Society and edited by Professor Laughton, distinctly states that when Torrington (Herbert) sighted the French fleet they were to leeward of him, and then "drawing into a line of

day Lord Torrington got near enough to observe with his own eyes
the strength of the French force, and even to count the ships with
some approach to accuracy. The prospect was not reassuring for an
Admiral who knew that there were no reserves behind him, and that
his country was divided against itself. The two fleets anchored for
the night, and on the morning of the 26th Lord Torrington wrote to
Nottingham as follows:—

It is unaccountable why the French shunned us: for though they
had many ships to leeward, and scattered, they had enough in a body
to have given us more than sufficient work. I do acknowledge my first
attention of attacking them a rashness that will admit of no better
excuse than that, though I did believe them stronger than we are, I
did not believe it to so great a degree. I find by their manner of working, that notwithstanding their strength, they act with some caution,
and seem to be willing to add to the advantage of force that of wind
too. Their great strength and caution have put soberer thoughts into
my head, and have made me very heartily give God thanks they declined the battle yesterday. And, indeed, I shall not think myself very
unhappy if I can get rid of them without fighting, unless it may be
upon equaller terms than for the present I see any prospect of. I find I
am not the only man of that opinion, for a Council of War I called
this morning unanimously agreed we are by all manner of means to
shun fighting with them, especially if they have the wind of us, and
retire, if we cannot avoid it otherwise, even to the Gunfleet, the only
place we can with any manner of probability make our party good
with them in the condition we are in.[10] We have now had a pretty
good view of their fleet, which consists of near, if not quite, 80 men-
of-war, fit to lie in a line, and 30 fire-ships, a strength that puts me
beside the hopes of success, if we should fight, and really may not
only endanger the losing of the fleet, but at least the quiet of our
country too; for if we are beaten, they being absolute masters of the
sea, will be at great liberty of doing many things they dare not attempt whilst we observe them, and are in a possibility of joining
Vice-Admiral Killigrew and our ships to the westward. If I find a possibility, I will get by them to the westward to join those ships; if not, I
mean to follow the result of the council of war. In the meantime, I

battle," he "bore down upon them." But this neither agrees with the wind as given
by Lord Torrington in his letter, nor with the movements he described himself to
have made. Speaker Onslow, in a note on Burnett's *History of his Own Times*,
says—speaking presumably of these Memoirs—that they give the best account of the
battle of Beachey Head which he had seen.

10. The Gunfleet is a bank running out from Foulness, north of the Thames, in an
E.N.E. direction, in part covering Harwich, and affording anchorage to a large fleet
behind it.

wish there might be speedy orders given to fit out with speed whatever ships of war are in the river of Chatham, and that the ships to
the westward proceed to Portsmouth, and from thence, if the French
come before the river, they may join us over the flats. This is the best
advice I can give at present; but had I been believed in winter, the
kingdom had not received this insult. Your Lordship now knows the
opinion of the flag-officers of both Dutch and English fleets, which I
desire you will lay before Her Majesty, and to assure her that if she
has other considerations, whenever she pleases to signify her pleasure, her commands shall be punctually obeyed, let the consequence
be what it will.[11]

Nothing could be plainer or more straightforward than this cool
exposition of the situation. As far as he could see, he was, with a
force 55 men-of-war, opposed to a force of 80; and though if it
were the mere winning or losing of a battle, the risk of one might be
properly run, yet, considering what was behind—the army over in
Ireland with the King, a large disaffected population ready to welcome the French, the considerable detachments of naval force,
under Killigrew and under Cloudesley Shovel, open to annihilation—the risk of being beaten became disproportionably great.
While if he could altogether avoid fighting, and merely wait and
watch, he would render the great French armament powerless, and
entirely defeat its ends. It could do absolutely nothing if Torrington
declined to be drawn into a battle, because the moment it attempted
anything by way of a landing, or an attack upon the shore, it would
give to the British admiral exactly that advantage which was required to made his attack successful.

But his letter makes it perfectly clear that he proposed to abandon nothing, unless he was forced to do so. He was ready, rather
than risk a battle at such immense disadvantage, even to retire behind the Gunfleet. For there, amongst the shoals, his fleet was secure; and while he was there, the very utmost the French could do
would be to lie off the Thames and blockade it. But their inability to
thread the intricate navigation of the entrance to the river was the
very circumstance which would enable reinforcements to reach him
"over the flats." In his mind, the Gunfleet shoal was to do for him
just what, more than a century later, the Duke of Wellington rightly
calculated that the lines of Torres Vedras would do for him.

Short-sighted people in 1690 and in 1810 thought just in the same
way. To them, a retirement behind the Gunfleet was an abandon-

11. Entick, p. 548.

ment of the country to the Allies of the ex-King; and the retreat upon Lisbon was to give up Portugal to the French.

But Torrington had no intention of making for the Gunfleet except in the last resort. If he could win past the French fleet to the westward, he might pick up Killigrew and Shovel, and then returning with his augmented force, he would be able to deal satisfactorily with de Tourville, who was just as much prevented from meddling with the shore when Torrington was west as when he was east of him. The plan then was (1) at all hazards to avoid fighting with the odds so greatly against him; (2) to endeavour to pass the French to the westward; and (3) if this could not be accomplished, and the French forced him to the eastward, then he would secure himself finally behind the Gunfleet, where it was difficult to attack him at an advantage, but whence he could issue at any moment, and therefore could hold the French completely in check. Where also he could be reinforced until strong enough to take the offensive.

Nottingham, at the elbow of the Queen, either could not or would not understand anything of this. "Sir William Jennings," [12] he wrote to Torrington, "is on board of the French Admiral, and examined some prisoners (whom they took off of Weymouth, and set on shore in the Isle of Wight) what the number of our fleet was; and they saying 90 sail of men-of-war, he was in a great rage, and threatened to hang them for lying, for that he was sure we had but 30 ships together; for the Dutch were not come, Killigrew in the Straits, and Shovel in the Irish seas; and that they came to destroy our fleet thus divided, first at Portsmouth, and then in the river. And they were extremely discouraged upon hearing the salutes, when they were told that it must be upon the arrival of the Dutch ships.[13] And we have further information that they are very ill manned. And though your lordship, that has seen them, may better judge of their number than we can by any advice from France, yet I have seen letters from one who, in company with others, was very near their fleet; and they all say, that they counted them twelve times, and could never make them more than 103 or 104 of all rates; of which they say positively there was not about 60 ships that could stand in a line." [14]

12. One of James's adherents.
13. Not impossibly it was this information reaching the French, and the hearing the salutes on the 24th, which disinclined them from coming to action on the 25th of June. It will have been observed that Torrington failed to count the French accurately, and somewhat over-rated their force. The French, perhaps, failed in the same way, proximity not being close enough for accurate counting.
14. This, it will be observed, was as much under-counting as Torrington's over-

The ships from Plymouth [Nottingham continues] sailed thence on Monday morning last, so that if they are not already with you they must be very near.

Sir Cloudesley Shovel sailed from Belfast at three of the clock in the morning of the 18th instant, so that he also cannot be far from you.

By letters from Vice-Admiral Killigrew, dated May 26th from Cadiz, I find he intended to sail in a few days, and return according to his orders.

So that upon the whole, if you should retire to the Gunfleet, the ships from Plymouth, if not joined with you and Sir Cloudesley Shovel, and all the ships returning from Ireland, and Vice-Admiral Killigrew, with that squadron and a rich fleet of merchantmen, will all be exposed to inevitable ruin. And besides, the French may have opportunity of going with their whole fleet, or sending such part as they may think fit to Scotland, where they are expected; and we have too good reason to apprehend disturbances.[15]

This would be a perverse enough misunderstanding of the situation, and of Torrington's view of it, if it stood alone. But the *non-sequitur* of the enclosure almost takes one's breath away. Nottingham was in the main only repeating what Torrington had put in his mind, but with the inferences turned inside out. The importance of joining, or at least of securing the safety of Killigrew and Shovel, was the matter which dwelt in the foremost place in Torrington's mind, and his main effort, as sketched out, was the endeavour to join them. If he could not pass the French to the westward, but could keep in observation of them to the eastward, his colleagues would be safe enough. For if de Tourville should go west after them, Torrington would follow him up; if he should detach force sufficient for their destruction, he would weaken himself so much that Torrington might engage him at an advantage.

It was just the same with regard to Scotland. If Torrington was forced back—in order to avoid a battle—to the Gunfleet, the French could neither proceed to Scotland in full force nor send a detachment there. First, because they would be unable to shake off Torrington; and, secondly, because if they weakened themselves by detaching, Torrington would fall on the remainder.

---

counting. There were certainly 70 ships fit for the line, and if the galleys were then with them, which, however, I doubt, there were 106 sail all told. Torrington might easily have been deceived if the 15 galleys, the 5 frigates, and the 16 fire-ships were all present.

15. Entick, p. 549.

The one thing certain, both from Torrington's words and Nottingham's, was that the French wished of all things for a general action with the odds in their favour, and this alone was sufficient to prescribe a refusal. The one point on which Nottingham could hang a grain of justification for the extraordinary enclosure which his letter contained, was his estimate of the relative forces watching each other. He assumed them nearly equal. Torrington and his brother admirals, looking at both fleets when they so decided, were of opinion that the odds were too great to give reasonable hopes of success. What right had any statesman or politician in London to treat as fallacious estimates of force so arrived at?

But Nottingham did it; for his letter, written in such haste that he was unable to take a copy of it, enclosed a positive order from the Queen to Torrington to bring the French fleet to action. The order ran:—

MARIE R.

Right trusty and well-beloved cousin and counsellor, we greet you well. We have heard your letter dated June 26, to our Secretary of State, and do not doubt of your skill and conduct in this important conjuncture, to take all opportunities of advantage against the enemy. But we apprehend the consequences of your retiring to the Gunfleet to be so fatal, that we chuse rather you should upon any advantage of the wind give battle to the enemy than retreat further than is necessary to get an advantage upon the enemy. But in case you find it necessary to go to the westward of the French fleet, in order to be better joining with our ships from Plymouth, or any others coming from the westward, we leave it to your discretion, so as you by no means ever lose sight of the French fleet whereby they may have opportunities of making attempts upon the shore, or in the rivers of Medway or Thames, or get away without fighting. And so we bid you heartily farewell.[16]

This order was, of course, Nottingham's, and its wrongheadedness may possibly show itself to the reader who has followed me thus far. There is no sign in it of an understanding of the possibly overwhelming consequences of a lost battle, for it assumes it to be a bad thing to let the French "get away without fighting." Nottingham must have got it into his mind, and carried it into the mind of the Queen and her council, that the well-tried Herbert and his colleague flag-officers were incompetent cowards, fearing a battle

16. Ibid.

where there were at least fair chances of success, and nothing to follow defeat if it should come. But as has often happened since, the
statesman was found on the quarter-deck, and the rash blunderer at
the seat of Government. There was absolutely nothing to be gained
by a battle which could not possibly be a decisive victory, and over
which from the great numbers engaged, and the limits placed on
manœuvring by the character of the ships and the lightness of the
wind, the admirals could have no real control. A complete victory
to the enemy on the other hand, would, at the very least, have sent
the Dutch King back to Holland, if it did not place this kingdom
under the orders of the Pope and of Louis. The sailors saw it all well
enough. The statesmen neither saw it then nor afterwards.

While Torrington's report of the 26th was on its way to town, and
while Nottingham's despatch and its ruinous enclosure were on
their way back, the British fleet had been pressed eastwards as far
as Beachy Head. Torrington received the Queen's order on the
29th, and at once sat down to acknowledge the receipt of it to
Nottingham.

> My Lord,
> I this minute received Her Majesty's orders, which I will (so soon
> as I can get the flag-officers on board), communicate to them: I am
> very certain that they all will, with myself, with great cheerfulness
> give due obedience to her commands.
> Now in answer to your Lordship's, I infer from the examination of
> the prisoners they took off Weymouth, and set on shore at the Isle of
> Wight, that the French are as strong as we take them to be; for were
> they not so strong, or under any consternation, I cannot think they
> would have put anybody ashore to bring us the news of it, but quietly
> have retired. For if they do not think they have the advantage, I am
> yet to learn what can move them to stay, having for several days had
> a fair wind to carry them off. And, my Lord, notwithstanding your
> advice from France, I take them to be 80 men-of-war strong. How
> they are manned indeed, I am not able to judge; but I am credibly
> informed by some French prisoners, who were taken in a small bark,
> that they are well manned, and that the Toulon ships are now with
> them. Had we had Killigrew with us, the match had been a little
> more equal. I cannot comprehend that Killigrew, the merchant ships,
> Shovel, or the Plymouth ships, can run much hazard if they take any
> care of themselves. For whilst we observe the French, they cannot
> make any attempt either upon ships or shore, without running a
> great hazard; and if we are beaten, all is exposed to their mercy. 'Tis
> very possible I reason wrong, but I do assure you I can, and will,
> obey. Pray God direct all for the best. I send your Lordship a copy

enclosed of your letter to me. Pray, my Lord, assure Her Majesty that all that can be done by men in our circumstances shall be done for her service.[17]

In accordance with the Queen's orders and this decision, Torrington, at daylight next morning, proceeded to draw his fleet into line. The wind appears to have been from the eastward, and very light, and the line was formed on the starboard tack, with the ships' heads to the northward. The Dutch formed the van, Torrington, according to usage, commanded the centre, and Delaval the rear. About eight on the morning of June 30th, signal was made to engage, the allied line bore down on the French to leeward, who lay to with their head-yards aback and waited for the onset.[18]

Here, I do not examine the tactics of the battle that followed. It is sufficient to mention that the Dutch in the van got into close action with the rear part of the French van, and were doubled on by the nine leading ships of the latter.[19] The British rear also got into action, but not so close, with the French rear. The ships in the French centre were to leeward of the van and rear, and Torrington in the British centre, attacked them only at long range, and left for some time a gap between himself and the Dutch. The Dutch were badly damaged, but saved themselves, or were saved by Torrington's orders, in consequence of their dropping their anchors when the

17. Ibid.

18. The composition of Torrington's fleet is given in the *Memoirs of Lord Torrington* (Byng), already quoted, and I have not met it elsewhere. The Dutch van consisted of 22 sail, as follows:

| Ships. | | Guns. | Ships. | | Guns. |
|---|---|---|---|---|---|
| 1 | of | 92 | 2 | of | 64 |
| 1 | „ | 82 | 1 | „ | 62 |
| 1 | „ | 74 | 4 | „ | 60 |
| 2 | „ | 72 | 2 | „ | 52 |
| 1 | „ | 70 | 5 | „ | 50 |
| 1 | „ | 68 | 1 | „ | 44 |

The English centre and rear of 35 ships:

| Ships. | | Guns. | Ships. | | Guns. |
|---|---|---|---|---|---|
| 1 | of | 100 | 1 | of | 66 |
| 1 | „ | 96 | 1 | „ | 64 |
| 5 | „ | 90 | 3 | „ | 60 |
| 1 | „ | 82 | 1 | „ | 54 |
| 1 | „ | 72 | 1 | „ | 50 |
| 16 | „ | 70 | 2 | „ | 48 |
| | | | 1 | „ | 36 |

19. *Memoirs Relating to Lord Torrington*, p. 46.

ebb made, which the French not perceiving, drifted away to the westward out of gun-shot.[20] One of the Dutch ships, from inability to anchor, drifted away with the French and was captured.

In the evening, Torrington weighed, and taking in tow the disabled ships, beat to the eastward against the light foul winds that prevailed, taking the precaution to drop his anchors when the ebb-tide made against him. The French followed, not in general chase, but in line of battle, the contemporary opinion being that the desire to maintain the fighting formation saved our fleet from destruction. At any rate, the council of war which sat on the 1st July, decided that things were so bad with them that if they were pressed by the French, it would be necessary to destroy the disabled ships and retire, rather than face a renewal of the fight.

The French pursued, but not strenuously, for four days, by which time the Allies had reached Dover, and had left the enemy so far in the rear that the pursuit was abandoned, and the French drew off to the westward. The Allies suffered losses in the pursuit, four Dutch and one English ship having either been burnt or run ashore in a disabled state.

Naturally, the alarm was great in England on the news of this defeat spreading. Immediate invasion was the least that was expected. But it should seem that Torrington was entirely right in his strategical judgment. The French made for their original destination, Torbay, where they anchored and landed a party to burn the village of Teignmouth, which was easily driven off by the hastily assembled militia. They also destroyed one or two vessels of little value in the harbour, and later retired to Brest; some ruined houses at Teignmouth, some burnt small craft, and a single captured man-of-war being the insignificant trophies of the great expedition.

Torrington's defence of his conduct was the strategical condition he had to contend with. He was greatly inferior to the French, but they were powerless for mischief as long as his fleet existed. When forced by the Queen's order to fight a battle which there was no hope of winning against ships not only more numerous but of greater individual force, it behoved him to take care that he ran no risks of being beaten.

20. Not only were numbers of ships against the Dutch, but the individual power of their ships was less than that of the French. The average force of the 22 ships forming the Dutch van was but 61.8 guns, while of the 25 leading ships of the French it was 64.7.

That our fighting upon so great a disadvantage as we did was of
the last consequence to the kingdom, is as certain as that the Queen
could not have been prevailed with to sign an order for it, had not
both our weakness, and the strength of the enemy, been disguised to
hear. . .

It is true, the French made no great advantage of their victory, tho'
they put us to a great charge in keeping up the militia; but had I
fought otherwise, our fleet had been totally lost, and the kingdom
had lain open to an invasion. What then would have become of us in
the absence of His Majesty, and most of the land forces? As it was,
most men were in fear that the French would invade; but I was always of another opinion; for I always said, that whilst we had a fleet
in being, they would not dare to make an attempt.

In my letter of the 29th June, the matter is stated pretty plain:
whilst we observe the French, they can make no attempt either on sea
or shore, but with great disadvantages; and if we are beaten all is
exposed to their mercy. This I dare be bold to say, that if the management of the fleet had been left to the discretion of the council of war,
there would have been no need of the excessive charge the kingdom
was put to in keeping up the militia, nor would the French have gone
off so much at their ease.[21]

So that, even though the beaten Allied fleet had come "to an anchor at the Nore in great confusion; and expecting that the French
might attack them, all the buoys were taken up, and other necessary
dispositions made as soon as they got there,"[22] yet the strategy of
the conditions was such as to leave and keep the great French fleet
powerless. If, indeed, the enemy had followed up and beaten the
fleet at the Nore absolutely, "all would have been at his mercy." But
"a fleet in being," even though it was discredited, inferior, and shut
up behind unbuoyed sandbanks, was such a power in observation
as to paralyze the action of an apparently victorious fleet either
against "sea or shore."

This is the part of the battle of Beachy Head which constitutes its
chief interest, but which is hardly touched by the different historians who have related the story. The first attempt of the French to
gain the command of the sea with a definite ulterior purpose failed,
because, as a fact, they were not enterprising or persevering enough
to secure the preliminary condition. They had beaten our fleet, yet
not to the point of annihilation which was necessary if the command of the sea was to be gained. Lord Torrington's acquittal by the

21. Torrinton's defence, Entick, p. 549.
22. *Memoirs Relating to Lord Torrington,* p. 47.

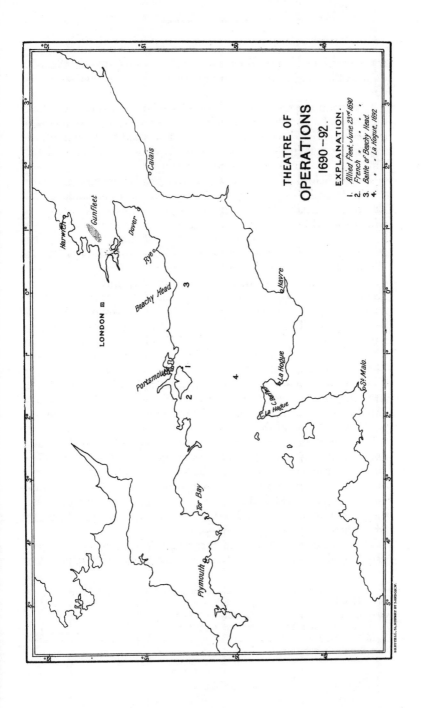

THEATRE OF
OPERATIONS
1690-92.

EXPLANATION.

1. Allied Fleet, June 23rd 1690
2. French " " " 1690
3. Battle of Beachy Head.
4. " " La Hogue, 1892

Harwich
Gunfleet
Calais
Dover
Rye
Beachy Head
LONDON
Portsmouth
Tor Bay
Plymouth
Havre
La Hogue
C. La Hague
St Malo

3
1
2
4

court-martial which tried him, in the face of very strong influences on the other side, is a significant reminder of the naval views of that day.[23]

Both countries had now studied in the school of experience. But if the French had hardly got to understand what sort of a command of the sea would be necessary before invasion could be thought of; the English had taken some warning as to the dangers of delay and parsimony in the preparation of naval defence.

The French plan for 1692 was as follows. By arrangement with the disaffected party in England, an attempt was to be made to land an army of 20,000 men[24] on the coast of Sussex, the arrival of which should be the signal for a general rising in the country on behalf of James. This army, assembling with the necessary sea-transport at La Hague, Cherbourg, and Havre, consisted of 14 battalions of English, Scotch, and Irish, and 9,000 French, was joined by the ex-King.[25] No doubt it was originally intended that the French fleet of 1692 should be as superior to that of the Allied English and Dutch as it had been in 1690, and equally beforehand in beginning hostilities. The authorities at Brest were ordered to prepare the whole of the ships there for sea, and orders were given that a contingent of 13 sail-of-the-line should join them from Toulon. Then the precedent of 1690 was taken up, and it was hoped that de Tourville—again in command—might be able to fall upon and destroy the British home fleet before it could be joined by the Dutch, and that then the invading military force might cross and encourage a successful rising of the Jacobites.

But two things happened, or rather three, which marred and rendered abortive the otherwise reasonable plans of the French. The Toulon contingent, approaching the Straits of Gibraltar on the 18th of May, was met by a gale of wind, which drove two of the ships ashore at Centa, and so dispersed and damaged the remainder that they were not able to reach Brest till the end of the month of July, by which time many things had happened.

The second misfortune which the French suffered was the persistent advice from English Jacobites, that many of the captains of

23. A matter not touched on by any of the historians, which would deserve comment if I dealt with the tactical part of the subject, is the non-use by Torrington of his fire-ships. I have not observed that anyone says a word about them.

24. Forbin, quoted by Lediard, vol. ii., p. 665.

25. Entick, p. 555. O. Troude, vol. i., p. 209. Troude says there were but 12,000 men, but this is a mistake.

the British fleet had been gained over to the cause of James, and would desert to the enemy at the first opportunity.

The third misfortune was that the Dutch were more prompt and earlier than usual in joining the English fleet, and that Louis' information on this head had failed him.[26]

James pressed upon Louis the certainty of his information with regard to the disaffected English captains, and the relative weakness of the English fleet alone; and in an evil hour for the French success, Louis sent orders to de Tourville to put to sea with the 45 ships of the line and the 7 fire-ships which were ready at Brest, and to fall upon the English before the junction of the Dutch, whether they were strong or weak. De Tourville sailed, but foul north-easterly winds delayed his progress up Channel, and facilitated the passage of the English down Channel, and the approach of the Dutch to join them. Cruisers were despatched after de Tourville, from Barfleur and elsewhere, to countermand the previous orders, but the despatches never reached him, and he went on towards the point where the army for invasion was assembled.

The English had, as I have observed, profited by experience. They do not seem to have had any accurate information of the French complete design, for they were, down to the last moment, proposing a descent on St. Malo, and the necessary troops were called together at Portsmouth for the purpose. But they were well aware that a great sea force early in the field was the double necessity under the knowledge that some design was in preparation in France. Admiral Russell was appointed to the command of the Home fleet as early as the 3rd of December 1691, and great activity was displayed in pushing on the fitment of the ships.

Look-out ships were sent out to observe the movements of the French, and as the ships grew towards readiness, two strong squadrons were despatched into the Channel with orders so curiously inconsequent as almost to show that the real designs of the French were quite misunderstood.

Sir Ralph Delaval had arrived in the Downs with a squadron in the beginning of March, after successful convoy service from the Mediterranean, and was now ordered to reconnoitre the French coast as far as Cape La Hague, with scouts out to give him due warning of the enemy's approach. Then he was to cross over to the Isle of Wight, whence, if no orders reached him, he was to return

26. O. Troude, vol. i., p. 209, *et seq.*

along the French coast to Dover, and again, if no orders reached him, he was to repair to the flats off the North Foreland.

Admiral Carter, with a considerable squadron, including 11 ships for the line, had orders on the 14th of April to sail to the Channel Islands, and to cruise near St. Malo for eight-and-forty hours, unless "an opportunity of doing service" should recommend a longer stay. Then he was to look in at Havre, and if no service could be done there, he was to return to Spithead.[27]

It is not very easy to understand what was in the mind of the authorities dictating these orders. Mere reconnoitring a part of the French coast, where either no heavy ships or the whole naval force of France might be expected to be met, could have been much better carried out by a few very light and insignificant ships; and it does not appear that mere collection of intelligence was the object. But if not, then what *was* the object? Dangers were run in separating such considerable bodies from the main fleet, and leaving them liable to be taken at a disadvantage. I do not perceive that value, compensating for the risk, was aimed at. And, indeed, this view seems to have been speedily taken, for countermanding orders to both Admirals almost immediately followed, resulting in general directions to Russell, Delaval, and Carter to concentrate south of the Isle of Wight.[28]

Admiral Russell, with the main body of the English fleet, arrived off Rye on the 8th of May, where some of the Dutch ships were already at anchor. The joined forces seem to have anchored thereabouts, and on the 10th a council of war decided, on considering the orders given to Sir Ralph Delaval, that it would be prudent to make a further delay off Rye, so as to secure his junction.[29] The fleet, however, sailed for St. Helen's on the 11th, and on the 13th, Delaval and Carter, who had already formed a junction at sea, joined Russell at St. Helen's.

The British admiral now found himself at the head of an enormous fleet. The Red squadron, under Russell, with Sir Ralph Delaval and Sir Cloudesley Shovel as vice- and rear-admirals, consisted of 5 first-rates, 3 second, 16 third, and 7 fourth. The Blue squadron, under Admiral Sir John Ashby, Vice-Admiral Hon. George Rooke, and Rear-Admiral Hon. Richard Carter, consisted of 1 first-rate, 7

27. Lediard, vol. ii., p. 656.
28. Lediard (ibid., note) considers that the first countermanding orders followed on intelligence that the French were preparing for sea (at Brest?). The dates were 20th and 23rd of April. Creasy, *Invasions of England,* says Russell was playing false, if so, many things are explained.
29. Burchett, p. 463; Lediard follows.

second, 18 third, and 6 fourth-rates. The English part of the fleet consisted thus of 63 ships of the line, carrying 27,725 men, and 4,500 guns. Besides these were 23 frigates and fire-ships.

The Dutch formed the White squadron, under Admiral Allemonde and two Vice-admirals, and consisted of 36 ships-of-the-line, namely, 9 first, 10 second, 9 third, and 8 fourth-rates. The division carried 12,950 men, and 2,494 guns. Attached to the division were 14 frigates and fire-ships. The total line-of-battle force was therefore 99 sail, carrying 40,675 men, and 6,994 guns. I suppose that never before or since has such a tremendous naval force been assembled under one admiral, and yet from want of proper intelligence, the French admiral at the head of less than half the force, was quietly sailing up channel to be destroyed by it.[30]

Russell seems to have had no advices of the near approach of the French. The Allies were full of the intended descent on St. Malo, and Russell's proposal was that, guarded by the whole fleet to the westward, the descent should be made by the troops prepared at Portsmouth. But as a preliminary a squadron of 6 light frigates was despatched towards Havre and that part of the French coast, to reconnoitre; and on the 18th of May the whole fleet weighed, and stood directly over towards Cape Barfleur.

It does not appear that either side was aware of the immediate proximity of the enemy. The weather was thick, and the wind light from the westward, and the Allied fleet stood on, on the starboard tack, till about 3 o'clock on the morning of the 19th May. Then guns were heard from the look-outs to the westward, and soon, out of the fog, two of them appeared with the signals flying denoting the presence of the enemy. Russell at once made the signal for the rear to tack, so as to meet the French if it should turn out that they were on the port tack. But as the sun rose, the weather cleared, and the French were seen to be forming their line on the starboard tack with their heads to the southward. Russell ran to leeward, and then, his line fairly well formed from S.S.W. to N.N.E., lay to and awaited the attack of the French, the Dutch White squadron forming the van, the Red squadron the centre, and the Blue the rear, as the signal to tack had been annulled.

What concerns us, now that we have brought the French fleet all but into contact with the Allied fleet of twice its force, is less any

30. Lediard gives the names and guns of 63 French ships, and says there were 55 small craft attached. But he admits he may over-state. Troude gives names of captains as well, and I accept his statement, the more so as Russell himself makes the number as under 50.

Ships of the Line in Action at the Close of the 17th Century

close investigation of its disastrous defeat which most inevitably followed, than those general reflections which naturally arise on such a complete failure of strategy. Let us first bear in mind that we have a set of conditions just opposite to those which had, two years before, surrounded the battle of Beachy Head. The superiorities of the attacking and defending fleets were reversed, and the attacking fleet was to windward, barred therefore from all chances of escape, because the propulsive force on which escape depended, was adverse. De Tourville had fallen into this horrible trap, not of choice, but from want of intelligence. Hoping, in the fog, that the enemy, of whose presence he possibly had warning for the first time by the sound of our look-out ship's guns, was at most the whole English, or the whole Dutch fleet, the lifting of the fog left him in face of a combination such as would have in any case kept him at Brest had he known of it. Close to him was the army of invasion and its transport. The cruising squadrons of the English had, up to this time, made it impossible for the force at La Hague to dream of moving. Now, it was quite certain that, whatever happened, the game of invasion was up. It was not a question of de Tourville's being beaten, it was only one of escaping total annihilation, if such escape were possible. The invasion project so far had come to this, that there had been all the expense of collecting a useless army in Normandy, besides the certainty that such a collection was about to involve the greater or less destruction of the French fleet.

We are not told how the tide was when the two fleets sighted one another. Had it been flood, de Tourville might have profited by the example of Torrington, and by dropping his anchors immediately, suffered the enemy to drift away from him. Had it been ebb, I know not what he could have done other than what he did do, that is, to put the boldest possible face on it, and bear down to the attack.

But of course it was hopeless. In the thick weather that again set in, it was impossible to say exactly what happened, but that the unhappy French were everywhere beaten and dispersed. The wind had shifted to the N.W. by W. in the afternoon, which facilitated the attempts of the French to escape south and south-west indiscriminately, which they did. Later on the wind changed to the eastward and freshened. Next day (the 20th May) Russell wrote that it had continued calm all night. There had, during the day's calm, been an engagement to the westward of him, "which he supposed to be the Blue." "I can give," he said, "no particular account of things; but the French were beaten, and I am now steering away for Conquet Roads, having a fresh gale easterly, but extremely foggy. I suppose

161

that is the place they design for.[31] If it please God to send us a little clear weather, I do not doubt but we shall destroy their whole fleet. I saw in the night three or four ships blow up; but I know not what they were." [32]

There was nothing now to be done but to pursue and destroy. Some of the beaten enemy made for St. Malo, and secured themselves; but some that escaped to Cherbourg and others to La Hague were fallen upon and burnt by Delaval and Russell himself. There were no less than 15 ships of from 60 to 104 guns destroyed, 3 at Cherbourg, and 12 at La Hague. The French attempt to gain the command of the sea had a second time failed, but now disastrously.

31. He was still 21 miles N.E. of Cape Barfleur when he wrote. Conquet Roads are close to Brest.

32. I have taken for illustration of battle at this date a sketch of a picture which hangs in the house of the Admiral Superintendent at Devonport, and of which no history exists, but to which I have had access through the kindness of Sir Walter Hunt-Grubbe, when he was superintendent. The painting has suffered from decayed portions of it having passed through the hands of some audacious master painter in the yard, but what has not been touched is of exceeding beauty and truth. It is impossible to say who was the artist, but internal evidence points irresistibly to the conclusion that it is nearly as old as the yard itself, which was founded in 1691, or is a copy of a picture of that date. The single reefs in the top-sails, the colouring of the hulls, the shape of the tops, shortness of the mast-heads, cut of the sails, and other things all fix the date of the ships represented as close to that of La Hague.

# CHAPTER SEVEN

I T IS PROPER that we should glance for a moment, before passing on, at the consequences likely to arise from a complete failure to obtain the command of the sea for an ulterior purpose: the consequences, that is, of making naval warfare a means rather than an end. In 1690 the French attempt had been frustrated by the sound policy of the Earl of Torrington operating under very disadvantageous conditions, but governed by a profound conviction of the tremendous risks which would be run if the rash adoption of any other policy should land the allied fleets in a serious disaster. In 1692 the French may be said to have adopted the opposite view. They were prepared to stake their maritime life upon a cast, and to stand the hazard of the die. De Tourville's orders were, practically, to go through with it without regard to consequences. The naval war was made subordinate to the military war which was ready to be launched from La Hague, and so overwhelmingly important did this military war seem, that any mere naval risk was not to stand for a moment in the way of it. So the die was cast, the battle of La Hague was fought, and the French navy was destroyed, scattered, and dispersed, and the consequences had to be taken, which, however, as will be related in the proper place, the French, by a return to the principles of legitimate naval war, were able in some degree to discount in 1693.

The Anglo-Dutch fleets may be said to have been quite unprepared for the absolute collapse which French maritime enterprise suffered on the defeat of de Tourville. Practically, the rest of the year 1692 and the whole of 1693 were spent in considering what was to be done, without coming to any definite conclusions. But in 1694 the notorious powerlessness of the enemy at sea determined an attack upon Brest by land and sea. There was, however, no heart in it, nor were the land forces nearly sufficient for so considerable an enterprise. It was in no degree surprising that on the failure of an attack on a fort in Camaret Bay the whole thing should have been abandoned; yet the cool audacity of the attack was a direct consequence of the defeat of La Hague, and the sense of Torrington's language in relation to a broken-up fleet—if it is beaten, all is exposed to the mercy of the enemy—came home to the mind of the English Government. They provided abundance of mortar boats—bombs, as they were then called—and laid in good store of shells.

This being done, Dieppe was heavily bombarded on the 13th July 1694. Havre was bombarded on the 16th, and burnt steadily for two days. An audacious endeavour was made to smoke the inhabitants out of Dunkirk with a certain inventor's "smoak-boats," in September.

The Allies quietly took up a permanent position in the Mediterranean, and wintering for the first time in these latitudes, lay across French trade, watched French ports, and hampered every effort of France by sea.

The year 1695 was but one series of bombardments. St. Malo, in July, was fired by "machines," and had 900 shells and carcases thrown into it. Granville was destroyed. Dunkirk was attacked again, but again unsuccessfully, in August. Calais was bombarded with 600 shells, and next year with 300 shells again; while further down the coast, Belleisle, Houat, and Haedic were ravaged and harried. Palamos, captured by the French land-ways, was, in August 1695, bombarded by the Allies sea-ways; and, in fact, it was from 1692 to 1697 a mere question with the victorious powers what sort of mischief might be most conveniently and economically carried out. The French navy was thrown into such a state of demoralization for those five years by the break-up off the coast of Normandy that most of what was done in the maritime war way was the work of private enterprise. These were the days of Jean Bart in the North Sea, as a private adventurer under Government control, and of the practice of hiring out as to contractors the ships, officers, and men of the Royal Navy of France.[1] Practically, it may be said that the failure of de Tourville to gain the command of the sea for the temporary advantage of getting the army across the Channel, involved

1. La guerre de détail, la guerre de course avait seule occupé la Marine de la France. Les bâtiments de l'état et les officiers de vaisseau étaient prêtés, sous certaines conditions, aux armateurs ou aux compagnies qui voulaient tenter ce gendre d'entreprises auxquelles, du reste, les ministres eux-mêmes ne dédaignaient pas de s'associer.—O. Troude, vol. i., p. 235.

the close of the naval war and the leaving every spot of French coast open to the descents of the enemy.

In the absence of any possible attempt to recover the naval position, France in 1695 was minded to try the feasibility of rushing an army across, in the absence of the British fleet. The practice of laying up the great body of the fleet in the winter seemed to offer such an opportunity, and preparations were made for embarking an army at Dunkirk, Calais, and adjacent ports in the month of February. But intelligence to this effect having reached the English Government, orders were instantly given, on the 21st of that month, to mobilise the navy. So expeditiously was the business conducted that Russell found himself, on the 28th, off Gravelines, at the head of 40 sail of the line of English ships, and 12 Dutch, beside fire-ships and small craft. The mere appearance of such a fleet put to flight all ideas of any descent.

The next attempt of the French was not made until 1744; and though it can hardly be classed as one where the command of the sea was sought, yet as the intention was to provide sufficient naval force to escort the army over, it cannot properly be passed by; the less so as the expedition was prepared in peace, and its discharge upon our shores was intended to form the declaration of war.

The preparations were made in the winter of 1743–44 with great secrecy; 15,000 troops in Flanders and Picardy were assembled at Dunkirk, Calais, and Boulogne, commanded by Count de Saxe, and accompanied by the Young Pretender and a body of his Scotch and Irish supporters. Transports for this force were collected at the ports, and a fleet of 18 sail of the line, under de Roquefeuille was fitted out at Brest and Rochefort, and entered the Channel on the 3rd of February.[2] The British Government does not appear to have been early apprised of the designs of France. The general preparations for carrying on the war with Spain, and guarding against a coming war with France were considerable, but more perhaps in the way of attack than of defence against a particular form of it.

But the *Phoenix* 24, Captain T. Brodrick, was watching Brest, and saw the squadron on the same day that it put to sea. She at once made sail for Plymouth, arriving there on the 3rd of February, and sent off express to the Admiralty with the news. The whole of the ships available were at once whipped up. Admiral Sir John Norris was placed in command; he started for Spithead, picked up the

---

2. According to Schomberg, 19 ships of 44 to 76 guns, and 4 of 26 guns. Vol. v., p. 207. O. Troude says simply 26 vessels. Vol. i., p. 296.

ships there on the 6th of February, and sailed for the Downs, where the whole fleet was ordered to rendezvous. There he soon found himself at the head of 49 sail, of which 21 carried not less than 60 guns, and 11 not less than 44, a fleet therefore greatly superior to that which was approaching under de Roquefeuille.

This was seen at the entrance to the Channel by the *Bideford* and *Kinsale,* which were in charge of a convoy for Jamaica, on the 3rd of February, the day on which the *Phœnix* had arrived at Plymouth. Captain Young, who commanded the latter ship, judged that a higher duty was before him; he quitted the convoy, and made all speed to Plymouth with the news. The Admiralty were thus kept well informed of the progress and strength of the enemy. At Dunkirk the embarkation of the troops was proceeded with, though it is said that the process could only be made tasteful to the remainder of the troops by the execution of a recalcitrant member of the body on the beach, and in presence of his comrades.

The French fleet met foul winds and weather, and did not reach the back of the Isle of Wight until the 17th. The Admiral sent forward a look-out ship to examine St. Helen's and Spithead, and on the report that nothing was there, conceived the remarkable idea that the British fleet had retired into Portsmouth harbour. He thereupon despatched Commodore Bareil with 5 sail to Dunkirk to hasten the embarkation, as if under the impression that the coast was clear. He himself fell into a three days' furious gale off the Isle of Wight, and suffered much damage; but on the 22nd of February the wind changed to the westward and the weather cleared. The French Admiral took advantage of the change and anchored that evening off Dungeness.

It is easy at this point to take notice of the daring, as well as of the rashness of such proceedings as these. They can hardly be counted as naval warfare, and more clearly represent naval gambling. To assume, as de Roquefeuille had done, that because there were no ships at Spithead, therefore Great Britain at an hour of peculiar danger and anxiety would leave her coasts so unguarded that a force of a score of line-of-battle ships might become master of the British seas, was to place an abnormal faith in the stupidity of the islanders. He was about to conduct an attack which had been long in preparation, and which was vital to Great Britain, and yet his force was relatively small, however looked at. It was true that England had a great fleet detached to the Mediterranean, and a considerable force in the West Indies at the time, but it was hardly to be supposed that she would have denuded her own shores to such an extent as not to be able to match de Roquefeuille's force. But unless she had done so, his position was perilous in the extreme. The method was not really an advance on that adopted in 1695, and which was so easily and so completely made absurd. The present attempt might just as easily turn out to be absurd, and something else, unless the very unlikely contingency of the absence of the British fleet could be calculated on.

And some such ideas were very forcibly impressed on de Roquefeuille's mind when he saw, the next day, the 23rd of February, the great fleet under Sir John Norris "tiding it round the South Foreland." At that moment, though the French were to windward, they were apparently embayed to the eastward of Dungeness, and powerless to escape from the superior fleet slowly approaching them. But fortune favoured the audacious squadron of the enemy. The tide failed Sir John Norris when he had got within six miles of the French, and the wind remaining foul and light, compelled him to drop his anchors. Upon ascertaining this respite, de Roquefeuille called a council of war, which determined that the sooner they got out of their critical position the better, and orders were accordingly given to weigh at sunset and to make sail with the tide at seven in the evening. This was done, and fortune still befriending them, a furious gale sprang up which drove them down Channel at the rate of 12 knots, and safely, though in some disorder, into Brest. Sir John Norris finding, when day broke, that the French had disappeared, returned to the Downs so soon as the weather permitted, and arrived there once more on the 27th of February, though somewhat damaged by the heavy gale.[3]

Thus absurdly ended an expedition in which the chances were so much against the attacking side that it could not be ranged under the head of legitimate naval warfare. The French were only fortunate in escaping intact; for any impartial judge acquainted with all the circumstances of the early days of February must have predicted certain ruin to the French fleet. The attempt was and was not one to gain command of the sea for the ulterior purpose of invasion. Undertaken while the two nations were as yet at peace, and prepared in secret, it was to operate by way of surprise, although it was all but impossible that surprise could be effective. The naval force was insufficient to completely break up and disorganize anything

---

3. The chief authorities for my description are Entick's *Naval History;* Hervey's *Naval History, 1779;* Campbell's *Lives of the Admirals; Batailles Navales de France,* O. Troude, 1867; Schomberg's *Naval Chronology,* 1815.

but a very small force of the British, and it had been shown in 1690 that anything short of complete demoralization of the defending forces would be of no avail to permit the invading army to cross. Therefore, if full thought had been given to the matter, it must have been considered that the English Government would prove so extraordinarily supine as to leave practically no force in defence of its shores. But it could not have been unknown to the French Government that there never was a time when the English Government could be less accused of supineness, for in the previous December it had carried a vote appropriating 40,000 men for the sea, and 52,000 for the army and marines. The whole idea of the expedition betrayed a want of comprehension of the naval problem which pointed to the sinister influence of the most ignorant.

War with France, being again formally declared in 1756, tended to put a stop to a sort of disgraceful panic fear of invasion which had possessed the country, and to turn attention towards direct measures for preventing such a thing. France on her part mistaking, with the instincts of a military nation, the true points of naval policy, was full of invasion projects, and notwithstanding the several lessons she had already received, was bent upon making the naval subordinate to the military view; bent upon attempts to gain the temporary command of the sea with the ulterior purpose of passing armies over it if not going further, and supposing armies could be effectually guarded, and safely landed, under the protection of a mere escort.

The success of a somewhat contrary policy resulting in the capture of Minorca, and the general ill success of every other operation, instead of turning the attention of men of influence wholly to the concentration of naval force in order to wrest the command of the sea from the English, seemed to have directed attention more closely than ever to the idea of a military invasion. It was the more strange that such ideas should have prevailed at a time when the impotence of the French navy to protect its own shores was so very marked. Rochefort had been in September 1757 the object of a cool attack, in the absence of any French naval force competent to prevent it. In the following April (1758) Hawke broke up, in the inner waters of the Basque Roads, the convoys destined for the protection and sustenance of the French North American Colonies; and in June Anson assisted at another rehearsal of a favourite naval play—the partial destruction of St. Malo. In August the whole of the public works of Cherbourg were demolished under the protecting wing of Commodore Howe.

So far as experience had gone, only one way of preventing this kind of thing had been discovered; this was the neighbourhood of a sufficient naval force. The establishment and maintenance of such forces, which it was understood were prepared to meet equal forces of the enemy face to face at sea, had hitherto been found sufficient to frustrate all intention of territorial attack. France had fallen into the belief that though she could not protect her own shores, she might attack those of her enemy with naval forces which were at least doubtful about their being able to obtain such a command of the sea as they might hold. There was, in effect, a doubt as to whether the forthcoming invasion was to be conducted by force or by stratagem; by open defiance or secret evasion. And when the time came for putting such of it as remained possible into action, there was a difference of opinion between the Minister of Marine and the naval commander on the fundamental principles which were to govern proceedings. Strangely and ominously, it was the naval commander who held the view which was opposed to the teaching of experience so far. I shall advert to this point a little further on.

In the beginning of 1759, the French had three main fleets in existence. There were twelve sail of the line at Toulon under Rear-Admiral de la Clue.[4] At Brest, under Vice-Admiral Marshal de Conflans, was a force which was counted up to 17 sail by the British scouts in June, and proved to be 20 or 21 sail of the line strong in November; and in the West Indies a squadron of 9 sail of the line under Rear-Admiral Bompart.[5]

This made up a total force of 38 sail of the line capable of being concentrated, had the command of the sea been aimed at, on the English force off Toulon, not exceeding 14 or 15 sail of the line; or on that off Brest, never exceeding 25 sail of the line, but seldom reaching that strength at any given moment.

Command of the sea as an end was not, however, thought of. Such concentration as was contemplated did not pass beyond the object of convoy or escort for the armies. One of these was collected with complete transport about Morbihan, a district comprising a group of estuaries opening into Quiberon Bay; it consisted of 19,000 men under the command of the Duke d'Aiguillon, and was originally intended to be convoyed to Irvine near Ardrossan on the Firth of Clyde, by Captain de Morogues with 5 sail-of-the-line and

---

4. I give the name as we generally hear it. M. Troude gives it as "de Laclue."
5. This is the usual spelling, but Troude spells it "Bompard."

frigates. Preparations were also made for the embarkation of another army at Havre, in flat boats and small craft, and a diversion was to be made by a third force sailing from Dunkirk under Thurot, acting against some point on the north-eastern coasts of England or Scotland, or possibly Ireland. Great differences of opinion existed in France on the methods to be pursued, and no doubt as the months went on, and the preparations became more and more complete, changes in the programme took place.

The English Government, animated by the genius of the elder Pitt, took a practical view of the situation. The Dunkirk invading squadron which consisted of 5 frigates, was watched by 12 sail of from 50 to 12 guns under Commodore Boys. Commodore Sir Piercy Brett lay in the Downs or Yarmouth Roads with another squadron of 8 sail, to guard against the chances of Thurot eluding Boys. An equal or superior fleet to that of de la Clue watched him in Toulon, and to Sir Edward Hawke was confided a fleet of 25 sail of the line and a powerful force of 50-gun ships and frigates[6] for the purpose of watching Conflans and guarding Morbihan, Rochefort and the Basque Roads, and preventing the unobserved escape of any French forces from these points.

This is not the place to discuss the causes of the advance which had been made in the powers of defence by naval force, as shown in this distribution of the British fleets. We have hitherto seen them, when the attack on our shores was imminent, concentrated close at home to await it. Now we see the points of resistance moved away from our own shores, and transferred to the immediate neighbourhood of the enemy's ports. The change was chiefly due, no doubt, to the improvements in naval architecture which had continually progressed, and also to the improved quality and quantity of the provisions carried, as well as to a better state of hygiene[7] on board ship. But, undoubtedly, the change was also due to altered conceptions of the principles of naval war and to a more general acceptation of Lord Torrington's maxim that an intact defending fleet was an absolute bar to territorial attack. To the superficial strategist, the absence of great fleets in the Bay of Biscay and the Mediterranean was leaving the shores of England exposed. To the sound mind of Pitt

6. Sixteen, according to Schomberg.
7. Hawke was able to maintain a winter blockade of Brest, but still bitterly complained of the badness of provisions, especially bread and beer, and had men constantly "falling down with scurvy," but this was a wonderful improvement on 1695, when the mere fitting out of a winter fleet put 500 men on shore sick, and still left the fleet unhealthy. See Burrows' *Life of Hawke, passim,* and Burchett, p. 541.

and the instructed intellects of his naval supporters and advisers, the mere existence of these fleets was full protection to the coasts of the United Kingdom in the first instance, and afterwards cover for the more direct destruction of the enemy's invading material, and immediate prevention of even the issue of invading forces from the watched ports. Not, of course, that danger did not arise, but that it came more from the division of the naval force into several groups, which might be incapable of supporting one another, than from any removal of the bulk of the naval force to the immediate neighbourhood of the enemy.

As a direct employment of the cover gained by the masking of the French fleet at Brest, Rear-Admiral Rodney, with a squadron of 60- and 50-gun ships and bomb vessels, proceeded in July to bombard Havre and to destroy the invasion flotilla. Shells were poured into the place for fifty-two hours, and the flat boats endeavouring to escape out of it were pursued, driven on shore, and afterwards ordered by the victorious admiral to be burnt by their own crews under penalty that otherwise the town of Port Bassin, where they had sought shelter, should suffer the fate of Havre.

The main naval object of the French was the junction of the fleet of de la Clue with that of Conflans at Brest, and the prevention of this was the special object of Admiral Boscawen off Toulon. The means employed were not at all the confining of de la Clue in his port, but rather the bringing him to action at sea. The underlying principle was plain enough. If the French fleet could be brought to battle, come what come would of it, all immediate idea of a con- centration at Brest must be given up. Even were Boscawen thor- oughly beaten, which was not at all likely considering the relative strength of the forces, a return to Toulon by the French to refit and repair would be imperative after the action. The success of the French plan, however, chiefly depended on de la Clue's avoidance of battle; he was not to be drawn out, and he trusted to time to force Bosca- wen to retire for a space.

The British Admiral kept watch till the beginning of July, and was then compelled by want of water and provisions, and by certain damage to some of his ships to fall back upon Gibraltar. The coast being so far clear, de la Clue weighed from Toulon on the 5th of August, with his fleet of 12 sail of the line and 3 frigates, in hopes of passing the Straits of Gibraltar unnoticed. But Boscawen had placed a look-out ship off Malaga, and another, the *Gibraltar,* between Es- tepona on the Spanish and Ceuta on the African shore. On the 17th of August, Boscawen's ships were still in the middle of refitting:

171

their sails were unbent, and some of them had their topmasts down.[8] Towards evening the French fleet drew near the straits, and running before a strong easterly breeze, found themselves off Cape Spartel at midnight, in a pitch dark atmosphere, and with no sign that they were in any way followed, perhaps with no belief that they had been even seen.

De la Clue was happy in the supposed success of his movements. No ship had shown a light, and the game was played and won; Boscawen was outwitted, the blockade of Brest and Morbihan would be raised, and the Scotch invasion at least would proceed. But there was a fatal flaw in his own conduct, of which he was far from perceiving the consequences. He had thought much of pushing on himself, and had been less careful of the order in which he maintained the fleet astern of him. He had made Cadiz the rendezvous of his ships, and when darkness fell and precluded the establishment of a fresh rendezvous, or even of any very definite communication of orders, by reason of the defective signal systems of those days, all the captains believed that Cadiz was the destination. Now at midnight, the course to Cadiz was, perhaps, N.N.W., while the course to pass Cape St. Vincent and proceed up the coast of Portugal was, perhaps, W.N.W. At midnight M. de la Clue began to think of pulling his fleet together, and began also to think that the rendezvous at Cadiz was a mistake. He would simply be blocked there, as he had been blocked at Toulon. He could never expect again such a chance as was now before him. He shortened sail to allow the fleet to close up; he exhibited his stern lights to show his position, and he made, or attempted to make, a night signal which would direct the fleet to continue to steer to the westward.[9] Then, fearing that Boscawen's look-out ships might see the lights, and assuming that his ships had all seen and understood the intended signal, he complacently extinguished his lights and made sail for Cape St. Vincent. At daylight he had but six ships with him, and it was not until 8 o'clock that the report of 8 sail to the eastward gave him hopes that the stragglers were rejoining. He was then 30 or 40 miles to the E.S.E. of Cape St. Vincent, and he took steps to let this remainder of his fleet come up with him.

8. Schomberg, vol. i., p. 232.
9. Troude, vol. i., pp. 373–79. M. de Lapeyrouse, quoted by Troude, says the Admiral made the signal to steer to the westward. But even as late as 1832 there was no such night-signal in the French navy; the nearest signal was "sail large" on the starboard or port tack.

Now let us see what had been going on in the English fleet during this time. I do not think I can more clearly or forcibly tell the story than by quoting *verbatim* the language of the journal of the Captain of the *Namur,* Captain Buckle, Boscawen's flag-captain.[10]

Friday, 17th August 1759, moored in Gibraltar Bay. Wind E.S.E. to East. First part moderate and fair, middle and latter part a fresh gale, and hazy. P.M., received a long-boat load of water. At 8 heard the report of several guns, soon after saw a ship in the offing with several lights, then we sent our barge, who returned and informed us that the ship we saw was the *Gibraltar,* who had seen fifteen large ships at the back of the hill. At 9 made the signal to unmoor. Bent the sails and hove up the best bower anchor. At 10 made signal and slipped; the long-boat being made fast to the end of the cable, got athwart hawse, broke the slip-rope and went adrift. At 11 Cabritta Point bore west, three or four miles. Brought to, and hoisted in the boats. Employed clearing the ship. At midnight made sail. At 1 A.M. out all reefs and set top gallant sails. Cape Spartel W. by S., seven or eight miles. At 6 saw seven sail to the westward. At 7 made the *Gibraltar's* signal to come within hail, and ordered him to make sail ahead and see what the strangers were. At 8 six Sweeds passed by to the southward. Made the signal for a general chase to the N.W. At 9 made the signal for the ships astern to make more sail, soon after repeated it. At noon all the fleet in chase.

Saturday 18th, at noon Cape St. Vincent N.W. by W., distant eight or nine leagues Winds East, E.N.E., and E.S.E. First part moderate and fair, middle and latter little wind. At 1 P.M. the strangers hoisted French colours, then we showed ours. Twenty minutes after made the signal to engage. At 50 minutes past made the *America's* signal to make more sail. At 2 repeated it; the enemy began to fire, as did the *Culloden* at 25 minutes past 2. At three-quarters past 2, the *America* backed her mizzen topsail and topgallant-sail and hauled up her mainsail. Then made her signal to make more sail. At 10 minutes past 3, made the *Guernsey's* signal to make more sail, which she not observing we soon after repeated it. At a quarter-past changed the chasing signal from N.W. to N.E. At 4 ran alongside the *Ocean,*[11] having a flag at the mizzen topmast head, and engaged her and two other ships of the enemy till quarter-past 7, when they made sail and shot ahead of us. The mizzen-stay being shot away the mast went overboard. The fore and main topsail yards likewise shot away, and all our sails and rigging much damaged; then the Admiral went on

10. The journal, with great numbers of others, is preserved in the Royal Victoria Yard, Deptford. The day begins at noon.
11. De la Clue's flag-ship.

board the *Newark* and hoisted his flag there. Soon after one of the French ships struck, being the *Centaur*, of 74 guns and 750 men, whom the *Edgar* lay by. We had six men killed in the action and upwards of forty wounded. People employed repairing the damages. At 10 Thomas Quinnell, Thomas Cattness, and John Williams, seamen, died of their wounds. At 5 A.M. saw our fleet in the S.W. and made sail after them.

Sunday, August 19th, 1759. Noon, Cape St. Vincent N.W. ½ W. three or four leagues, winds West, N.W. by N., N.N.E., N.N.W., North, light airs and fair. At 2 P.M. saw three of the French ships at anchor to the eastward of Cape St. Vincent, and one on shore without any masts, being the *Ocean*, of 84 guns, who struck to the *St. Alban's*, as did one of the others to the *Warspite*. At 7 saw one of the remaining two on fire. The *Warspite* brought her prize into the fleet, being the *Temeraire* of 74 guns and 750 men. Unbent the foresail and fore-topsail and bent new ones. At half-past 9, the ship (that) was on fire blew up. At 10, saw the *Ocean* on fire. At midnight our ships brought in the other French ship, called the *Modeste* of 64 guns and 700 men. A.M. got up a new main topgallant mast and yard. Employed setting up a pair of sheers to raise the mizzen-mast. N.B.— The ship which blew up was the *Redoubtable*, of 74 guns.

Monday, August 20th, Cape St. Vincent distant twelve leagues. Winds N.W., N., N.E. Moderate and clear. At 4 P.M. Cape St. Vincent bore N.W. by N., eight or nine leagues. Admiral Boscawen returned from the *Newark* and hoisted his flag here. Raised the mizzen mast, and stepped it on the upper deck.

Such was the first battle of St. Vincent, as described in the cool and terse language of the official record. It is easy to understand what had happened in the French fleet. M. de la Clue, who paid with his life the forfeit of his error, small as it might have seemed at the time, had not been justified in assuming that his signals at midnight on the 17th had been seen and their purport understood. However he might have thought of it, his captains had no opportunity of looking into his mind and noting what was going on there. Five of the line-of-battle ships, and all the frigates, missing the rest of the fleet, had obeyed their orders and proceeded to Cadiz. The ships, which de la Clue did not see till 8 A.M. on the 18th, and which he for a time drew near to, supposing them to be friends, were in fact the leaders of Boscawen's fleet, which were even then preparing for a general chase. The danger of playing fast and loose with a rendezvous had even then been fully recognized in the English navy, and it is highly improbable that any English admiral would have acted as de la Clue did. The importance attached to the thing is well illustrated in this very journal of Captain Buckle, in which a new rendezvous being given out on the afternoon of the 20th, and a lieutenant from each ship summoned to receive it, the names of the officers thus made responsible are entered.

The result of the error was a loss to the French of two line-of-battle ships burnt, and three captured, out of the total of seven. Two made their escape on the night of the 18th, and one reached Rochefort and the other the Canaries in safety. Poor de la Clue was landed badly wounded, and died of his wounds soon afterwards. The conjunction of the Toulon and Brest fleets was entirely abandoned, and those French ships which had got into Cadiz, only thought themselves too happy in escaping to Toulon as late as the 17th of December.

There was still the combination of Admiral Bompart's squadron with that of de Conflans, and against this Hawke was taking all possible steps. He was primarily concerned in a close watch upon Brest, in order that the fleet there should not be able to put to sea unwatched and unfollowed. The secondary object was as close a watch on the invading force assembled at Morbihan. But the greater danger was the junction of the Toulon fleet with the Brest fleet, and even after he had heard from Boscawen of the result of the battle of the 18th and 19th of August, he saw no cause to relax his vigilance. Boscawen wrote on the 20th, and did not then know that the half of the French fleet was in Cadiz, and capable of being masked. So that when Hawke in the latter end of August heard that Bompart had actually sailed from America, there was a possible combination at or near Brest of an exceedingly serious character. Bompart might make for Rochefort, and the moiety of de la Clue's fleet also, as a preliminary, and if Brest were opened, by heavy weather driving Hawke off, a junction might prove to be easy. He had not force enough to watch Rochefort as well as Brest. "If," he wrote on the 28th of August, "M. Bompart's destination should be Brest, I shall do my utmost to interrupt him. But should he be bound to Rochefort I must not think of him"—for the reason that a detachment to Rochefort, though enough to meet Bompart's nine sail of the line, would leave him too weak even for Conflans, certainly too weak for the missing ships of de la Clue's fleet and that of Conflans' together.[12]

But later on, when Hawke was probably relieved of all apprehension on the score of the ships shut up in Cadiz, he did despatch

12. Burrows' *Life of Hawke*, p. 380.

Admiral Geary with a squadron to bar Bompart's entry into Rochefort, while another squadron, under Captain Duff, lay in Quiberon
Bay watching Morbihan. And then, on the 10th of October, the Admiralty having informed him that Bompart was not likely to sail for
Europe at present, Geary was recalled.

Hawke's plans were thus very simple; he would watch Brest as
long as the weather would let him, and when driven off he would
invariably make for the then safe anchorage of Torbay, where the
store-ships and victuallers could always meet him, and where the
whole efforts of the fleet would be concentrated on getting ready to
put to sea the instant the wind changed.

On the same 10th of October Hawke, being off Brest, wrote:—

> Their lordships will pardon me for observing that from the present
> disposition of the squadron I think there is little cause for alarm
> while the weather continues tolerable. As to Brest, I may safely affirm
> that, except the few ships that took shelter in Conquet, hardly a ves-
> sel of any kind has been able to come out of that port these four
> months. We are as vigilant as ever, though we have not as much
> daylight. . . . It must be the fault of the weather, not ours, if any of
> them escape.[13]

The fault of the weather, however, showed itself immediately, for
on the 11th so heavy a westerly gale sprang up that the fleet sought
shelter in Plymouth, whence Hawke wrote on the 13th:—

> Yesterday and this day, the gale rather increasing, I thought it
> better to bear up for Plymouth than run the risk of being scattered
> and driven to the eastward. While this wind shall continue, it is im-
> possible for the enemy to stir. . . . The instant it shall be moderate, I
> shall sail again.[14]

Then next day, he says:—

> Their lordships may rest assured there is little foundation for the
> present alarms. While the wind is fair for the enemy's coming out, it
> is also favourable for our keeping them in; and while we are obliged
> to keep off, they cannot stir.[15]

The Admiral got back to his watch, now from the lateness of the
season become one of desperate anxiety and hazard, by the 23rd of
October, and the commanders of the inshore squadrons, breaking
down in health as they were from the strain, are only warned that

13. Ibid., p. 383.
14. Ibid.
15. Ibid., p. 384.

there must be less relaxation than ever. By the beginning of November, Hawke was informed that Conflans was under orders to put to sea and engage the English fleet at once; but probably the Admiral's wisdom doubted the fact, as there was no such superiority of numbers on the French side as would lead to hopes of victory. This, however, might be as it would, for on the 9th of November another westerly gale, which had been blowing three days, so increased that it drove the English fleet back into Torbay again, whence it was not possible to put to sea finally till the 13th.

It is necessary, as we now approach the *dénouement,* to look at the French part in this momentous drama. I have already said that there was a doubt over the whole of these invasion operations, as to whether they were to be carried out by force or strategem. Indeed, considerable doubt has existed in my own mind as to whether I can properly class them as an attempt to gain the command of the sea with an ulterior object. The military preparations occupy so great a field, when I look across the Channel, that I cannot make up my mind whether there was anywhere in France such a real idea of gaining the command of the sea, as there had been in 1690 and 1692. The plans seem disjointed and mixed, without a consciousness running through them that the invading forces must pass unprotected through an enemy's country, unless that water-country was first conquered. The French idea of the whole matter departs from simplicity, and is difficult to realise. Neither de la Clue, Conflans, nor Bompart, seem to have been clear about what they were going to do—de la Clue, by his fixing a rendezvous at Cadiz, when he should have wanted to push on to Brest at all hazards and speed; Bompart by his delayed return; and both he and Conflans by their subsequent conduct. As far as Conflans was concerned, he certainly had no clear ideas of what was before him.

> The timidity of our navy afflicts and humiliates me (wrote the Marshal de Belle-Isle to the Duke d'Aiguillon); above all, after the state in which I saw it at the beginning of the century. The King must give positive orders to M. de Conflans. He will not desire anything better, according to what I hear; but this is not enough. Many sad reflections arise upon it, but we may possibly hope that when things are once decided and ordered, they will stand on their honour.[16]

Conflans distinctly proposed to escort the convoy with his whole fleet.

---

16. Troude, quoting the Archives of the French Marine, vol. i., p. 381.

The Marshal (Berryer, the Minister of Marine, wrote to the Duke d'Aiguillon) is not a sufficiently good tactician to have any hopes of holding the enemy in check by his skill, and I regard a battle as inevitable; then it would be much better to fight it before the convoy puts to sea. If we gain the victory, we shall easily push it over; if it is doubtful, it will still facilitate the passage over; if our fleet is destroyed, the army will not be lost.[17]

But de Conflans was urgent with his own views, and the Minister of Marine at length submitted. Yet is the Marshal's conduct inexplicable, for between the 9th and the 14th of November, when the coast was clear by reason of Hawke's absence in Torbay, Bompart arrived with his squadron and passed into Brest without difficulty. Notwithstanding that, and apparently without seeing how much this reinforcement of nine sail of the line[18] should have strengthened the views of the Minister of Marine and weakened his own, Conflans put to sea with his original 21 sail of the line on the 14th of November. His destination was Quiberon Bay, whatever he might have intended to do when he got there; but a strong easterly gale carried him 180 miles west of Belleisle.[19] Calms and light air then fell upon the fleet, so that when the wind changed to the westward at 11 P.M. on the 19th of November, de Conflans was still 70 miles S.W. ¼ W. from the island. He then filled and stood on, intending to go to the southward of the island, and to pass up Quiberon Bay next day. The wind, however, began to blow so strong from the W.N.W., that it was necessary to shorten sail in order not to overrun the distance. At daybreak on the 20th, several sail were seen ahead, and the signals were made to close up and clear for action. As the light came, seven or eight of these ships were made out to be the squadron of Captain Duff, which had been lying in Quiberon Bay watching the armament, and were now making all speed to escape from the superior fleet of the French. De Conflans thereupon made the signal for a general chase.

The same easterly wind which had carried de Conflans out of Brest, on the same day took Hawke out of Torbay,[20] and on the 15th he learned from Captain McCleverty of the *Gibraltar,* the same offi-

17. Ibid.
18. The seamen of Bompart's squadron, as being more experienced, were substituted for those of de Conflans, but this only implied that the whole thing had been hopeless before. What was wanted was a superior fleet, and Bompart's ships would have made one.
19. De Conflans to the Duke d'Aiguillon, quoted by Troude, vol. v., p. 402.
20. Schomberg, vol. i., p. 327; Hervey, vol. v., p. 184; Hawke's despatch.

cer who had had the honour of announcing de la Clue's approach to Boscawen, that the French fleet had been seen seventy miles to the N.W. of Belleisle, steering to the S.E.[21] Hawke thereupon shaped his course for Quiberon Bay, but the wind beginning to blow hard from S. by E. and S., drove the English fleet, as it was driving the French, far to the westward. On the 18th and 19th wind and weather mended, and Hawke pushed on to pass Belleisle on his left hand. The *Maidstone* and *Coventry* frigates were sent ahead to look out, but nothing was seen until half-past eight on the morning of the 20th when the *Maidstone* made the signal for seeing a fleet. Hawke at once made the signal to form line abreast.

This was the moment when de Conflans, full of his chase of Duff, and hailing the *Tonnant*, "that he was resolved to attack the enemy smartly and without any order,"[22] found himself perfectly satisfied that no superior force could be present, and yet counting 23 ships of the line, clearly British, which had just hove in sight to windward "in very good order."

Marshal de Conflans had issued, before he left Brest, a curiously verbose order as to how he proposed to meet the enemy, and especially how he would be satisfied with nothing short of engaging at musket range. The plans were very elaborate, but they all seemed to hinge on the point that the meeting of the fleets would take place in a particular way. Nothing was provided for the case now before him. So little had such a meeting been contemplated that there were no look-outs astern, although it was from the northward and westward alone that any hostile force could be expected to make its appearance. Yet there was but one thing before the French admiral; that was to turn and give the British battle in the open sea. To do anything else was to give up bodily the whole plan of invasion, and to leave it open to the enemy to shell the expedition to pieces in Quiberon Bay, as another branch of it had already been shelled to pieces in the Roads of Havre. The very best that could happen if de Conflans did not give battle at sea, was that the whole of the French would henceforth be blockaded in Quiberon Bay, a much easier task than their blockade in Brest.

But the whole plan from beginning to end was confused and without definite principle, and it was not possible to turn round full of principle at a moment's notice. Quiberon Bay is studded with rocks and shoals; the thought uppermost in de Conflans' mind was

---

21. Schomberg, vol. i., p. 327.
22. De Conflans' despatch, quoted by Troude.

that if he could only get his ships into the Bay before those of the British, these rocks and shoals would prove in some sort a protection to the French; at any rate their danger would be less to the latter than to the former. Out of it all came the short story as told by Sir Edward Hawke:—

> All the day we had very fresh gales at N.W. and W.N.W. with heavy squalls. M. Conflans kept going off under such sail as all his squadron could carry and at the same time keep together; while we crowded after him with every sail our ships could bear. At half-past 2 P.M., the fire beginning ahead, I made the signal for engaging. We were then to the southward of Belleisle; and the French Admiral headmost, soon after led round the Cardinals,[23] while his rear was in action. About 4 o'clock the *Formidable* struck, and a little after, the *Thésée* and *Superbe* were sunk. About 5, the *Héros* struck, and came to an anchor; but, it blowing hard, no boat could be sent on board her. Night was now come, and being on a part of the coast among islands and shoals, of which we were totally ignorant, without a pilot, as was the greatest part of the squadron, and blowing hard on a lee shore, I made the signal to anchor, and came to in 15 fathoms of water. . . .

The French fleet, in short, was totally broken up and destroyed. Of the 21 sail of the line that had left Brest a week before, 2 were driven ashore and burnt; 2 were sunk; 1 was wrecked off the Loire; 1 was taken; 11 saved themselves by throwing all their guns and stores overboard and escaping into the shallow waters of the river Vilaine; while 8 only made good their retreat to Rochefort.

This terrible but decisive battle necessarily put the finishing stroke to the collapse of the French plans, which had indeed set in as soon as they came to be formulated. It is only necessary to add to the narrative the statement that M. Thurot's expedition proved itself the most successful of all, inasmuch as on the 12th of October he escaped to sea with his squadron, taking advantage of a gale which drove Commodore Boys off his station. His good fortune followed him so far as to permit him to gain the neutral port of Gottenburg in Sweden, and afterwards that of Bergen in Norway, where the squadron lay till next year.[24]

23. A peninsula and then a group of islands surrounded by rocks—of which Houat and Haedick are the chief—run down from the N.W. to the S.E. and form the Bay of Quiberon; the Cardinals are the rocks at the extreme S.E. point.
24. Naval history has hitherto been so written that simple as the story of the operations of 1759 is respecting the invasions proposed, it is hardly to be drawn from any single narrative. My sketch leaves much unexplained which it would be of the highest interest to enlarge upon and to seek for in those MS. authorities where alone

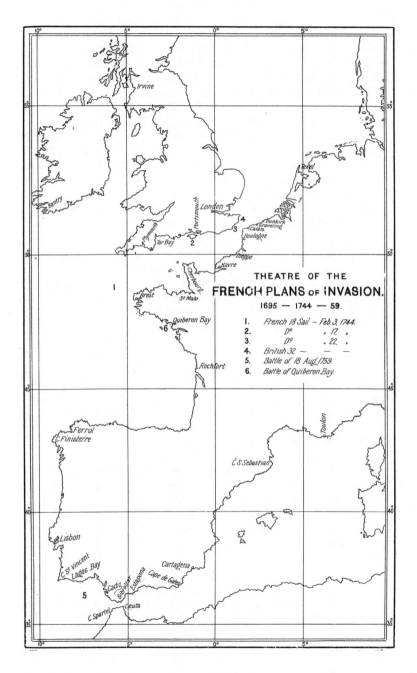

THEATRE OF THE
FRENCH PLANS OF INVASION.
1695 — 1744 — 59.

| | |
|---|---|
| 1. | French 18 Sail ~ Feb. 3, 1744. |
| 2. | D⁰ " 17, " |
| 3. | D⁰ " 22, " |
| 4. | British 32 — — — |
| 5. | Battle of 18 Aug. 1759. |
| 6. | Battle of Quiberon Bay. |

181

When from the singularly abortive character of all these plans on the part of the French in the year 1759, we turn to the question of whether they failed through bad management, faulty principles, or want of enterprise, I think we can say that while the first and last elements were present, they could hardly be absent when attempts to set up and enforce such faulty principles were also present.

I think it becomes more and more clear as we proceed, that the sea is not, and cannot be made, neutral ground. For the purposes of passage it is almost always in the hands of one side or the other in war, and if undisputed passage across it is desired by one side, it must be obtained by conquest of the water territory.

France in the year 1759, was, it seems to me, entirely mistaken on this fundamental principle. The only chance she could ever have had of successful invasion must have come after, and not side by side with, conquest at sea. With squadrons at Toulon, Brest, Rochefort, and the West Indies, which were all possible to her, she had so magnificent a strategic position that, barring mismanagement and the chapter of accidents, there was a possibility of her beating the British fleets in detail, as it was a necessity of the position that their naval forces should be divided.

This being so, it should have been her sole object to make such combinations as would have enabled her to fall on British detached fleets with superior force. If she were able to effect this purpose, and to gradually weaken her opponent thereby, there would be no possible difficulties in the way of invasion on any scale thereafter. But her attention, which should have been thus simply directed, was split up into two parts, one in preparing to invade, and the other in preparing fleets of which the employment was doubtful. Had she concentrated her mind wholly on the defeat of the British by sea, who is now to say that she might not have affected her purpose supposing her enterprise to correspond with her resolution? If her enterprise was unequal to the task, surely it must have been much more unequal to conveying armies across, and landing them in the face of naval forces admittedly superior. Or if it be said that it was hoped to escape the notice of these superior forces at sea, where was

---

the answers are to be found. But such things are altogether beyond the scope of my present purpose. I have drawn my narrative from comparisons of Schomberg's *Naval Chronology* 1815; Campbell's *Lives of the Admirals* 1813; Hervey's excellent but little known *History of the Navy* 1779; O. Troude's *Batailles Navales de la France* 1867, and above all, for what relates to Hawke, Burrows' *Life of Lord Hawke*, beyond measure the most interesting naval work of our time.

the advantage of adding great naval forces to accompany the transports? So that in whatever way the French plans be regarded, we see a want of clear comprehension of the strategical problem, and cease to wonder at the want of principle which governed every detail of the proceedings.

It was manifestly weak to prepare the transports, as in the case of Havre, in so exposed a position as to leave them open to destruction by shells and carcases.[25] No less clear was de la Clue's mistake in making Cadiz the rendezvous when everything depended on his evading Boscawen, and making all speed to join de Conflans. Out of this primary error arose the others, which led directly to the catastrophe of Lagos Bay.

Why de Conflans should ever have made for Quiberon Bay is at present to me an unfathomed mystery. His clear plan was to have engaged Hawke as far as possible from the army transports, which were already in possession of a stout convoy under de Morogues. Had he followed Hawke up into Torbay and there engaged his attention, de Morogues would have had a clear field up the St. George's Channel. But drawing Hawke down upon the transports was an effective means of preventing their sailing; and as already observed, to withdraw from the security of Brest to the open position of Quiberon Bay, was to court the destruction which came upon him. And, then, the final error of not proceeding to meet Hawke with the 9 sail of Bompart's squadron incorporated with his own, is but the key-stone of the series. If anything would have given the project success, it would have been the display of 30 sail of the line east of Ushant, and even the defeat of such a force might have crippled Hawke for the time so as to compel him to let the army pass.

No doubt this history, like so much other naval history, requires re-writing. Explanations of steps in themselves inexplicable might then be forthcoming, but it is hardly possible that we should not still pronounce that the plain principles of naval warfare were everywhere disregarded by the French nation in the year 1759.

25. The bombardment lasted 52 hours, during which 1,900 shells, and 1,100 carcases were thrown into the place.

# CHAPTER EIGHT

I T WAS TWENTY YEARS after the failure of 1759, before France made another attempt to gain the command of the sea for the purpose of transporting an invading army across it. But the state of things was such on the approach of the year 1779, that she began, as it were, to see her way to another undertaking of the same nature, but bolder and grander. I think we cannot have avoided observing how very marked is the difference between the attempt to gain the command of the sea as an end and as a means, when we have before us the practical effect as exemplified in the Dutch wars and these successive failures on the part of France. Looking back on the ground we have passed over, it does seem as if there were a possibility that had France thought nothing of invasion, but had devoted herself wholly, as Holland did, to wresting from us the command of the sea, she might always have maintained a better naval position than she actually did. But wasting her energies on a double design, she fell more and more at the opening of each war, into the position of an assuredly inferior naval power, which could only look to better her position by some stroke of fortune much more to be hoped for than expected.

Nothing ever seems to have turned the French commanders and statesmen from the repetition of these hitherto abortive double measures. In 1767, two French officers were in this country drawing up plans for invading it in the manner most likely to be successful. Their report proposed a sudden descent during peace time, as only parallel with the common practice very freely indulged in by this country, of making war by sea long before its formal declaration. The army to be prepared was to consist of 40,000 infantry, 6,000 dragoons, and 4,000 light troops (cavalry) with a proportionate detachment of artillery. The light cavalry were to embark with their horses, but the heavy cavalry were to pick up their mounts as they penetrated up country. The selected point of landing was Deal beach.[1]

It must be supposed that these reports were laid up in the archives at Paris awaiting opportunity, but as there could have been no hopes of carrying out such a scheme in absolute secrecy, so that the immense force could be slipped across without convoy or protection, it ultimately fell into the old groove, with the hope that it might be carried out when the command of the sea could be temporarily secured on purpose.

It was not till 1779 that opportunity seemed to offer, when France, allied with our revolted colonies in North America, and pressing Great Britain heavily as a consequence, drew Spain to her side. It then became possible to show, by combining the fleets of both powers, a greatly superior force than any which this country could at the moment produce. But France, as usual, was unable to pursue the simple policy of attempting to gain the command of the sea. The project was now, in fact, three-fold. The fleets were to be combined as one object, an attack on Gibraltar by Spain was a second, and 40,000 men were assembled along the coasts of Normandy and Brittany, ready to cross the sea and invade the country, as a third.

In the spring were collected at Brest more than 30 sail of the line, and 10 frigates, and at Cadiz and other Spanish ports were about 36 sail of the line and 10 or 12 frigates. After some weeks warning, the whole available force of England came to only 37 sail of the line and 24 frigates, fire-ships, and small craft.

The French fleet, unhindered and almost unwatched by us, quitted Brest on June 3rd, to join the Spaniards on their own coast, but a month elapsed before the junction even began to be effected. Spanish pride was hurt at the idea of serving in a fleet commanded by a French admiral—d'Orvilliers—and the ships were slow in making their appearance. It was not till the 2nd of July that 8 ships of the line and 2 frigates under Vice-Admiral Don Antonio Darce, joined the French from Ferrol, and twenty more days passed before the remaining division joined from Cadiz, consisting of 28 sail of the line with 7 frigates and small vessels, under Vice-Admiral Don Luis de Cordova. This made a total force of 66 sail of the line and 14 frigates and small vessels; but the force was not united, as

1. See Lord Mahon's *History of England*, vol. v., App. xix. Sir E. Creasy notices it in his *Invasions of England*.

Cordova took 16 sail of the line under his separate command as a "squadron of observation."[2] Tactically the division was sound enough, as it was known that the combined portion was of greater force than any likely to be met in the Channel, and the neighbourhood of a fresh fleet would almost make victory over the English secure. But possibly national jealousy and not tactics was the moving principle. d'Orvilliers on his side did a superficially wise thing in separating 5 line-of-battle ships, under La Touche Treville, to form a light squadron.

All was therefore well outwardly with this immense armament in the first week in July, and presumably the 40,000 men were ready and waiting for the order to embark and cross. Let us see how England stood in the way of preparation.[3]

On June 16th, proclamation was made to begin hostilities against Spain, and on the same day Sir Charles Hardy sailed from St. Helens with the 37 sail of the line and 24 smaller vessels already mentioned. He stood away at once to the westward and was cruising off Ushant, 30 or 40 miles to the westward of it, until the 26th. Then he stood away north, and was to the westward of Scilly till July 2nd. On that day he was twenty miles nearly due south of the Land's End, making his way to Torbay, where he moored on the 6th and remained till the 14th.

On quitting Torbay, on the 14th of July, Sir Charles again stood to the westward, and again cruised to the northward and westward of Ushant for two or three days. On the 23rd he was back again on the English coast, and was cruising between Plymouth and Scilly until the 11th of August, without apparently any intelligence whatever.

On the 12th of August he was 34 miles S.S.E. of Scilly, with a westerly wind which continued to blow for several days. Sir Charles not only maintained his position against it, but was getting farther to the westward. On the 15th his position was well to the northward, Scilly bearing about E. by N. 47 miles.[4]

The whole of these movements seem rather aimless and vague, in the absence of information regarding the combined fleets. If it had been intended to intercept the enemy in his way up Channel, the position off Ushant might have been maintained with look-outs to

2. I am following Troude, vol. ii., p. 31. Schomberg's numbers are slightly different.

3. It was not a good omen that on the 11th July there were 1,035 sick, and 174 convalescent in the French fleet alone, and since leaving Brest they had lost 48 men by death, and sent 412 to hospital at Corunna. See ibid., p. 33.

4. I have taken the positions from the Flag-Captain's journal, now at the Royal Victoria Yard, Deptford.

the northward, or the position off Scilly might have been held with look-outs to the southward. But in the absence of assigned reasons, it is a complete puzzle to discover why Sir Charles Hardy should at one time have taken the one position and at another time the other. If, again, the invasion was apprehended, and the great strength of the enemy's fleet was known, this cruising to the westward with such a very inferior force would appear to have been exactly what the enemy would have most wished for. It placed him in the position of forcing battle, and then, on the defeat of the British force, the carrying out of the plan of invasion. The only reasonable strategy for Sir Charles Hardy was that adopted so long before by Lord Torrington, a policy of observation and threatening; and such a policy would have left the British fleet at Torbay if not at St. Helens, with abundant scouts—of which we must remember Sir Charles had 24—to give the earliest information of the enemy's approach. What is at any rate clear, from a glance at the map, is that the approach to the Channel was quite open from the 12th of August, and as the wind was then and until the 19th from the westward, this leaving of the Channel uncovered, was deliberate.[5]

We have seen that it was not until the 22nd of July that the French and Spanish fleets were combined at and off Ferrol, probably some time was occupied in the different arrangements for proceeding, and for dividing of the fleet already mentioned. After that, sail was made for Ushant, and after sighting it, a course was shaped for the English Channel. The great fleet, besides suffering heavily from sickness, as mentioned, was already short of water and provisions.[6]

The intention of d'Orvilliers was to proceed in the first instance to Torbay, to anchor there and to more equally distribute the provisions remaining in the fleet, as well as to receive the supplies which had been demanded from Brest. Following out this intention, the great fleet swept up Channel, and on the 15th of August was in sight of Plymouth without having seen a sign of a British look-out ship or a shadow of opposition. The English historians who record these transactions think it was "by some unaccountable event" that the

5. It is a misfortune that the naval history of this time is the most defective of any. Entick closes his with the execution of Byng, Harvey with the appointment of Sir C. Hardy to command the Channel fleet in 1779; Schomberg, Beatson, and Campbell have but a few notes, the latter supposing that there never was anything serious contemplated by the enemy. Schomberg supposes the strong easterly winds forced the enemy out of the Channel, and prevented Sir Charles Hardy from getting in; an entirely erroneous idea. Troude and Chevalier are a little better.

6. Troude, vol. ii., p. 33.

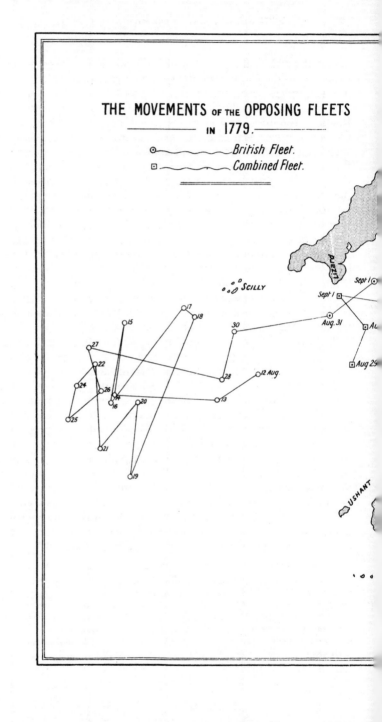

THE MOVEMENTS OF THE OPPOSING FLEETS
IN 1779.

⊙———— British Fleet.
▫———— Combined Fleet.

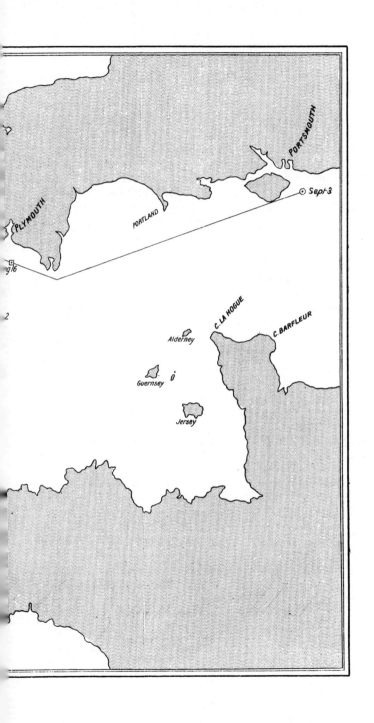

PLYMOUTH

PORTLAND

PORTSMOUTH

⊙ Sept-3

□
g16

2

Alderney

C.LA HOGUE

C.BARFLEUR

Guernsey ȯ

Jersey

combined fleet was able to evade that of Sir Charles Hardy. A glance at the map shows us that there was nothing unaccountable in the matter, but that, as we have already seen, the way might be said to have been specially left open for d'Orvilliers to approach. As early as the 12th of August Hardy had passed to the westward of any reasonable strategical position, not driven thither by stress of weather or want of wind. The westernmost strategical line was the Ushant-Lizard line, and if the guarding of the Channel were the object in view, no position to the west of it was a right one. But it is clear that from the 12th to the 20th of August, at least, Sir Charles Hardy was always where he should not have been, and d'Orvilliers was quietly sailing up Channel to the southward of him. On the 15th of August, the enemies were 120 miles apart, the combined fleets off Plymouth, and the British fleet nearly 50 miles beyond Scilly.

On the outside of things, it is not easy to imagine a position of greater peril to this country than was now exhibited. There was enough Franco-Spanish force to have allowed of such a division as would have kept Sir Charles Hardy in check, and, if necessary, to have brought him to action at a great disadvantage, while leaving an ample strength to convoy the troops over and protect their landing. Or, if still safer tactics were employed, it would have been easy to have completely destroyed Sir Charles Hardy's fleet by means of the overwhelming odds at hand, and then with all ease and leisure to have passed over as many armies as might have been necessary for the subjugation of the United Kingdom.

It was not until the 19th of August that a change of wind to the eastward put it out of the power of Sir Charles Hardy to return immediately to his proper position, and it was not until the 20th that he got any news of the enemy. The easterly wind, however, reached the combined fleets before it did that of the British. The wind was easterly off Plymouth on the 16th, and the strength of it was so gradually increasing that Torbay was no longer a safe anchorage, and the idea of going there had, in fact, to be given up.[7] This not only prevented the combined fleets from going to the eastward of Plymouth, but as the wind increased, tended to drive them to the westward. It was probably on this account that one of Sir Charles Hardy's ships was able to report to him on the 20th that she had seen 15 sail

---

7. I get the winds from the minutes of the court-martial on the officers of the *Ardent*, 64, which ran into the midst of the combined fleet, and was captured on the 16th, nine miles from Plymouth.

to the N.E. The *Porcupine* was ordered to chase in that direction, but she returned without seeing anything of the enemy.

And now set in a period of aimless cruising on both sides, Sir Charles being generally 60 to 80 miles to the south-westward of Scilly, and d'Orvilliers, apparently with his fleet somewhat scattered, south of the Lizard. The winds were fresh from the East, N.E., and S.E., not seemingly either in direction or force so persistent as to prevent Sir Charles Hardy from making some easterly progress had he been so minded, nor yet to prevent d'Orvilliers from holding his own.

On the 28th of August, Sir Charles Hardy had crept up to a position south of Scilly, and about 22 miles off; the wind was light, and the weather growing from hazy to thick, and very thick. Thus it was on the 29th, when the following entry appears in the captain's journal:—"6 P.M., the bumboat informed us she had counted 28 large ships to the S.E., which she was certain were part of the combined fleet." It still continued very thick, but Hardy was able to make signals for calling in the cruisers. On the 30th it was moderate and clear, and at noon the British fleet was in the position marked on the chart; a part, at least, of the combined fleet were also where I have noted their position, for 16 sail of them were in sight from Hardy's flagship near that spot at 7 A.M. Hardy, it will be observed by his position on the 31st, S.S.W. from the Lizard, was making no attempt to approach the combined fleet, which, in its turn, was but languidly following up the British. At half-past four on the morning of the 1st September, the *Duke* made the signal for seeing the enemy to the S.W., and then Hardy, apparently for the first time, made sail to reconnoitre. At five they counted 60 sail of large ships, and later were near enough to distinguish some of the flags displayed. Two frigates were now sent down to reconnoitre more closely, but some of the enemy's ships appearing to bear down on them, they were recalled. At noon on September 1st, the admiral had been informed by signal from some of his look-outs that the enemy was in superior force; the whole of his own fleet was in company, steering to the eastward, the enemy being visible astern. At half-past 5 P.M., 38 sail of the enemy's fleet were still visible to the westward, but only from the mast-head. They were still in sight at 5 A.M., on the morning of the 2nd of September, and continued so all the forenoon. At 11 A.M., Hardy anchored his fleet 6 miles S.W. of the Ramhead, on account of the ebb tide making, and so as to widen his distance from the enemy. After this, no more mention is made of them, except that

191

after the fleet weighed next evening, one of the lookouts reported 7 sail to the S.W. Hardy made sail to the eastward, and anchored at Spithead next evening.

The French account is in agreement with all this. Finding, when as far up Channel as Torbay, on the 17th of August, the wind strong from the eastward, not only was it necessary to beat up to it, but it became an impossible anchorage as entirely open to that wind. The weather continued bad for several days. On the 25th, d'Orvilliers, having had precise intelligence as to Sir Charles Hardy's fleet, called a council of war to deliberate on the situation. It was shown that some ships had 300 sick, and neither doctors nor medicines on board; that others were so short of water that they were obliged to borrow from day to day from their neighbours; that several, and notably the *Bretagne*, were provisioned only till the 25th of September. The council of war unanimously decided either to seek the British fleet in the Soundings, or to wait for it there. The council further decided that it would be necessary in any case to terminate the cruise on the 8th of September, and that then, conformably to the orders received by the Spanish admiral, the Allies should separate as soon as convenient. The combined fleet thereupon made sail to the westward for the Soundings.

The British fleet does not appear to have been seen until the 31st of August, and was followed up languidly as described, until the 1st of September, when, believing it to be 18 or 20 miles to windward, and in a position to enter Plymouth, and having also intelligence of the appearance of a great number of sail to the westward, which afterwards turned out to be a Dutch convoy, the pursuit, if such it can be called, was finally abandoned, and the great fleet steered for Brest.[8]

Thus ended quite the most promising attempt for our enemies, and the most threatening for us, of these attempts to gain the command of the sea for the purpose of invasion. My authority attributes its complete failure to the delay of the Spaniards in forming their junction with the French. Such delay bred sickness, want of provisions and water, but more, perhaps, loss of temper and heart in the business. But I think while we admit the want of enterprise in not bringing to an issue so fair an opportunity, we must allow that a fatal double purpose reigned in the combined councils. Had there been but the single idea under which we have seen that the Dutch always acted, it is almost inconceivable that with such an ample

8. See Troude, vol. ii., pp. 33–36.

force, Sir Charles Hardy's fleet would not have been sought, found, and possibly mastered early in August. The half idea of acting by way of invasion in the face of Hardy's fleet, and the other half idea of attacking the fleet, left divided decisions, and councils thinking more of getting home again. There is really no clear explanation of what the fleet meant to do, but whatever intentions it may have had were paralyzed by the neighbourhood of the very inferior fleet of the British.

I pass now to consider the preliminaries which led up to the greatest, most persistent, and best-arranged of all the attempts of France to gain the command of the sea for an ulterior object.

The period from 1797 to 1805 was one during which the naval operations in the Channel, in the North Seas, off the coasts of France, Spain, and Portugal, in the Mediterranean, and even, perhaps, in the West Indies, were all dominated more or less by a single idea; that of gaining sufficient command of the sea to get an army across the Channel.

Although preparations for the great business were in progress as early as the autumn of 1796 certainly, and though some attempt at systematic invasion was as early as that date expected in England, it remained for the mind of Napoleon to comprehend the whole field of war, and to see the immense possibilities of the strategic position held by France and her Allies or subordinates.[9] In 1796, though the beginning of the great Boulogne flotilla had been made, and ideas of repeating on a greater scale the method of invasion adopted by William the Conqueror—embarkation from one beach, and disembarkation on the other in a host of small vessels—were current, the immediate proposals for invasion were of a more desultory kind: invasions which were to be carried out by comparatively small bodies of troops, sustained and supported by squadrons of ships not sufficiently large to attempt gaining command of the sea, but only capable of repelling the attack of comparatively small squadrons.

These ideas were focused in the expedition of Hoche from Brest

9. Lord Grenville writes to the Marquis of Buckingham, January 30th, 1794, "The French seem certainly disposed to try their scheme of invasion. . . . Our best defence is unquestionably our water-guard, which is very strong, and will, I think, every day get stronger.—*Memoirs of the Court and Cabinets of George III.*

Lord Malmesbury landing in France, in 1796, on the abortive peace negotiations of that date, notes in his diary: "October 19th. Calais. Report of an intended invasion." On the 20th he has "Troops at St. Valery. Gun-boats of a new construction at Boulogne; 25 men, 2 24-pounders, and 2 horses; to slip out on rollers."—*Diaries and Correspondence of James Harris, First Earl of Malmesbury.* Vol. iii., p. 276.

to Bantry Bay in December 1796, and the intended expedition of the Dutch from the Texel to the North of England, or Scotland, which, after lying ready for many weeks, was broken up and abandoned in the autumn of 1797. It is by no means necessary at this stage to discuss these plans in detail, but a brief notice of them is desirable, as it cannot be doubted but that their failure produced in the mind of Napoleon the conviction that naval war could not be carried on in that way with any hopes of success against the United Kingdom, but that an absolute command of the sea was a prior necessity if invasion were to be carried out at all.

The attempt of Hoche, which became abortive from a variety of causes, was nevertheless a proof of the inefficiency of the blockade of Brest in the face of an enemy ready from moment to moment to put to sea. But on the other hand, the inner life of Hoche's forces, naval and military, as told by the rebel Theobald Wolfe Tone, the long delay after all was ready for a start, and the weary watching of the signal stations from day to day for the announcement that the coast was clear, are equally a proof of the extreme difficulty of getting to sea unobserved, and the likelihood that an expedition might break up simply as a consequence of the delay.[10] This moral is even more strongly pointed by the result of the intended invasion from the Texel, and it is again Wolfe Tone who gives us the inner life of the blockaded fleet and its difficulties.

The Dutch fleet consisted of 15 sail of the line, 10 frigates and sloops, and 27 transports, carrying some 13,500 men. Two things were wanting to enable them to pass to sea: a fair wind and an absent enemy. The two never came together; provisions and stores wasted and disappeared; the troops were disembarked, and the whole expedition given over.[11]

These two failures were hardly a part of any general scheme. The troops embarked were mere flying columns, intended to trust them-

10. The embarkation of the troops was going on at Brest on November 17th. On the 23rd, Tone "could not imagine what delays them now." On the 25th Colonel Shee tells him they will be off in six days. Tone himself embarked on December 1st, Hoche and the staff embarked on the 12th. The fleet put to sea on the night of the 16th, and next morning 25 out of the 43 sail that should have been in company were missing. See *Life of Theobald Wolfe Tone*. Washington, 1826.

11. All had been some time ready to start when Tone arrived on July 8th 1797. From that time till September 3rd, when he left the fleet, knowing that the expedition had collapsed, the days were passed in watching the weather-cock and the British fleet, which was generally in easy view from the anchorage. The Dutch seem to have been perfectly well informed of everything as it went on in England; of the mutiny, and of the exact strength of Duncan's force from day to day.

selves to their own resources, and to the supposed friendliness of parts of the invaded populations. They were without hopes, or should have been without hopes, of communications with their own country after landing.

But could nothing be done beyond these desultory failures? France, in 1797, was not France alone, but for the purpose of those naval operations by which the invasion of England might be made possible was perhaps France, Holland, and Spain; with it might be other naval powers thrown in, such as Russia and Denmark.

The whole coast, from Nice along the French and Spanish shores of the Mediterranean, out into the Atlantic as far as the river Guadiana, was hostile; then, after the interval of the Portuguese coast, the hostile line began again at the river Minho, and was traced round the Bay of Biscay, along the Channel coasts of France, out into the North Sea, along the coast of Holland as far as Oldenberg. Then, after a short interval of the coast of Hanover, began the doubtful shores of Denmark and of the Baltic.

Along this line, the principal hostile ports where the enemy could collect and arm, and whence he might be expected to issue, were Toulon, Cartagena, Cadiz, Ferrol, Rochefort, Brest, and the Texel. In 1796 it was understood that the Spanish Alliance with France might array against us the following line-of-battle fleets, distributed somewhat as given below:—

| | | |
|---|---|---|
| Toulon | 15 | French |
| Cartagena | 18 | Spanish |
| Cadiz | 3 | Spanish |
| Ferrol | 26 | Spanish |
| Guarnizo [12] | 7 | Spanish |
| Brest | 21 | French |
| Texel | 21 | Dutch |
| Newfoundland | 7 | French |
| Havannah | 18 | Spanish |

In many respects, especially on the Spanish side, this was no doubt a paper force, but a grand total of 136 sail of the line was one from which many deductions might be allowed and yet leave a very imposing array behind them.

A glance at the chart will show the immense strategical power in the hands of the French Government, moving all these forces from such a central position as Paris. Blockade at this time, though much

12. A port on the north coast of Spain, now of no importance.

195

more complete than it had been, was still but an intermittent power, subject to the vagaries of the weather and to the necessities of provisioning and watering the blockading ships in sheltered spots, which could generally be found at only a distance from the port to be watched. However heroic and persistent the attempt of the blockading forces might be, it was always uncertain whether a watched force might not be able to escape unseen, and to bury itself at sea, no one knew where.

Under such circumstances, a superior force on the side of the British might prove very inferior in defence. If it concentrated on the shores of the United Kingdom, it might certainly prove a sufficient defence against invasion, but then it abandoned not only the commerce of the Empire, but most of its outlying territories. If it was divided into numerous squadrons, each employed in watching one of these great war ports from Toulon to the Texel, what was to prevent even several squadrons of the enemy from escaping, forming a junction, and falling in vastly superior force upon any selected one of the British squadrons at the moment most inopportune for it? Paris could despatch orders to Brest, Rochefort, and Toulon, so that they would reach those ports certainly and simultaneously, in a few days. Horse expresses to Ferrol, Cadiz, and Cartagena, were in a measure certain and speedy.[13]

London was at the extreme end of the chain of forces to be moved and governed. It was impossible to warn blockading squadrons simultaneously. The Toulon squadron could not possibly know till weeks had passed what news had been given to the squadron off Brest on a certain day. And even when messages were sent and reached the intended spot, it was never certain that the ships would not have been driven off by a gale of wind, or have fallen back to some point on the strength of a true or a false alarm.

But Great Britain's duties and necessities were such that she could never guarantee having superior forces stationed off each port. Speaking generally of the date mentioned, her line-of-battle forces were in quantity and distribution as follows:—

> In the North Sea............26
> In the Channel .............29
> On the coast of Ireland...... 2
> In the Mediterranean........31
> In the West Indies ..........20

13. Napoleon at Boulogne received a dispatch from Lauriston at Ferrol on the 22nd of August, which probably left the latter place on the 10th.

North America.............. 5
At the Cape of Good Hope.... 8
In the East Indies............ 5
126 [14]

So that not only were the total forces nominally 10 sail short of the numbers set out by the enemy, but the British Colonial necessities took away from the European war theatre 38 sail of the line against the 25 only which were withdrawn from the enemy's European forces.

Speaking in general terms, then, and not troubling ourselves with those changes of distribution which were so constantly going on that it is difficult to be accurate at any given moment, the position was this. There was a possibility of the French finding 111 sail of the line at command, strategically disposed in secure ports in Europe, and capable of reinforcement by 25 sail more from the other side of the Atlantic. There was a probability that as a defence against these, the British would be able to bring no more than 88 sail, broken up into squadrons generally inferior to the forces in port opposed to them, and everywhere open to be overwhelmed by concentrations initiated and ordered from Paris, of which the British could have no conception whatever until it was too late.

Some sort of picture of this kind must have early presented itself to the mind of Napoleon, as it possibly did to other Frenchmen, as early perhaps as 1796. The central idea which grew out of it was the formation of a great army along the shores of France nearest to those of England, from Ostend to Etaples, the provision of a special kind of transport in the form of gun-boats, flat-boats, and horse-boats, repeating in some measure the characteristics of that flotilla which had brought over in a former age the army of Duke William.

Very possibly this flotilla had been originally destined to move alone, or at least that there had been no original idea of making use of the full strategical resources of the alliance in the sudden concentration from different points of an immense naval force in the Straits of Dover, sufficient to hold the waters against all comers and to cover and protect the crossing and landing.

On the other hand, the possibilities of these strategic combinations were already well known on both sides of the Channel. What is not so easy to understand is the object of many of the combina-

14. This total includes all ships with guns on two decks, one ship having but 44 guns.

tions made and operations undertaken previous to the time when Napoleon, as Consul and Emperor, took the matter wholly into his own hands.

The first combination was a powerful one, had it been employed directly to wrest the command of the whole sea from our hands, that is, had it been engaged in for the simple object of destroying and capturing our ships. Langara, shortly after the declaration of war by Spain, that is in October 1796, passed into the Mediterranean from Cadiz with 19 sail of the line and 10 frigates. At the time there were 7 sail of Spaniards at Cartagena, and 12 sail of French at Toulon. Langara picked up the 7 sail at Cartagena and then effected his junction with the French at Toulon, where the combined fleet amounted to 38 sail of the line and 18 or 20 frigates.

Sir John Jervis commanded a fleet in the Mediterranean of no more than 15 sail of the line, while Mann had been watching Cadiz with no more than 6 sail. Instead of joining Jervis, as he should have done, this officer took on himself to fall back into the Channel, leaving Jervis wholly in the power of the combined fleet, had its objects been simple and definite. No attack or attempted attack was made on him, and he fell back to Gibraltar and Lisbon, leaving the Allies masters of the Mediterranean sea.

Of course, had real command of the sea been aimed at, the Allies should have fallen on Sir John at all hazards, following him out of the Mediterranean, if necessary, with that object. But with an infirmity of purpose which requires explanation, the combination made was broken up, and the Spaniards alone and undesignedly fell into the hands of Jervis on the 14th of February next year, and suffered the penalty, off Cape St. Vincent, of deliberately neglecting the first principles of war.

Equally wasteful of naval force, and unmeaning as to any possible advantage to be gained, was the battle of Camperdown at the other end of the strategic line on the 11th of October following. The Dutch fleet of 15 sail had, as we have seen, landed all the troops and abandoned the idea of invasion, so that when it was determined to put to sea in the face of a known superior fleet of British ships, the enterprise was objectless. In the Mediterranean, the French and Spanish admirals, with a fair chance of breaking up Jervis's force, neglected to do it, and lost their opportunity. In the North Sea, the Dutch, without any hopes beyond destruction and bloodshed, proceeded to engage the British force. Both mistakes were equally grave and obvious, so that there is some difficulty in understanding whether there was any single intelligence actuating the operations.

All the possibilities, and both these errors, were necessarily in the mind of Napoleon, when, a month before he sailed for Egypt—that is in the middle of April 1798—he wrote his celebrated Memorandum on the Invasion of England, and supposed that the expedition he was about to undertake was to be directly instrumental in securing a superior naval force in the Channel.[15]

He calculated then, that by the month of September there might be 35 sail of the line at Brest, and 400 gun-boats at Boulogne, with troops at hand that had spent the whole summer in becoming inured to these vessels and sea life in them. The Dutch at the same time, he thought, would have sufficiently recovered the blow of Camperdown to be ready with 12 sail of the line in the Texel. There were in the Mediterranean 12 French sail of the line, which might be augmented to 14 by September, and there were also in French hands 9 sail of the line which had belonged to the Venetian Republic. The 14 French ships Napoleon thought might go to Brest, so as by the month of October or November to show a force of 50 sail of the line in the western part of the Channel beside the 12 sail in the eastern part. It might then be possible to carry out the invasion upon three selected points of attack:—namely, 40,000 men coming by long sea to be landed at some point to be determined; 40,000 men to cross in the invasion flotilla, and 10,000 men to be landed in Scotland by the Dutch.

The expedition to the East would oblige England, Napoleon thought, to send 6 additional sail of the line to India, and perhaps 12 frigates to the entrance of the Red Sea. She would be obliged to have 22 to 25 ships of the line at the entrance to the Mediterranean, 60 before Brest, and 12 before the Texel. Napoleon, or his copyists for him, fall at this point into some loose arithmetic, for he says this would make a total of 300 ships of war,[16] without counting what the British already had abroad, or the ten or twelve 50-gun ships and score of frigates which she must keep to oppose the invasion flotilla. "The invasion of England," he said, "put in practice in this manner, in the months of November and December, would be almost certain. England would waste herself by immense efforts, but these would not secure her from our invasion."

This was the theory of it, but Napoleon did not perceive that he was about to violate a clear rule of naval war in the first instance in

15. "Soldiers! you are one of the wings of the army of England!" Address to his trops, see *Victoires, Conquêtes, &c.*, vol. x., p. 375.
16. James translates "line-of-battle ships" in error. The mistake was great enough as it stood.

his own person, and that the whole arrangements were too vague and indeterminate, even without the absurd arithmetic, to promise any success. If, as he somewhat wildly conceived, the passage to India was open to him through Egypt, and that it was by means of evasion and not by command in the Mediterranean sea that he hoped to get there, he should have left the 13—not 14—sail of the line safe under the batteries of Toulon. Taking them with him, he deliberately exposed them to the fate they met at the hands of Nelson in the following August. And if he, by his occupation of Egypt, had compelled the British to send ships to India, they could now afford to do it, having captured and destroyed 11 of their opponents at home.

The enemy also wasted his forces in subsidiary attacks, almost bound to be failures if the matter had been rightly considered. Thus in August 1798 Commodore Savary took a body of 1,150 troops, under General Humbert, on board a small squadron escaping from Aix, which landed in Killala Bay in Mayo and duly surrendered soon after. A larger expedition under Commodore Bompart sailed from Brest for the North of Ireland on the 16th of September. He was followed up by British look-out frigates, and news of his progress was duly sent on to the Commander-in-Chief on the Irish coast. As a consequence, Sir John Warren met him off Lough Swilly, on the 11th of October, and captured the main part of his squadron.

But the invasion flotilla itself was under considerable difficulties. The British in command of the sea were interfering with it all along the line. In July 1795, Sir Sydney Smith had made a beginning by capturing and garrisoning the little Islands of Marcouf which lie four miles off-shore south of Cape Barfleur. The islands were found a convenient spot for interfering with the flotilla arrangements, and were held against attack both without and with assistance from the sea.

On May 19, 1798, Ostend was shelled; 1,140 troops were landed, who destroyed the canal lock and gates, and several gun-boats in the basin, though they were afterwards obliged to surrender to the superior force which the French had had time to collect.

On the 30th and 31st of the same year, a frigate and corvette belonging to the flotilla were driven on shore by the British near Havre, and the frigate was burnt.

In June 1800, a British squadron attacked the frigates lying in the anchorage of Dunkirk, and one of them, the *Desirée*, was cut out and brought away.

And then, as the time seemed to be approaching when decided

steps were to be taken with regard to the flotilla, Lord Nelson was placed, in July 1801, in command of the operations against it, which was followed by the shelling of Boulogne on the 4th of August, and an audacious attempt to break up the flotilla there on the 15th.

The operations of 1799 were on a great strategic scale, but yet they only serve to show how divided purposes and diverse aims fritter away the golden opportunities in naval warfare.

By the month of April, France had 25 sail of the line at Brest under Bruix, watched by a force under Lord Bridport which did not exceed 16 sail of the line. The French were industriously spreading reports there that they had now a design on Ireland; and taking advantage of Bridport's withdrawal to a distance, and of thick weather occurring simultaneously, put to sea on the 25th of April with the whole force of 25 sail of the line, and were off, no one knew where. Bridport, after despatching cruisers to Lord Keith, off Cadiz with 15 sail of the line, and to Lord St. Vincent at Gibraltar, and also homewards to convey the news, fell back himself to Bantry Bay, where he was presently reinforced, and found himself a match for the enemy, and at the head of 26 sail of the line.

But Ireland was at the moment far from the thoughts of the French. On the 3rd of May, Lord Keith, at the head of his 15 sail of the line off Cadiz, was made acquainted with the fact that the Brest fleet was coming down on him, having been most probably joined by 5 Spanish ships which had sailed from Ferrol. The 17 or 18 Spanish ships in Cadiz which Lord Keith was watching, shewed no signs of movement, yet practically he was being brought into the presence of a fleet of 48 sail of the line, to which he could oppose no more than 15.

The fleets were in sight of one another on the 4th and 5th of May, but it was then blowing a westerly gale, which would have prevented the Cadiz Spaniards from coming out, had such been their intention, and the result was that the French, who had not, after all, been joined by the Ferrol Spaniards, ran before the gale into the Mediterranean.[17]

Lord Keith then, after counting, as he supposed, 22 sail of the line in the harbour of Cadiz, fell back and joined Lord St. Vincent at Gibraltar. Despatches of warning were then sent off to Duckworth, who had 4 sail of the line at Minorca; to Nelson at Palermo, whose

---

17. Troude says, vol. iii., p. 157, that Bruix was ordered to join the Spaniards at Cadiz, but that the state of the weather, with his untrained crews, forbid him either to fight or to make for Cadiz.

12 sail of the line and 4 Portuguese ships were scattered over the Mediterranean, at Naples, at Alexandria, and at Malta.

On the 11th of May, Lord St. Vincent, meeting combination by combination, and endeavouring at any rate to guard Minorca as the point most obviously threatened, made for that island with his 16 sail of the line, where, being joined by Duckworth's 4, he now found himself at the head of 20 sail of the line.

The withdrawal of Lord Keith from Cadiz enabled the Spaniards to send 17 sail of the line to sea on the 14th of May, and these, notwithstanding some mishaps in a gale of wind, found their way safely into Cartagena on the 20th, just a week after the Brest fleet had put into Toulon.

As a consequence of these circumstances, Lord St. Vincent was driven to place himself between Toulon and Cartagena, in order that, by preventing a junction between the French and Spanish ships, he might avoid the risk of finding himself in presence of a combined fleet of more than double his strength. But he was in this difficulty. Either the Spaniards from Cartagena, or the French from Toulon, might suddenly issue forth and strike at the greatly inferior force of Nelson on the coast of Sicily. When this contingency presented itself so forcibly to the mind of St. Vincent as to make him weaken his own fleet by 4 sail of the line in order to strengthen Nelson at Palermo, we can well understand the straits he was in, even if he knew, which he probably did, that a reinforcement of 5 sail of the line was close at hand to join him. Having made these arrangements, Lord St. Vincent, whose health was completely shattered, gave up the command to Lord Keith and prepared to return to England.

The general station of the British fleet was now off Cape St. Sebastian, and there, on the 30th of May, Lord Keith heard that the French fleet of 22 sail of the line, under Admiral Bruix, had put to sea from Toulon on the 27th. Lord Keith now took the strange step of proceeding to Toulon himself; I say the strange step, because if the thing to be feared were the junction at Cartagena, this movement left it open more than ever. To close with the port of Cartagena, with the hope of meeting and fighting the French before they could be succoured by the Spanish, had an obvious promise of advantage, which drawing near to Toulon after the French had left it could certainly not have had.

While the obvious course was not taken by the British, the French missed a course equally obvious; that was, to make a *détour* to the eastward, and passing round Lord Keith's fleet, make for Cartagena from the westward rather than from the northward. Occasions took them to Vado Bay, near Genoa, and this especially favoured the eastern *détour*, which was not taken.

Lord Keith stood past Toulon as far as Fréjus, where, on the 5th of June, he heard that the French were at anchor in Vado Bay, and at once made sail in that direction. He reached within 90 miles of the place, where, on the 8th, he received imperative orders from St. Vincent, who had not yet quitted Minorca on his homeward voyage, to return to Rosas Bay, near Cape St. Sebastian, for the purpose of intercepting the French fleet. This order is one of those which we meet sometimes, and must admit to be inexplicable, for how Lord Keith was thus to intercept a French fleet known to be at sea, and supposed to be steering for Cartagena, a glance at the chart fails to give the slightest hint. It is still more perplexing that Lord Keith, with his good information as to the presence of the French only 90 miles from him in Vado Bay, and with his knowledge that St. Vincent could not be aware of this, should have so promptly obeyed the order, in so far as it concerned his abandonment of that pursuit of the French, but not in so far as concerned his proceeding as directed to Rosas Bay. For he steered, in point of fact, for Minorca. On the day that he turned thus to partly obey St. Vincent's orders, the French fleet weighed from Genoa, to which point they had meantime moved, for Cartagena; but instead of steering the safe course well to the eastward, it followed directly on Lord Keith's track, sighting Toulon, and the pursued became the unconscious pursuer.

The result of this backward movement of Lord Keith's was that the blunder of Bruix in sighting Toulon brought him no harm.[18] He crossed the path of Lord Keith behind him, and got safe into Cartagena on the 23rd of June. On the 24th, then, there was a force of some 40 sail of the line ready for sea in that port.

Meanwhile, Lord Keith, after rather aimlessly wandering about in the Gulf of Lyons for weeks, was compelled to fall back on Minorca for water. There he was joined on the 7th of July by a detachment from the Channel, which augmented his force to 31 sail of the line; and there he learnt how, a fortnight before, that which it should have been his sole aim to prevent had occurred, and that the combined French and Spanish fleets were in his rear at Cartagena; not

18. James reads the French accounts as if Bruix was credited with the determination to attack the British, of whose advance he had heard. Troude, vol. iii., p. 158, says distinctly that Bruix was forbidden to fight until joined with the Spanish, and that he weighed to avoid the British.

only this, but that on the 24th of June this same combined fleet had sailed, and was on its way out of the Mediterranean.

So here was failure upon failure. The very reinforcement which had been detached from the Channel was a dead loss. It had been taken away from the point to be defended, and sent to a point where no attack was to be apprehended; 40 sail of the enemy, and a proportion of frigates, were bowling away to take the command of the Channel and carry the great invasion scheme into execution rolling up the feeble British squadrons as they went, and the only force of a size even to observe him was a fortnight behind the enemy. There was nothing for it but to follow with all speed, and this Lord Keith set himself to do.

The combined fleets, with the fine start which fortune and error more than skill had given them, got into Cadiz on the 12th of July, and were out again on the 21st, making a goodly show of 59 sail, of which 40 were of the line.

Lord Keith's fleet having only partially watered at Port Mahon, was obliged to put into Tetuan to complete with that necessary, and so did not reach Gibraltar until the 29th of July, just three weeks behind the Franco-Spanish fleet, and a week after it had quitted Cadiz for Brest.

While these early and aimless movements had been carried out by the British in the Mediterranean, Lord Bridport had been lying unemployed in Bantry Bay with his 26 sail, waiting for the fleet which never came his way. And thus the retirement north-west of one part, and the retirement south-west of the other part, rendered it an easy matter for the 5 Spanish ships which had got out of Ferrol at the end of April to find their way into Rochefort. But here fortune, which had so far befriended the enemy, deserted him. These 5 ships were never able to rejoin their companions in Brest, and though there were 90 pendants flying there, the little reinforcement of 5 Spaniards was forced back into the port it had sailed from, and lay in Ferrol for the remainder of the year.

The condition of things was now, however, that there was a force at Brest absolutely overwhelming should any ulterior ideas of invasion set it in motion, and far away at the other end of the line the genius which was alone supposed competent to wield it was hurrying back to France, where he did not set foot until the 9th of October, which may account for the quiet which subsisted all along the line till the close of the year.

The British were fortunate at the northern end. In spite of the losses of Camperdown, the Dutch fleet remained very strong. There were 8 sail of the line in the Texel, 6 at Amsterdam, and 8 in the Meuse, besides frigates and small vessels. But it was known, on the other hand, that there was a large and growing party in Holland absolutely inimical to Republicanism and French domination. The fleet was less willing than it had been to waste its strength in the endeavour to achieve an object for which it had no liking. The result of these conditions was that when, in the months of August and September, an English land force possessed itself of the Helder, the 8 line-of-battle ships and 2 frigates which were lying in the Texel surrendered to Admiral Mitchell as representing the Prince of Orange, without firing a shot.

The simile which occurs to my mind as best illustrating the various operations all along the enemy's coast, from Toulon to the Helder, is that of a smouldering fire, every now and then breaking out in a fresh quarter, and as often being stamped out by the firemen who were watching it. It was all over at the close of 1799, and all through 1800 it remained apparently subdued, but to be alone likely to break out at Brest, where its real strength lay.

But while men turned their attention in this direction, the fire suddenly blazed in a place altogether beyond the bounds of the old fire. There sprang up a confederacy between the Northern Powers—Russia, Denmark, and Sweden—against England, which was nearly the most alarming incident that had yet developed itself in the course of the great struggle. It is not necessary here to dwell upon the policy and events which brought about the battle of Copenhagen, and broke the confederacy up as rapidly as it had been formed.

This being done, the enemy concentrated his endeavours upon augmenting and improving the invasion flotilla, and in preparing, by exercise and experiment, as far as they could be carried out in the face of constant interruption from crowds of British cruisers, for the day when the great force might cross. The Peace of Amiens, however, put an end for the time to the whole of the operations of every kind, and left this country still uninvaded, still secure, and still in command of the sea.

As I observed on introducing the consideration of the operations on both sides from 1797 to 1805, they were more or less governed by the invasion idea. It is quite possible that the control of this idea may have been more indirect than direct, but I have felt that if this is even so, some brief study of them is a necessary introduction to the undoubted invasion movements of 1805.

I think that if the outline story I have told be regarded not so much by way of detail as of general effect, it will be seen that the

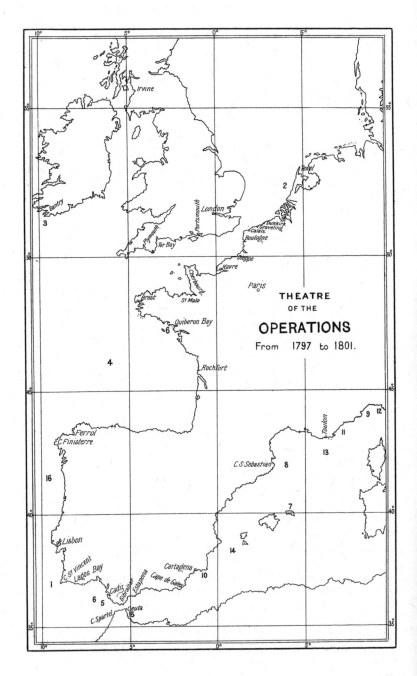

THEATRE
OF THE
OPERATIONS
From 1797 to 1801.

206

enemy's views were indefinite and generally fallacious throughout; that, having a strong position, he misused it, and that the main cause of his misusing it was the prevalence of the double idea of command of the sea and of something to follow it, as if the command of the sea were not itself all in all. There was, I think, in the mind of the enemy the inconsequent belief that though he might not be strong enough to gain and to hold the command of the sea by direct and simple attack on the forces which then held it, he might be strong enough to achieve purposes which only the command of the sea could enable him to achieve.

And with his mind fixed on these remote and misty purposes, he failed to play the simple but powerful game which a great strategical position and many fortunate chances put into his hands.

We begin with the Franco-Spanish combination in the Mediterranean in 1797, when, by the strange defection of Admiral Mann, St. Vincent was left with only 15 sail face to face with 38. Unless we credit the Allies with a condition of panic fear which should have kept them in their ports, we have nothing to fall back on but some more or less indefinite ulterior purposes for an explanation of why St. Vincent was not instantly fallen upon, or at least followed up

---

REFERENCE TO CHART OF THEATRE OF THE OPERATIONS, 1797 TO 1801.

1.—Place of Battle of St. Vincent, Feb. 14th, 1797.
2.—Place of Battle of Camperdown, Oct. 11th, 1797.
3.—Position of Lord Bridport's Fleet (16 sail of the line) on April 30th, 1799.
4.—Position of French Fleet (25 sail of the line) at same date.
5.—Lord Keith's Fleet (15 sail of the line) in presence of French Fleet, on May 4th, 1799.
6.—French Fleet at the same date.
7.—Duckworth's Squadron (4 sail of the line) at same date.
8.—Lord St. Vincent's Fleet (now 21 sail of the line) on May 30th, 1799, with news that the Spanish Fleet (17 sail of the line) was at Cartagena, and that the French Fleet (22 sail of the line) had left Toulon three days before.
9.—French Fleet in Vado Bay on same date.
10.—Spanish Fleet at Cartagena, same date.
11.—Position of Lord Keith's Fleet (20 sail of the line) on June 8th, 1799, when he turned back in obedience to Lord St. Vincent's order.
12.—Position of French Fleet (22 sail of the line) at same date.
13.—Position of Lord Keith's Fleet (19 sail of the line) on June 19th.
14.—Approximate position of French Fleet (22 sail of the line) at the same date, on its way to Cartagena.
15.—Lord Keith's Fleet (now 31 sail of the line) in pursuit of the Combined Fleets on July 26th, putting into Tetuan for water.
16.—Approximate position of the Combined Fleets (40 sail of the line) on their way to Brest, at same date.

and fallen upon, when such very superior force was available. It seems impossible to suppose that had there been a single eye to conquest at sea, such as we have seen to pervade the whole of the Dutch operations in those earlier wars, St. Vincent could have escaped disaster.

And then how can we account for the waste of Spanish force off Cape St. Vincent on the 14th of February? The histories tell us that the Spanish fleet was really bound for Cadiz, and consequently the meeting with the British was for it an untoward accident. But it is exceedingly difficult to believe that any accident could have taken the Spaniards so very far west of their intended port. The battle of St. Vincent appears more likely to have arisen out of the vague and unsettled views which seem to have characterized the whole proceedings of the Allies.

In like manner there is no explanation forthcoming which bears sound sense in its wake for the waste of Dutch force at the battle of Camperdown. It was *apropos* of nothing, and could lead to nothing more than mutual loss and bloodshed, and the causes of it seem to lie more amongst passionate reactions after the collapse of the invasion idea, than amongst any of the cold designs of a reasonable State policy.

In a somewhat wild way, Napoleon's adventure to Egypt with a "wing of the army of England" was intended to have a direct effect on ultimate command of the Channel, but in drawing the fleet with the land expedition, Napoleon was repeating the mistake of Medina Sidonia, and the intended mistake of Conflans. Force enough to cover the landing, which would probably have been a frigate force, was all that was necessary. The French may be said to have courted the fate which overtook them at the Nile, which was a much less severe one than would have overtaken the whole force had Nelson only followed up the sight he got of them on the evening of the 22nd of June, after leaving Cape Passaro.[19] Had the French line-of-battle fleet been left at Toulon, Nelson would probably have been unable to quit his watch of them, and the whole course of affairs might have been changed. At the most, the proper employment of the French line-of-battle force would have been masking the British near Gibraltar or Cadiz.

Passing on to the exit of Admiral Bruix from Brest in April 1799, and the movements and combinations that followed, a single eye to the destruction of any one of the three British squadrons, Lord

19. Nelson's *Despatches*, vol. iii., p. 43.

Keith's, Duckworth's, or Nelson's, must certainly have brought about an attack which should have promised success. Bruix arranged his orders as Minister of Marine and carried them out as Commander-in-Chief. What those orders actually were has not yet, I believe, been shown, but they certainly involved a number of possibilities. Possibly Keith was to be attacked; so, possibly, was Minorca and Duckworth; so also, possibly, was Nelson. Possibly Malta was to be relieved. Possibly Napoleon, in Egypt, was to be succoured. Something of the total failure to do anything whatever no doubt followed on the want of seamanship, which was general in both of the Allied fleets; but, to my mind, much more lies on the shoulders of the false notions of naval warfare which pervaded the minds of the Continental nations. If there had been a single design of crushing the 15 sail of Lord Keith off Cadiz, with the 25 sail outside him and the 17 or 18 sail inside him, might it not have been carried out? Though a gale of wind was blowing, it was not necessary that it should have carried the French up to and past Cadiz; care might have been taken to delay the approach, by lying-to till the wind abated. Or when the junction was ultimately effected at Cartagena, what was there but these same ulterior purposes to have prevented the carrying out of any decided programme which had for its object the destruction of British naval force in the Mediterranean?

And then, the last movement of all, the combined return to Brest, was clearly a false one. The strength of the strategic position consisted wholly in the division of the Allied fleets in secure ports whence, under direction from a central station, they could issue and strike in combination on the isolated squadrons which their presence in port compelled the masters of the sea to keep in watch upon them. It was their sudden issue and their unexpected stroke which gave them their power; as soon as their fleets were concentrated in one port, the danger to the masters of the sea had passed away, for they could concentrate too, and were no longer open to unexpected attacks by superior forces. Quite possibly this knowledge only arrived to those who were directing the movements of the Allied fleets when too late, and when it was clear that by their concentration in one port they had ceased to become of any account during the remainder of the war.

# CHAPTER NINE

WHEN NAPOLEON dismissed the British ambassador at the outbreak of hostilities in 1803, he informed him frankly that his main object would be to invade the country, but at the same time expressed a sense of the recklessness of the idea, and a belief that a great disaster to the French arms might follow the attempt. Ostensibly, from the outbreak of war in May 1803 until the 23rd of August 1805, every naval preparation and every naval movement had to do with obtaining the command of the Channel for a sufficient time to allow an immense army, embarked in an immense flotilla of small vessels, to cross from the French to the English coast.

Lord St. Vincent was then at the head of the Admiralty, and the nature of the situation as it was understood in England, together with the naval arrangements for meeting it, may be shortly stated.

At Toulon and Cadiz there were known to be of French not more than 10 sail of the line, 4 frigates, and 2 smaller vessels. To look after them was Nelson, with 14 sail of the line, 11 frigates, and 21 smaller vessels.

At Ferrol were 5 sail of the line and 2 frigates, and to mask them were despatched of British ships, 7 sail of the line, 2 frigates, and 2 smaller vessels.

At Rochefort, and near it, were 4 sail of the line, 5 frigates, and 2 smaller vessels. To watch them were stationed 5 sail of the line, 1 frigate, and 1 smaller vessel.

At Brest, the enemy mustered 18 sail of the line, 6 frigates, and 1 smaller vessel. Lord Cornwallis was here with 20 sail of the line, 5 frigates, and 6 smaller vessels.

This coast and these ports were furnished with the naval forces of the enemy in the usual character. From St. Malo to the Texel, the ports, besides containing the usual war vessels, were full of the invasion flotilla, which had now been in preparation for about eight years and was in a pretty forward state.

In the Texel were 4 Dutch sail of the line, with a frigate and 120 of the flotilla vessels; and in the various ports, as far as Dunkirk, there was 1 line-of-battle ship, 4 frigates, 7 smaller vessels, and 645 of the invasion flotilla.

To watch these various ports, the British stationed 9 sail of the line, 7 frigates, and 14 small vessels.

In the more westerly ports, including Boulogne, Havre, Cherbourg, &c., the enemy had 2 frigates, 7 smaller vessels, and 120 gun brigs for the service of the invasion, and about 1,450 of the flotilla itself.

The British watched these with 2 sail of the line (small 50's), 14 frigates, and 40 smaller vessels.

As an inner defence, 6 sail of the line, 4 frigates, and 19 smaller vessels were stationed in the Downs. Six frigates, and 11 smaller vessels were stationed to guard the coasts of Ireland, while at Hollesley Bay, at Yarmouth, the Humber, Leith, and generally along the coasts of England and Scotland were 4 line-of-battle ships, 2 frigates, and 20 smaller vessels.[1]

In July 1804, the French plans were drawing to completion, and Vice-Admiral Latouche-Treville was appointed to command the entire force. Napoleon then began to sketch out roughly and vaguely what was before his Commander-in-Chief to accomplish. Apparently, this object was more direct than it afterwards became, Latouche-Treville was to complete his squadron at Toulon, and to man it by disarming corvettes, by pressing men at Marseilles, and by embarking 1,600 soldiers to serve afloat. He was to reflect on the great enterprise which he was about to carry out, and before Napoleon signed his definitive orders he was to let him know what he considered to be the most effective way of executing them.

The squadron at Rochefort, according to Napoleon, consisted of 5 sail of the line and 4 frigates, ready to weigh at a moment, and there were only five of the enemy's vessels before the port.

The Brest squadron was 21 sail of the line, under orders to harass the enemy, and oblige him to keep a great number of ships before the port. The enemy had six ships before the Texel, blockading the Dutch squadron of 3 ships of the line, 4 frigates, and a convoy of 30 ships, on board of which Marmont had his army embarked.

Between Etaples, Boulogne, Vimereux, and Ambleteuse, there

1. See Tucker's *Life of Earl St. Vincent*, vol. ii., p. 218.

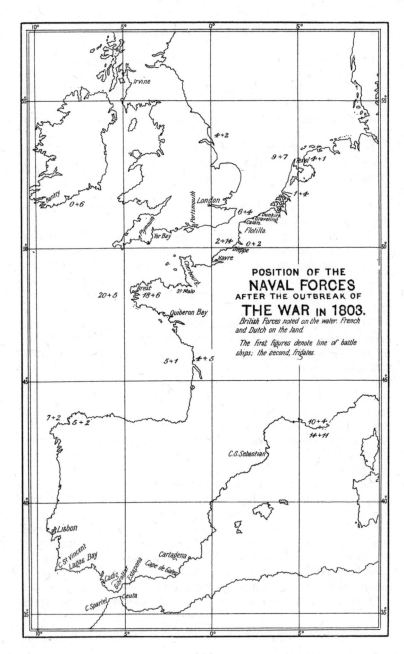

Irvine

4+2

9+7  Texel 4+1

1+4

Bantry

0+6

London  6+4  Dunkirk
Portsmouth                Graveling
Plymouth                  Calais.
Tor Bay                   Flotilla.

2+14  0+2
Dieppe
Havre

Cherbourg

Brest  St Malo
20+5  18+6

Quiberon Bay

5+1  4+5

**POSITION OF THE**
## NAVAL FORCES
AFTER THE OUTBREAK OF
# THE WAR IN 1803.

*British Forces noted on the water. French
and Dutch on the land.*

*The first figures denote line of battle
ships; the second, frigates.*

7+2
5+2

10+4
14+11

C.S.Sebastian

Lisbon

C.St Vincent
Lagos Bay

Cadiz  Estapona  Cartagena
Gibraltar  Cape de Gates

C.Spartel  Ceuta

212

were 1,800 gun-boats, gun-vessels, *péniches,* &c., carrying 120,000 men and 10,000 horses. "Let us be masters of the Straits for six hours," was Napoleon's dictum, "and we shall be masters of the world."

The enemy had before Ostend, before Boulogne, and in the Downs, two 74's, three 64's, and two 50's. Until now, Cornwallis had not had more than 15 sail of the line with him, but all the reserves in Portsmouth and Plymouth would be sent to reinforce him before Brest. The enemy had at Cork four or five war-ships, not to mention frigates and small vessels, of which there were great numbers.

> If [said Napoleon to Latouche-Treville] you evade Nelson, he will go to Sicily, or to Egypt, or to Ferrol. I do not think it will be necessary for you to go to Ferrol. Of the five vessels now in port there, four only are ready; the fifth, however, will be ready by the middle of August; but I think that Ferrol is too clearly pointed at; it is so natural to suppose that if your squadron passes out of the Mediterranean into the ocean, it is intended to raise the blockade of Ferrol. It appears better, therefore, to pass wide of it, and to arrive off Rochefort. This will make your squadron up to 16 sail of the line and 11 frigates, and then, without anchoring, without losing a single instant, whether in passing round Ireland, keeping well clear of it, or in executing the first plan, to present yourself before Boulogne. Our Brest squadron, 23 sail of the line strong, will have an army embarked, and will be always ready to sail; so that Cornwallis will be compelled to hug the coast of Brittany to prevent its escape. For the rest, to fix my ideas on this operation, which has its risks, but of which the success offers such immense results, I wait for the plan which you have mentioned to me, and which you will send me by the return of my courier. You must take on board as much provisions as possible, so that under no circumstances shall you be hindered.
>
> At the end of the month a new line-of-battle ship will be launched at Rochefort, and one at Lorient. It may be possible that they will be ready; there is no question about the one at Rochefort, but if the one at Lorient should be in the Roads and has not been able to pass out before your appearance off the Isle d'Aix, I wish to know if you think you should go out of your way to pick her up. Nevertheless, I think that if you get out with a good northerly wind, it is preferable on all grounds to carry out the operation before the winter; for, in the bad season it is possible you may have more chances of arriving, but there may be several days such that advantage cannot be taken of your arrival. Supposing that you can put to sea before the 29th of July, it is probable that you will appear before Boulogne in the course of Sep-

213

tember, when the nights are already reasonably long, and the weather does not continue bad for any time.[2]

The Toulon squadron, however, did not get to sea as Napoleon hoped. Latouche-Treville died on the 10th of August, but as late as the 28th no successor had been named, and Napoleon was hesitating between Bruix, Villeneuve, and Rosily, and considering it most urgent to come to a decision which ultimately dictated the choice of Villeneuve.

Presumably the delay had put aside all thoughts of proceeding according to the plans of Latouche-Treville during this year; not only so, but the plans seem to have become entirely altered, and the main design of gaining the command of the Channel began to take a co-ordinate place, if not indeed a subordinate place, with designs against St. Helena and the West Coast of Africa, against the British possessions in the West Indies, and against Ireland.

> We have [said Napoleon, writing to Decrès, the Minister of Marine, on the 29th of September 1804] three expeditions to carry out.
>
> First Expedition.—(1) To put Martinique, Guadaloupe, and St. Lucia, in a position of safety under all circumstances. For this purpose a reinforcement of 1,500 men is required, with 4,000 muskets and 100,000 cartridges. (2) To take possession of Dominica and St. Lucia, which will materially assist in placing Guadaloupe and Martinique in safety. A thousand men will be required for the garrison of these two islands. Total for the first expedition, 3,500 men. The Rochefort squadron is destined for this expedition, which will be commanded by General of Division Lagrange.
>
> Second Expedition—(1) To take Surinam and the other Dutch colonies; I think we cannot send from Europe less than 4,000 men for this service, who cannot reasonably be expected to be more than 3,600 when we shall have completed the conquest. (2) To take succours to St. Domingo. For this, 1,200 men, 2,000 muskets, and 25,000 cartridges will be required. If the Dutch colonies resist, and we lose more men than we expect, the succours to be taken to St. Domingo will be less. Total for the second expedition, from 5,200 to 5,600 men.
>
> Third Expedition.—To take St. Helena, and to establish a station there for several months. For this purpose 1,200 to 1,500 men will be required. The expedition to St. Helena will take 200 men to the support of Senegal, will retake Goree, will follow up all the British establishments along the coast of Africa, which will be put under contribution and burnt.

2. *Précis des Evénemens Militaires.* Par M. le Comte Mathieu Dumas, vol. xi., p. 198.

For this purpose, the fleet at Toulon, comprising 11 or 12 sail of the line, including the ship which is at Cadiz, will start first. Reaching the ocean, it will detach 2 ships of the line, 4 frigates, and 2 brigs, the best sailers, for the expedition to St. Helena (these 2 line-of-battle ships, 4 frigates, and 2 brigs will carry 1,800 men, of whom 200 will be left at Goree and Senegal), and 9 or 10 sail of the line and 3 frigates, carrying 5,000 or 6,000 men will proceed direct to Guiana, where they will find Victor Hugues, and then proceed to Surinam.

As soon as it is known that the fleet at Toulon has put to sea, the Rochefort squadron will receive orders to sail. It will proceed direct to Martinique, take possession of St. Lucia and Dominica, and put itself under the orders of the commander of the squadron destined for Surinam. This squadron, now consisting of 14 or 15 sail of the line and 7 or 8 frigates, will put all the British islands under contribution, take all the prizes possible, presenting itself before every road-stead, arrive before St. Domingo, put ashore there 1,000 or 1,200 men, arms and ammunition according to requirement, carry out its return to Ferrol, raise the blockade of our 5 sail of the line, and with 20 sail of the line proceed to Rochefort.

It appears to me that all is ready for these expeditions. To the squadron at Toulon, to the expedition to Surinam and to the squadron at Rochefort, there should be added a certain number of brigs and small vessels, as much for the service of the expeditions as to be left at Martinique and Surinam. Thus, supposing the expeditions should be able to start during Brumaire (October 22nd to November 20th), it may be hoped that before Germinal (March 20th to April 19th) our fleet may effect its return to Rochefort.

Admiral Villeneuve will command the expedition to Surinam; Rear-Admiral Missiessy will command that to Martinique; choose a good rear-admiral to command that to St. Helena. . . .

The English will find themselves attacked simultaneously in Asia,[3] Africa, and America; and accustomed as they are for so long to feel none of the effects of war, these successive shocks at their various centres of commerce will make them experience the evidence of their weakness. . . .[4]

I have made you acquainted with the manner in which I regard my three expeditions—Surinam, Demarara, Esquibo, St. Helena, and Dominica. In this dispatch I give you my views on Ireland. One of the six transports must be withdrawn and replaced by the armed store-ships *La Pensée* or *La Romaine;* the *Ocean* must be completed by working, if necessary, by torchlight. I think it is the only way of being able to carry 18,000 men, of which 3,000 are cavalry, artillery, engineers, and non-combatants, and 15,000 infantry; 500 horses, of

---

3. Alluding to the operations of Admiral Linois.
4. *Précis des Evénemens Militaires,* vol. xi., p. 205.

which 200 are for the cavalry, 200 for the artillery, and 100 for the staff. Less than this would not form a *corps d'armée*.

The place of landing which you indicate, appears to me the most convenient. The north of the Bay of Lough Swilly is, in my view, the most advantageous point. We must quit Brest, pass round Ireland, out of sight of the coast, and make it again as a ship coming from Newfoundland would. In speaking thus, I speak politically, not nautically, for the currents must decide the point at which the land is to be attacked. Politically, it would be better to threaten [*s'exposer*] to attack Scotland than to attack farther south. This plan will disconcert the enemy. Thirty-six hours after anchoring they must put to sea again, leaving the brigs and all the transports. . . . On all these matters I am in accord with you; but the landing in Ireland is only a preliminary act. If it were an operation by itself alone, we should run great risks. The squadron should then, after strengthening itself with all the good seamen in the six transports, enter the Channel and appear before Cherbourg, there to receive information as to the situation of the ships before Boulogne, and cover [*favoriser*] the passage of the flotilla. If, on arrival at Boulogne, the winds should be unfavourable for several days and oblige the squadron to pass the Straits, it should proceed to the Texel. There it would find 7 Dutch sail of the line with 27,000 men embarked; it should take them under its escort, and convey them to Ireland.

One of these two operations ought to succeed, and then, whether I have 30,000 or 40,000 men in Ireland, or whether I am both in England and Ireland, the success of the war is with us.

When the squadron shall have left Brest, Lord Cornwallis will go to watch for it in Ireland. When he knows of the landing in the north, he will return to await the squadron at Brest. We must not return thither. If, in leaving Ireland, our fleet should find the wind favourable, it might double Scotland, and so present itself at the Texel. When it leaves Brest, the 120,000 men will be embarked at Boulogne, and the 25,000 in the Texel. They should remain embarked during the whole period of the expedition to Ireland.

It is in this way that I look on the expedition to Ireland. Thus I approve the whole of the first part of the project up to the landing in Ireland. I shall await the report which I have asked you for, to come to a decision on the laying up of the other parts of the flotilla.

The second part of the project should be the subject of your consideration, and that of the Admiral.

I think that the starting of the expedition from Toulon, and of the expedition from Rochefort, should precede the departure of that for Ireland; for the escape of these 20 ships will oblige them (the English) to dispatch more than 30. The departure of 10,000 or 12,000 men, which they will well know to have gone, will oblige them to send troops to the most important points. If things turn out according to our wishes, I desire that the Toulon fleet should put to sea on October 12th; that of Rochefort before November 1st; and that of Brest before November 21st.[5]

In these two despatches of Napoleon, written on the same day, we have a second set of plans, in which on the one side the expeditions to the West Indies have their objective there, and apparently little or no connection with the invasion project, which is made to hang upon the success of a considerable landing in the north of Ireland.[6] But shining through both schemes there is the principle of an endeavour to occupy the attention of the British in distant quarters, so that a comparatively small naval force will suffice to command the Channel for a time long enough to permit the flotilla to cross.

We have seen that the July plan, under which the Toulon fleet was directly to act as cover to the flotilla, has wholly disappeared. We must now note that the Irish plan of September, above sketched, was also given up, possibly in view of the approaching Spanish alliance, possibly because it was found not so easy for the Brest fleet to get to sea unwatched, as it had been supposed.

A convention was agreed to on the 4th of January 1805 between the Emperor and the King of Spain, in which the former set out the forces under his hand as follows:—

In the Texel, 30,000 men, with the necessary war-ships and transports.

At Ostend, Dunkirk, Calais, Boulogne, and Havre, a flotilla and transport suitable to 120,000 men and 25,000 horses.

At Brest, a fleet of 21 sail of the line, several frigates and transports, prepared to embark 25,000 men in camp at Brest.

At Rochefort, 6 sail of the line and 4 frigates, anchored in Aix Roads, and having on board 4,000 troops.

At Toulon, 11 sail of the line, 8 frigates, and transports, having on board 9,000 troops.

Spain was asked to provide:—

At Ferrol, 8 sail of the line, or 7 at least, and 4 frigates, designed to combine their operations with the 5 French sail of the line and 2 frigates which were then in that port; 2,000 infantry, and 200 artil-

---

5. Napoleon to Decrès, September 29th, 1804. Ibid., p. 212.
6. James (*Naval History*, vol. iii., p. 213) assumes that Napoleon intended that Villeneuve, after his return to Rochefort, should join the Brest fleet so as together to cover the invasion. I cannot find any grounds for such an assumption.

lery, with 10 guns, were to be assembled, and the whole were to be ready for sea on the 20th of March, or, at latest, by the 30th of March.

At Cadiz, 15 sail of the line, or at least 12, were to be prepared ready to sail on March 30th, with 2,000 infantry, 100 artillery, and 400 cavalry, without their horses.

At Cartagena, 6 sail of the line were to be ready by the same date.

The Spanish ambassador, while signing the convention, was of opinion that though the ships could be got ready by the time named, they would neither be manned nor provisioned so soon.

Villeneuve's instructions were now modified to admit of his being joined by the Spanish ships at Cadiz, and also, as it appears, in abandoning the St. Helena expedition. Otherwise, the views of the Emperor, as expressed in his dispatch of 29th September 1804, regarding the Toulon and Rochefort squadrons, remained in force. The destination of the Brest squadron, now under Vice-Admiral Ganteaume, was however altered, and Villeneuve was to expect to meet it in the West Indies.[7]

The first moves under these conditions were made in January. Villeneuve at Toulon, with his 11 sail of the line and his 6,500 troops, taking advantage of Nelson's absence at the Madalena Islands,[8] put to sea on the 17th of the month. Missiessy, evading the blockading squadron of Sir Thomas Graves, got away with his 5 sail of the line and his 3,400 troops eight days later, and made straight for Martinique, in the West Indies. He ravaged the British West India Islands with ease and impunity, and loaded himself with their spoils.[9]

7. James has not noticed this. But it is clear from several of the Emperor's dispatches. On the 21st April 1805, he wrote to Decrès: "The non-departure of Ganteaume troubles me much." On the 23rd of April he says he has sent a courier to Brest, to inform Ganteaume that Nelson had gone to seek Villeneuve in Egypt, and he says: "Pray God that my courier may not find him at Brest!" On the same day, having heard that Ganteaume had not yet sailed, he expresses his impatience, and recommends sending out a succession of advice brigs and schooners to keep Villeneuve informed, and to recommend him "to do all the harm he can to the enemy, pending the arrival of General Ganteaume. . . . You perceive that the squadron of Admiral Ganteaume arriving, the force will be augmented by more than 2,000 men, which will keep me master in all those countries." It was only when the impossibility of Ganteaume's avoidance of Cornwallis became manifest that the plan was changed, and that Villeneuve was to relieve him by raising the blockade. On May 8th, Napoleon settled that if Ganteaume could not get out before the 20th of May he was not to attempt to move, but to wait for the appearance of Villeneuve. See *Précis des Evénemens Militaires*, vol. xi. *Pièces Justificatives*, passim.

8. A group forming part of the southern shore of the Straits of Bonifacio.

9. 100,000 fr. from Roseau (Charlotte-town), 192,000 fr. from St. Kitts, 89,000 fr. from Monserat. Troude, vol. iii., p. 334.

But early in March, at Martinique, he got a piece of news which told him that Villeneuve's move had miscarried; and also orders to return to Europe. He made sail there and then, and, being the luckiest of all the French admirals, voyaged home as he had voyaged out, without the least check or impediment, and anchored in Aix Roads on the 20th of May.

But his move had been an absolutely useless one, so far as the general current of the game went. He had taken a pawn and returned to his own square. Allemand succeeded him in the command, and thenceforward that squadron had no influence on events.

Ganteaume, with his 21 sail of the line and his 3,500 troops, made more than one attempt to get away from Brest, but the British, being augmented to an equal or even superior force to his own, and he himself being under necessarily positive orders not to get into action, he never made a real move, but lay blocked on his own square from the first to the last.

The interest of the game at once centres on the false move which Villeneuve made from Toulon on the 17th of January, and it must be told how it came to be false.

Nelson had a horror of the Gulf of Lyons and the coasts about Toulon. He knew no spot so subject to gales of wind, and was in a constant dread of being caught with disabled ships by the enemy issuing from Toulon. Discovery had been made of an excellent anchorage, thereupon named Agincourt Road, sheltered by the Madalena Islands. The Road was not 200 miles from Toulon, and there Nelson, on the 11th of January, had retired to refit and provision, leaving a couple of frigates to look out on Toulon. On the 19th, one of these frigates ran off Madalena, and reported, by signal, that Villeneuve was at sea. The British fleet was under way in a couple of hours after the receipt of the signal, and running down the east coast of Sardinia.

No one on the English side had yet fathomed Napoleon's plans. Nelson's mind was full of his old trials and difficulties—Naples, Sicily, and Egypt; these were, with him, the only places to which the enemy could be bound, and though he did not entirely exclude from his mind the possibility that Villeneuve meant to pass out of the Mediterranean, he did not give that possibility its full weight.[10]

It blew a furious south-westerly gale on the 20th of January, so that, though the ships were sheltered by a weather shore, they were under storm sails. I am not clear how it was that this circumstance,

10. Napoleon's prescience of Nelson's views and probable proceedings, mentioned on a previous page, is a striking illustration of his genius.

combined with others, did not put Nelson's mind into the right channel, and so save him a weary and heart-breaking journey. The gale ceased and the wind shifted, but Nelson was still off the south end of Sardinia, dispatching his limited numbers of frigates in all directions in search of intelligence. But there was none until the 26th, and then word was brought that on the 19th one of Villeneuve's line-of-battle ships, with her topmasts gone, had been seen making for shelter off the west coast of Corsica. The inference to be drawn from this piece of news was not drawn, and Nelson steered for Stromboli, off which island he spent a wakeful night on the 28th, watching its fires of unusual brilliancy. Still persuaded that history was repeating itself in his case, and being assured of the safety of Naples, he passed on to Palermo and Messina. Then, admitting the possibility of an alternative, and finding no evidence beyond a total absence of intelligence, he stood over to the Morea, and afterwards saw the land of Egypt on the 4th of February.

He now found himself utterly wrong. Not in Egypt, not in any part of the Eastern Mediterranean was the prey he was sighing for. This was worse than the first visit to Egypt, for he had pushed on there this time without a shred of real evidence to guide him. No one had seen or heard of the French fleet east of Sardinia, and it was now certain that it had never been in that direction at all. There was nothing for it but to retrace his steps, with all the speed possible. At Malta, on the 19th of February, Nelson learnt that Villeneuve, having put to sea on the 17th of January, had passed but a very little way to the southward when he was met by the furious south-westerly gale which Nelson had felt off the east coast of Sardinia, and had been driven back into Toulon, where he had anchored on the 20th.

Nelson's return journey was pursued, and on the 27th of February he anchored at Cagliari to water his fleet. On the 12th of March he was off Toulon again, making sure that the enemy was actually in port. A few days later he detached a single line-of-battle ship to Barcelona, to give colour to a report that he was off the Spanish coast, while he himself turned to the south-eastward to Palmas Bay, in the south of Sardinia, where the victuallers and store ships had been ordered to assemble to supply the wants of the exhausted squadron.

There, or in a neighbouring anchorage, the British lay from the 27th of March till the 3rd of April. They then weighed and stood to the southward. The next day, when the squadron had made but very little way, the wind shifted to the N.N.W., and very soon one of the frigates which had been left to watch Toulon, the *Phœbe,* hove in sight with the signal flying that the enemy was again at sea.

Nelson, still full of Sardinia, Naples, and Egypt, hove to midway between Sardinia and the African coast for the night, spreading his look-out ships north and south, to prevent the French passing to the eastward without his knowing it. The other frigate available, the *Active,* had been left by the *Phœbe* to follow up the French and bring word of their movements. She missed them on the night of the 31st of March. They were then sixty miles only from Toulon, steering S.S.W. for Minorca. This news had no effect on Nelson's preconceptions. He was back at Palermo on the 10th of April, but the absence of intelligence there at length awoke him to the possibility that the design of the French had never been eastwards at all, and that they might already have passed out of the Mediterranean, have swallowed up Sir John Orde's detachment off Cadiz, and have done whatever mischief it was their intention to do. But the wind now turned and blew from the westward, and then on the 16th of April Nelson received certain intelligence that on the 7th of April the French had been seen off Cape de Gata, steering towards the Straits of Gibraltar.

On the 18th Nelson made up his mind to follow the French fleet, wherever it had gone to. He now learnt that Villeneuve had actually passed the Straits on the 8th; but, owing to the persistent foul wind, the British did not see Gibraltar until the 30th, and it was not till the 4th of May that they were able to anchor at the usual watering-place, Tetuan, on the African coast, to fill up with that necessary. A change of wind next day brought out all Nelson's eagerness, and with ships unsupplied he made sail for Lagos Bay, where it was expected to meet victuallers and store ships. That anchorage was reached on the 10th of May, and there Nelson learnt that Villeneuve's destination was certainly the West Indies. Nelson, remarking that "Salt beef and the French fleet was preferable to roast beef and champagne without them," started after the enemy for Barbados on the 11th of May.

I may now usefully bring together chronologically the movements of this duel, up to the time of Villeneuve's arrival in the West Indies.

*March 29th.*—Villeneuve sails from Toulon.[11] Nelson is at anchor in Palmas Bay.

*March 31st.*—The *Phœbe* and *Active* see the French fleet thirty-five miles south of Toulon; they follow it, steering S.S.W. till sunset, when the *Phœbe* leaves the *Active* to follow up the French, and

---

11. Troude says 30th; and that the troops carried were reduced to 3,350 men. Vol. iii., p. 340.

herself makes for Palmas Bay to report to Nelson. Nelson still at Palmas Bay.

*April 1st.*—The *Active* having steered S.W. during the night, finds herself alone in the morning, and makes sail after Nelson. Villeneuve having been under the impression—created by Nelson's *ruse* of sending a ship off Barcelona—that he was off the Spanish Coast, now learns that he was off the south end of Sardinia on the 27th of March; he thereupon alters his course so as to pass inside of the Balearic Islands. Nelson moves from Palmas Bay to Pula for water.

*April 3rd.*—Nelson puts to sea with the intention of proceeding to Toulon. Villeneuve is steering for Cartagena.

*April 4th.*—Nelson is off the south end of Sardinia; the wind has shifted to N.N.W., and the *Phœbe* makes her report. Nelson spreads his ships between the south point of Sardinia and the coast of Africa.

*April 6th.*—Villeneuve arrives off Cartagena; offers to escort the six Spanish sail there to Cadiz; the Spaniards decline. Nelson still watching between Sardinia and Africa.

*April 7th.*—Villeneuve, with a fresh easterly breeze, starts for the Straits of Gibraltar. Nelson makes for Palermo.

*April 8th.*—Villeneuve passes through the Straits, and anchors at Cadiz. Nelson on his way to Palermo.

*April 9th.*—Villeneuve sails from Cadiz with 12 French and 5 Spanish sail of the line, leaving a sixth Spanish line-of-battle ship, which had been on shore, to follow. Nelson still on his way to Palermo.

*April 10th.*—Villeneuve at sea, on his way to Martinique. Nelson off Palermo, with no news.

*April 16th.*—Villeneuve at sea. Nelson, beating to the westward round the south point of Sardinia, gets news that the French had passed the Straits on the 8th.

*May 4th.*—Villeneuve within nine days' sail of Martinique. Nelson anchors in Mazarri Bay, Tetuan.

*May 5th.*—Villeneuve within eight days' sail of Martinique. Nelson sails from Mazarri Bay, with no more news.

*May 10th.*—Villeneuve within three days' sail of Martinique. Nelson anchors in Lagos Bay.

*May 12th.*—Villeneuve within a day's sail of Martinique. Nelson sails from Lagos Bay for Barbados.

*May 13th.*—Villeneuve arrives at Martinique. Nelson is within two days' sail of Madeira.

Nelson was in sight of Madeira on the 15th of May. The fleet had been going 10 knots, and he thought they had been very fortunate since quitting Cape St. Vincent, and would be in time to secure Jamaica, which he considered the objective of the French. Others thought of Surinam and Trinidad; but no one had any conception of the great strategic plan which was formulated, or the least idea that Nelson might be doing that which more than anything else tended, on the face of things, to further Napoleon's schemes. The points most against the Emperor were Nelson's speed and its moral effect.

It would appear that Villeneuve's orders must have been modified between his first and second sailing from Toulon.

> I have re-read [writes the Emperor to Decrès on the 30th April] with attention the instructions given to Admiral Villeneuve. I suppose that he will arrive at Martinique the 15th of this month,[12] and that then he will leave to proceed to St. Domingo, from thence to the bay of St. Iago on June 9th, remain there 20 days, and afterwards go to Cadiz.[13] If Admiral Mazon sails before the 10th or 15th of May he will take him orders to wait 35 days, and then to proceed by the shortest route to Ferrol. Admiral Mazon will not arrive before the 4th or 9th of June, and Admiral Villeneuve would have to wait till the 19th of July, and would not appear before Ferrol until the 18th of August. . . . If Admiral Mazon has not yet sailed, you must write to him that in the letter which Admiral Mazon takes it is said that he should remain 35 days; but it was hoped that Admiral Mazon would have left a fortnight earlier; that my intention is that he should not stay at Martinique beyond July 4th.[14]

On the 8th of May, Napoleon drew up two sets of draft instructions for Villeneuve; and it is only for the first time in these instructions that the idea of gaining the command of the Channel seems to take that overwhelming position which, if it really occupied the Emperor's mind, was all along its due.

> The direction which you should take after your junction at Ferrol depends on so many different circumstances, that I can only leave it to your experience at sea and your zeal for my service. In fact, many things have come to pass since your departure for Martinique; the knowledge of the enemy's force which you have drawn to America, the strength of the squadron at Ferrol, and of the enemy's fleet before the port, the condition of your fleet, are so many necessary elements regulating imperiously your ulterior destination.

12. Floréal. That is the 5th of May.
13. I can find no explanation for this curious statement, which seems contradictory to most of what had gone before and came after.
14. *Précis des Evénemens Militaires*, vol. xi., p. 237.

The principal end of the whole operation is to give us, for some days, a superiority before Boulogne. Masters of the Straits for four days, 150,000 men embarked in 2,000 vessels will entirely complete the expedition. To achieve this great end, immediately after your appearance at Ferrol you will have four courses open to you.

The first, to proceed to Rochefort, and to join the 5 sail of the line which I have in that roadstead.[15] I have sent instructions to the *Regulus,* which is at Lorient, to join you, and thus with 25 French and 15 Spanish sail of the line, to make your junction with the Brest squadron, and then with 60 sail of the line to pass into the Channel.

The second plan is to pass by the Rochefort squadron, which engages the attention of an equal number of the enemy, and to direct your steps as promptly as possible on Brest to effect your junction with Admiral Ganteaume.

The third plan would be, after your junction with the squadron at Ferrol, to pass round Ireland to join with the squadron in the Texel, seven sail of the line strong, with its convoy, and to proceed before Boulogne.

The fourth plan appears to be to make for the Lizard, and when 30 leagues off it to take advantage of a westerly wind to run along the coast of England to avoid encountering the squadron which blockades Brest, and to arrive at Boulogne four or five days before it.

For either of these operations, in taking account of the provisions which you will find on board the French and Spanish ships, and those which you will find at Rochefort, you will be sufficiently provided; and having long foreseen your expedition, I have caused a great quantity to be prepared at Brest, Cherbourg, and Boulogne.

If you adopt the plan of forming a junction with the Brest squadron, you should endeavour to do so without fighting; but if this proves too difficult, arrange to fight as near Brest as possible, and to this end deceive the enemy by false movements, should he, on learning your arrival at Ferrol adopt the plan of advancing 20 leagues or so to encounter you. If, on the contrary, you adopt the plan of passing round Ireland, you should pass out of sight of the coast, and keep your route as much from the knowledge of the enemy as possible, who will for a time believe you have returned to the Mediterranean, which report we shall not fail to use all means to spread.

Admiral Ganteaume, with 21 sail of the line provisioned for six months, is anchored outside the Goulet, between Bertheaume and Camaret, under the protection of batteries mounting more than 100 guns. From the moment of your arrival at Ferrol, he will be ready to

15. Nevertheless on the 13th of May, when he believed that this squadron had returned from the West Inidies, Napoleon was urgent on Decrès to send it back again. Ibid., p. 260.

sail; he is more ready to do so than from any other position inside the Goulet. . . .

If you pass round Ireland, you will go to the Texel. Positive instructions have been sent there, as well as in relation to the position of the enemy in these waters.

If by events occurring in America, or in the course of your cruise, you should find yourself in a position which does not permit you to carry out your instructions, and that you might not be able to think of any new operation, you will despatch the squadron of Admiral Gourdon with three or four of the fastest Spanish ships from Ferrol, to undertake a cruise in conformity with the accompanying instructions: Our intention is that you should raise the blockade of Rochefort, and that you should give the accompanying instructions to Captain Allemand, whose exit you will cover; and that this being done, you should take my fleet to Cadiz with the Ferrol ships; that you cover the entry into Cadiz of the squadron from Cartagena; that you occupy the Straits; that you ravage the Roads of Gibraltar, and that you should complete there with provisions.[16]

I do not know when the text of the instructions, according to this draft, reached Villeneuve. It is possible that the orders may have gone out by the *Didon* frigate, which out-sailed Mazon's squadron, and was with Villeneuve at Martinique before the 4th of June. Otherwise it does not appear that he could have received them before his arrival at Vigo. That he had them at some time seems clear, from an observation in his letter of explanation after bearing up for Cadiz.

I proceed now to complete the narrative.

On the 29th of May, being within a week's sail of Barbados, Nelson detached a frigate to warn Admiral Cochrane, supposed to be with 6 sail of the line at Barbados, of his approach. On the 3rd of June he heard for certain of Villeneuve's arrival at Martinique, and the next day he anchored at Carlisle Bay, Barbados. Here he found Cochrane, but with only 2 sail of the line, the remaining 4 having been detained at Jamaica by Admiral Dacres. There was not a doubt in the minds of the authorities but that the French had gone south to attack Tobago and Trinidad. And when the general in command offered to embark himself, with 2,000 troops, to frustrate the French design, Nelson, though with much hesitation, accepted the offer.

The squadron, now of 12 sail of the line, sailed from Barbados for Trinidad on the 5th of June, and on the 7th arrived at the Gulf of

16. Ibid., p. 250.

Paria, only to learn that the French were not there, and that there were no tidings of them. Instantly the steps were retraced. On the 9th Nelson, off Grenada, learnt that the enemy had passed Dominique on the 6th, and was steering north.

Following north, the British admiral was at Antigua on the 12th. He disembarked the troops there, and passed a moment in debate as to what was to be done. First, he must not quit the West Indies until he was certain the French had left; secondly, this meant inaction, and waiting for intelligence which was generally wrong, and had already proved to be the ruin of his hopes; thirdly, were there not good grounds for supposing that Villeneuve had already turned homewards? A frigate from France had certainly communicated with Villeneuve on the 31st May, and from that moment all had been hurry. Nelson believed that the *Furet* had informed Villeneuve of his being on passage after him.[17] If Barbados was the point of attack, why had it not been made long ago? If Tobago or Trinidad had been the objects, these two might have been approached before this, and neither to reach them nor St. Lucia, St. Vincent, or Grenada, was it necessary to stand to the northward in the first instance. If any of the islands were in view, the game the French fleet was playing was incomprehensible.[18] What impression could they hope to make on Jamaica with only 4,000 or 5,000 men? But if they did mean Jamaica, what was to prevent their steering thither direct from Martinique? Some thought they might be going to Porto Rico to wait for reinforcements; but the season was past, and if 15 sail of the line were coming out to join them, there would be no need to hide themselves.

The admiral's opinion was as firm as a rock that some cause, orders, or inability to perform any service in these seas, had made them resolve to proceed direct to Europe, sending the Spanish ships to the Havannah.[19]

But, fourthly, if they were not on their way home, they certainly would be presently, if they believed that Nelson was still in the West

17. The *Didon* was the frigate spoken of. She met Villeneuve at Fort Royal, Martinique. Villeneuve seems to have first learnt the arrival of Nelson from prisoners taken out of the sugar ships captured on the 8th of June near Antigua.

18. Troude leaves it partly incomprehensible, as he makes Villeneuve take on board 700 troops at Martinique, and 600 at Guadaloupe, and still proceed north to Antigua, with the intention of attacking Barbados. Vol. iii., p. 346.

19. I have given Nelson's reasoning almost verbatim. It all seems conclusive enough, except the answer to the Porto Rico probability. There must, I think, have been some decisive matter in the news received at 8 P.M. on the 12th of June, and which he gave to Captain Bettesworth to take to the Admiralty.

Indies; and it might be a month before his departure would be known.

Good or bad, Nelson's reasoning generally concluded in favour of action. He sent Bettesworth in the *Curieux* to the Admiralty, to inform them of what he believed, and what his intentions were.[20] He quitted Antigua finally on the 13th of June, taking one of Cochrane's ships with him, and thus bringing his force up to 11 sail of the line. He made straight for Cape St. Vincent, and was in sight of it on the 17th of July.

Villeneuve, meanwhile, as we know, had arrived at Martinique on the 13th of May, 21 days before Nelson arrived at Barbados. He lay there till the very day Nelson arrived at Barbados, when having embarked a number of troops, he put to sea with the combined fleet.

It is not easy to say exactly what he intended to do, or why he had spent so long a time inactive—except for the capture of the Diamond Rock by a detachment—in the harbour of Fort Royal. The English accounts are silent as to his intentions. The French account, which I generally follow, says distinctly that an attack on Barbados was intended, in consequence of the certainty that neither Ganteaume nor Missiessy could join him at Martinique. But why should he then have stood away to the northward? However this may be, he did actually stand away east of Monserat and west of Antigua. On the 8th of June he captured a valuable fleet of sugar-laden ships off Antigua, and from them he learnt that 14 sail of the line had arrived at Barbados. This arrival, in the French Admiral's opinion, made it impossible to think of an attack either on Barbados or on any other British possessions in the West Indies. To return to Martinique, in order to wait the specified time for the arrival of the squadrons from Europe, seemed likely to produce no other result than to increase the number of sick on board, which was already considerable.[21]

His resolution was taken immediately. He put the whole of the West Indian troops into four frigates, with orders to land them at Guadaloupe. He sent two more frigates to convoy the prize sugar ships to the nearest port, and directed the whole six to rejoin him at

20. Brenton, in his *Life of St. Vincent*, has an anecdote of Nelson, the point of which rests on the assumed fact that Bettesworth disobeyed his orders in going to England. Nelson's memo. of June 12th, 8 P.M., is conclusive against the fact and the story.

21. Villeneuve thought that with Cochrane's ships there would be 16 against him; the number, as we have seen, was exaggerated. Troude, vol. iii., p. 346.

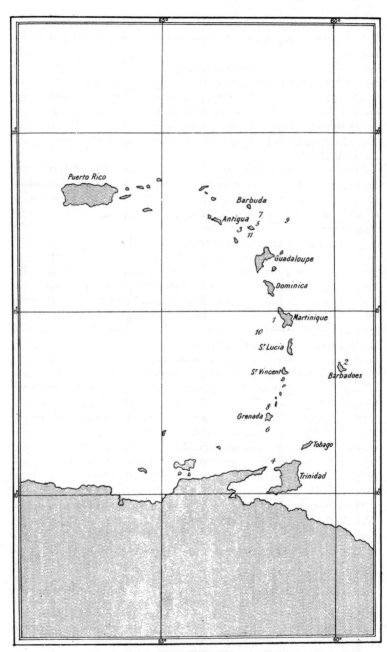

Chart of the West India Islands

228

a rendezvous 60 miles N.E. of Corvo, in the Azores. He then made sail for that rendezvous himself.

The condition of things in Europe was now this: Ganteaume, with his 21 sail of the line and his troops, had been trying all these months to get away, but being too closely watched by Cornwallis with 18 or 20 sail had been unable to do so, and was still in the Roads of Brest.

Missiessy, with his squadron, it will be remembered, had returned from the West Indies, and had got safe into Rochefort on the 20th of May. There he found orders waiting him which might have been put in force had he returned earlier. They were to the effect that if he could get away by the 15th of May, he was to return to the West Indies and join Villeneuve. If, however, the latter had left, he was to follow him direct to Ferrol, and to put into port there if Villeneuve was not met. If Ferrol was blockaded, this would presuppose the non-arrival of Villeneuve, and Missiessy was to cruise in the offing for a sufficient time to allow for Villeneuve's arrival, and to return to Rochefort if he failed to appear.[22]

The late arrival of Missiessy, and the extensive repairs which his ships required, prevented his being soon ready for sea, and fresh instructions were issued to him.

He was now directed to make a demonstration on the coast of Ireland, in order to distract the attention of the British, and to cause them to detach forces to that coast. He was, however, to keep away from the coast until the 4th to the 9th of July, burning or sinking every neutral or enemy's ship which might otherwise give note of his whereabouts. Between those dates he was to appear off the Shannon and Cape Clear, then to disappear again at sea, and finally to rendezvous 120 miles west of Ferrol from the 29th of July to the 3rd of August pending the arrival of Vice-Admiral Villeneuve, under whose orders he was then to place himself. If this meeting did not take

22. Ibid., p. 334.

EXPLANATION OF CHART

1.—Villeneuve leaving Martinique, June 4.
2.—Nelson arriving at Barbados, same date.
3.—Villeneuve, June 7.
4.—Nelson, same date.
5.—Villeneuve, June 8.
6.—Nelson, same date.
7.—Villeneuve, June 9.
8.—Nelson, same date.
9.—Villeneuve steering for Western Islands, June 10.
10.—Nelson, same date.
11.—Nelson sailing for Cape St. Vincent, June 13.

place before the 13th of August, Missiessy was to proceed to Vigo. If, however, Ferrol was found to be not blockaded when Missiessy appeared off it, he was to take the division formed there under his orders, and remain at a convenient rendezvous near at hand.[23]

On the 26th of June, the health of Missiessy had so broken down as to make it necessary that he should resign his command to Commodore Allemand.

This officer, with his 5 sail of the line, was now blockaded at Rochefort by Rear-Admiral Stirling with an equal force.

In Ferrol were still the Franco-Spanish squadron of 10 sail of the line, but now increased to 14 sail, and these ships were watched by Vice-Admiral Sir Robert Calder, with only 10 sail of the line.

It is easy to see how portentous to the issue of the war Villeneuve's return across the Atlantic in June 1805 actually was. Before the 11th of July, the only thing known to Cornwallis and his outlying squadrons was that Villeneuve had actually arrived at Martinique about two months before, and that Nelson was on his way after him; but what was about to happen, and when Villeneuve would appear in European waters, was entirely hidden from knowledge. Only it was, on the face of things, probable that Nelson's arrival in the West Indies would drive Villeneuve home again.

But if Villeneuve reached Ferrol at the head of 18 or 20 sail of the line, what could Calder do, except retire? Such retirement would release the Ferrol ships, and Villeneuve's fleet would be augmented to 34 sail of the line. There was then nothing to prevent him from appearing off Rochefort, driving Stirling away, and augmenting his fleet to 39 sail of the line by the addition of Allemand's squadron.

Cornwallis, off Brest, would only have some 28 sail of the line under his command when Calder and Stirling had fallen back and joined him. Would it be possible for him to face Villeneuve's 39 sail of the line, when Ganteaume was pressing out of Brest with 21 sail of the line behind him? It would have been a desperate venture, but, short of power to beat both fleets in succession, there was nothing to prevent Villeneuve's sailing leisurely up the Channel from Ushant at the head of his 60 sail of the line, and covering the passage of Napoleon's vast array to the shores of Kent and Sussex.

Such speed had been made by Bettesworth in the *Curieux,* that Cornwallis got news of Villeneuve's being on his way home, and Admiralty orders thereupon, on the 11th of July, five days before Nelson reached Cape St. Vincent.

23. Ibid., p. 335.

In obedience to the order, he sent to Admiral Stirling to raise the blockade of Rochefort, and to join Calder off Ferrol.

Calder, with his force thus augmented to 15 sail of the line, was ordered to take his post 100 miles west of Ferrol, and to wait for Villeneuve, who was supposed to have not more than 16 sail with him, whereas, as we have seen, he was at the head of 20 sail of the line. Calder was on this station when Nelson arrived at Cape St. Vincent.

It will be well here to repeat the former process of assembling together the contemporary events, in order to get a clearer view of what was actually taking place.

*June 4th*, 1805.—Villeneuve sails from Fort Royal, Martinique, with 20 sail of the line. Nelson arrives at Carlisle Bay, Barbados, and is joined by 2 sail of the line, making 12 in all.

*June 5th*.—Villeneuve on his way to Antigua. Nelson sails for Trinidad.

*June 7th*.—Villeneuve to the eastward of Antigua. Nelson arrives at Paria Bay, Trinidad; finds he has been misled, and turns his head north.

*June 8th*.—Villeneuve passing round the north part of Antigua, hears of the Sugar Convoy to the N.N.E.; chases and captures 15 sugar ships valued at 500,000 francs; hears also of Nelson's arrival at Barbados, and supposes him to have 16 sail under his command. Nelson is approaching Grenada.

*June 9th*.—Villeneuve, north of Antigua, puts the West Indian troops into six frigates to be landed at Guadaloupe. Nelson, off Grenada, learns that Villeneuve was seen to pass Dominica on the 6th.

*June 10th*.—Villeneuve sails for the rendezvous off the Western Islands. Nelson is steering north for Antigua.

*June 12th*.—Villeneuve is at sea on his way home. Nelson, at Antigua, disembarks his troops; receives important intelligence at 8 P.M.; despatches Bettesworth in the *Curieux* to the Admiralty, and sails, on 13th, with 11 line-of-battle ships for Cape St. Vincent.

*June 30th*.—Villeneuve, at the rendezvous off Corvo, is joined by his frigates. Nelson is at sea on his way home.

*July 3rd*.—Villeneuve re-captures a Spanish galleon valued at 15,000,000 francs, which had been taken by the British privateer *Mars*. Nelson still at sea.

*July 17th*.—Villeneuve within five days' sail of Calder's rendezvous. Nelson arrives off Cape St. Vincent.

Nelson had now been chasing and continually missing Villeneuve for three months and thirteen days. His last run after him had covered more than 7,000 miles of sea, at the rate of 93 miles a day. There was now the choice before him of going east to Cadiz, or north to Ferrol, and under the spell of ill-fortune which ever pursued him he chose the former route. Collingwood was watching Cadiz, but Nelson did not now meet with him; they only coresponded on the state of affairs, while Nelson put first into Gibraltar for stores and refitting, and then into Tetuan for water. He finally weighed from this latter place, with the intention of going north, on the 24th of July.

Collingwood had been writing to Nelson, putting to him the dangers of the position, and the probable plans of Napoleon. He penetrated parts of the Emperor's apparent design, but he considered Ireland the main point about to be struck at. Nelson now received a second letter, in which Collingwood said:—

> The flight to the West Indies was to take off the naval force, which is the great impediment to their undertaking. The Rochefort squadron's return confirmed me. I think they will now collect their forces at Ferrol—which Calder tells me are in motion—pick up those at Rochefort, who, I am told, are equally ready, and will make them about 30 sail; and then, without going near Ushant or the Channel fleet, proceed to Ireland, when the Brest fleet—21, I believe, of them—will sail either to another part of Ireland or up the Channel; a sort of force that has not been seen in those seas perhaps ever.

On the 25th of July, Nelson saw Collingwood, and talked matters over with him. He learnt then, also, that the Franco-Spanish fleet had actually been seen about half way between the West Indies and the Azores, steering for Europe on the previous 19th of June.

Nelson stood again to the northward. He was 400 miles west of Lisbon on the 3rd of August. He crossed the Bay of Biscay without intelligence, and without meeting anything worth notice, and then finally joined the squadron of Cornwallis off Ushant on the 15th.

Meanwhile, this is what had been happening elsewhere. Calder was, as we have seen, on his rendezvous 100 miles west of Ferrol, with 15 sail of the line, in hourly expectation of seeing an enemy's fleet only larger by one line-of-battle ship than his own. His health was bad. The constant anxiety of his situation was wearing him down. But he was able, zealous, and willing. He had been captain of the fleet under Jervis on Valentine's Day, and was not a likely man to fail.

The morning of the 22nd of July was very thick, with a light breeze from W.N.W. Calder's ships were on the starboard tack, standing therefore, no doubt, under very easy sail to the south-westward. The *Defiance* was stationed as a look-out ship nine or ten miles to windward of the main squadron, and between eleven and twelve o'clock in the forenoon, during a momentary lifting of the fog, this ship signalled an enemy's fleet to the south-west. This was Villeneuve's 20 sail; they were in three columns, steering straight for Ferrol, and nearly straight for the British fleet.

Calder thereupon formed in line of battle, and Villeneuve did the same; but the fog was too dense for either fleet to see what was done by the other, or even to count their numbers. As a fact, they were presently in the position of passing one another on opposite tacks, starboard side to starboard side, and as much as seven miles apart. It was not until 3 P.M. or thereabouts, that the *Sirius* frigate, having been sent to reconnoitre, reported by signal the exact number—20—of the enemy's sail of the line.

Calder thereupon made the signal to "engage the enemy," and immediately afterwards the signal to tack, the object being the natural one to close with the enemy on the same tack with him, but to leeward. It was still too foggy to see what was going on, but when the *Hero*, which was Calder's leading ship, got a little nearer, she found that the combined fleet itself had tacked, and was standing to the S.W. The *Hero* immediately tacked, and was followed by the rest of the British ships in succession. So the battle was joined very much in the old way. Both fleets were on the starboard tack, the British to leeward, engaging with their starboard guns, while the combined fleet engaged with their port guns. But what between the fog and the smoke, it was difficult to say what was happening, or almost what was being fired at.

In this somewhat confused state, the firing went on as steadily as was possible, till about 8 o'clock, when it was found that two Spanish ships, the *San Rafael* and the *Firme,* had struck to the British fleet.

It was growing dark at half-past 8, and the fleets were drawing rather apart. Calder made the night signal to discontinue the action, but the general state of things was such that the firing did not altogether cease till an hour later. It had lasted altogether about four hours and a half, and it had left the two Spanish prizes in the hands of the British, at a loss of 39 killed and 159 wounded, while the combined fleet had suffered a loss of 476 in killed and wounded.

Calder's squadron now lay-to all night with their heads to the S.W., repairing damages, and the combined fleet remained in the same condition.

At daylight on the 23rd of July it was almost as foggy as ever; the two fleets were some 17 miles apart, and each was in more or less disorder. The British were hampered by the presence of the disabled prizes, and also by one of their own ships, the *Windsor Castle,* which was also disabled. Yet it was so thick that Calder could hardly tell what the situation of his fleet really was, and a movement to close up his ships was taken by Villeneuve to be a sign of weakness, who bore up with an intention, which he did not carry out, of reopening the engagement. Being to windward, Villeneuve always had the opportunity, had he wished it, of bringing on the action again. Calder could certainly make attempts in that way, but only at some disadvantage.

Villeneuve, however, was from his orders necessarily disinclined for more decisive action. His purposes would have been much better fulfilled had he never seen Calder at all, even if he had beaten him.

Calder, on his part, had to remember that there were 14 ships from Ferrol, and 5 from Rochefort, which might be close upon him. The combined fleet was still 18 sail strong, while his own, on account of the disabled *Windsor Castle,* was reduced to 14 sail. The odds were heavy, when 19 additional enemies might be in sight as soon as the fog lifted.

The two fleets passed out of each other's view on the 24th of July.[24] Villeneuve made for Vigo, and anchored there on the 26th.[25] Calder conveyed his prizes towards the Channel, then steered back for Ferrol, and finding on arrival off the port on the 29th of July that Villeneuve had not put in there, he resumed the blockade of it, and awaited orders.

24. At 6 A.M. on the 23rd, according to nautical time.
25. "In the first moment after the battle, Villeneuve was almost happy that he had met the English without experiencing a disaster; but having left the scene of action, and having had time for reflection, his discouragement and habitual melancholy deepened into a profound grief. . . . To complete his misfortune, the wind which for two days had been favourable had now become contrary again. To the sick, whose numbers had increased, the wounded had now to be added. There were not the necessary refreshments for them, and there was only water for five or six days. Thus situated, he again wanted to proceed to Cadiz, Lauriston again opposed this course; they split the difference and ran into Vigo." Thiers' *History of the Consulate and the Empire* (Authorized Translation), vol. v., pp. 236–37.
Troude, vol. iii., p. 356, makes Villeneuve's decision to rest entirely on the wind, and his anxiety to land his sick and wounded. When the wind set in from the N.E. he steered for Cadiz; then after six hours, on a change to S.S.W., he made for Ferrol; then, on a change back to N.E., for Vigo.
James (*Naval History,* vol. iv., p. 16) dates the arrival at Vigo as given in the text, but Troude (vol. iii., p. 356) makes it the 28th.

On the next day, the 30th of July, Villeneuve sailed from Vigo for Ferrol, but now with only 15 sail, having left three behind him at Vigo.[26] On the 1st of August a strong south-westerly gale sprang up, which drove Calder away to the north-east, and enabled Villeneuve to pass into Ferrol unobserved. And thus, in spite of his mishaps and difficulties, the French admiral again found himself at the head of a fleet (29 sail of the line) so numerically superior to anything he was likely to meet, that had the quality been equal to the quantity, what had passed would have been mere incidental circumstances, in no degree troubling or hindering the main action of the great plan which was now working towards the *dénoûment*.[27]

Calder had detached Stirling with 4 sail of the line to resume the blockade of Rochefort, and now, when the wind moderated, and he reappeared off Ferrol on the 9th of August, with only 9 sail of the line, and found 29 enemy's ships ready to leave port, there was no possible course open to him but to fall back and join Lord Cornwallis off Ushant, which he did on the 14th.

There was still one thing wanting to complete Villeneuve's arrangements before he proceeded to roll up the blockading fleet at Brest, to set Ganteaume free, and to sweep into the Channel in his company unopposed. When Stirling should get to Rochefort, he was sure to find it empty, for Allemand had put to sea directly after the blockade had been raised nearly a month before. Villeneuve was bound, if he could, to pick up Allemand before he went on, and he seems to have had some idea of doing it off Cape Ortegal.[28] How-

26. The *Atlas*, French, and the *America* and *España*, Spanish. They had not suffered much in the action, but were said to be slow sailers, and likely to delay the fleet. They remained as hospital ships to accommodate the 1,200 sick and wounded which were discharged from the combined fleet. Villeneuve was only too glad of any excuse to be quit of the Spanish ships. "They have always," he wrote to Decrès, "brought us to the lowest depths of misfortune." *Consulate and Empire,* vol. v., p. 238.

27. It was in this sense that Napoleon affected to write to Villeneuve at Ferrol, endeavouring to encourage him in the belief that all was as it should be (see the letter of August 13th at p. 242, ibid.). Villeneuve, however, was not to be encouraged. "I am about to sail," he wrote to Decrès from Ferrol. . . . "No doubt it is thought that sailing hence with 29 ships, I am considered able to fight vessels of anything like the same number; I am not afraid to confess to you that I should be sorry to meet with 20. Our naval tactics are out of date; we only know how to range ourselves in line, and that is precisely what the enemy wishes for. I have neither time nor means to agree upon another system with the commanders of the vessels of the two nations. . . . I foresaw all this before I left Toulon; but all my delusions did not vanish until the day on which I saw the Spanish ships which are joined to mine . . . then I was obliged to despair of everything." Ibid., p. 240.

28. Allemand's various orders, as stated, do not correspond with his acts. According to Troude (vol. iii., pp. 335–36), he should have made Ferrol as soon as he

ever this may be, Villeneuve sailed on the 11th of August, and was on the 13th and 14th off Cape Ortegal. The Rochefort squadron was, in fact, then close to him, but not actually seeing him, made for Vigo, and anchored there on the 16th of August. Villeneuve's latest orders from Napoleon had urged him to proceed to Brest, and give battle to the British fleet off that port at all hazards, even at the loss of his own fleet, in order to enable Ganteaume to put to sea. That was all that was necessary, in the opinion of the Emperor, to allow the 150,000 men in the 2,000 vessels lying ready, from Etaples to Cape Grisnez, to cross the Channel.[29] I must allow the French Admiral to make his own statement in explanation, or justification, of the fact that on the 15th of August he bore up and steered for Cadiz.

> I was observed, on the day I quitted Ferrol, and the next morning also, by the frigates and by 2 sail of the line of the enemy, which I chased by the fastest ships in the fleet without being able to approach them. Having found the winds from the N.E. set in, and having stretched to the W.N.W. during the whole of the 14th and 15th without any appearance of change; having no confidence in the state of the armaments of my ships, or in their speed, or in the precision of their manœuvres; the reunion of the forces of the enemy, their knowledge of all my proceedings since my arrival on the coast of Spain, left me no hope of being able to carry out the great object for which the fleet was destined. In struggling longer against foul winds, I should experience irreparable damage and inevitable separation, the Spanish ship *San Francisco de Asis* having already lost her main topmast. Convinced that the state of affairs was essentially changed since the issue of His Majesty's orders, who, in directing the main part of his naval forces on the Colonies, had for his object to divide those of the

---

was free to put to sea, and only to cruise if he was prevented from doing so. At Vigo, he found orders from Villeneuve to rendezvous at the Penmarks. James (vol. iv., p. 27) says Allemand did not find any instructions at Vigo.

29. Troude, vol. iii., p. 357.

---

PLATE III.

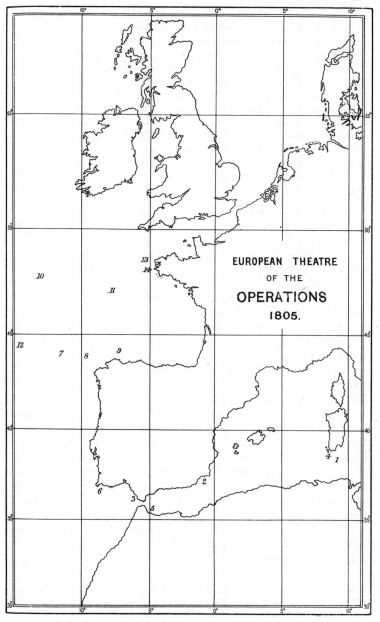

EUROPEAN THEATRE

OF THE

OPERATIONS

1805.

enemy by drawing his attention to his distant possessions, in order to surprise him, and to strike at his heart by their sudden return to Europe and their combined reunion; that this plan not having succeeded, being, in fact, upset by the time which had elapsed, and by the calculations to which the speed of the squadron had given occasion, the enemy was placed in a position to defend it; and that the junction of his forces, at this moment was greater than under any preceding circumstances, and was such that they might prove superior to the united fleets of Toulon; seeing, therefore, no chance of success in this state of affairs, and, conformably to my instructions, I determined, on the third day after my departure, on the evening of the 15th, being then 80 leagues W.N.W. of Cape Finisterre, to bear up for Cadiz.[30]

Let me now, finally, set out the contemporary events side by side, that the flow of the story up to the *dénoûment* may be the better comprehended.

*July 22nd.*—Villeneuve's and Calder's fleets in action west of Ferrol; Allemand's squadron within a day's sail of the spot. Nelson anchors in Mazarri Bay.

*July 24th.*—Villeneuve and Calder lose sight of each other. Nelson sails from Mazarri Bay.

*July 26th.*—Villeneuve anchors at Vigo. Calder convoying his prizes to the northward. Allemand at sea looking for Villeneuve. Nelson off the coast of Portugal, steering to the northward.

*July 29th.*—Villeneuve at Vigo; Allemand at sea, looking for him. Calder off Ferrol, with 13 sail; Nelson below the latitude of Lisbon, with 11 sail, steering to the northward.

*August 1st.*—Calder driven from Ferrol to the N.E. by a gale of wind. Villeneuve sails from Vigo with 15 sail, and anchors at Corunna; is now at the head of 29 sail; Allemand still at sea looking for him. Nelson still south of Lisbon.

*August 9th.*—Villeneuve still at Corunna; Allemand still at sea. Calder arriving off Ferrol with 9 sail, finds Villeneuve there, and falls back to join Cornwallis off Brest; Nelson within six days of Ushant.

*August 11th.*—Villeneuve quits Corunna with 29 sail; Allemand in the neighbourhood of Cape Ortegal with 5 sail. Nelson within four days of Ushant.

30. Ibid., p. 360. He says (vol. iii., p. 551) that before leaving the West Indies, Villeneuve received orders which would have justified his going to Cadiz. I am disposed to think, however, that he was relying on the latter part of Napoleon's draft of May 8th, already quoted.

*August* 13*th.*—Villeneuve off Cape Ortegal, standing W.N.W., with 29 sail; Allemand close to, but not in sight. Nelson, 11 sail, within two days of Ushant; Calder, 9 sail, within one day's sail of Ushant.

*August* 15*th.*—Villeneuve, being 240 miles W.N.W. of Cape Finisterre, with a N.E. wind, bears up for Cadiz; Allemand within one day's sail of Vigo. Nelson joins Cornwallis off Brest.

*August* 16*th.*—Villeneuve on his way south; Allemand anchors at Vigo. Nelson on his way home with only *Victory* and *Superb.*

While these transactions were in progress at sea, Napoleon had been apparently fully persuaded of the ultimate success of his plans, and fully determined to push his army across, so soon as the sails of the combined fleets should appear. He arrived at Boulogne on the 3rd of August, reviewed a line of infantry nine miles long, and said: "The English know not what awaits them. If we have the power of crossing but for twelve hours, England will be no more."[31] He heard of Calder's action about the 13th of August, and on that day wrote to Villeneuve the commendatory letter already noticed, in which he said:—

> The English are not so numerous as you seem to imagine. They are everywhere in a state of uncertainty and alarm. Should you make your appearance for three days—nay, even for 24 hours—your mission would be fulfilled. Make the moment of your departure known to Admiral Ganteaume by an extraordinary courier. Never for a grander object did a squadron run such risks. . . . For this great object of forwarding the descent upon the power which for six centuries has oppressed France, we may all die without regretting the sacrifice of life. . . . England has in the Downs only 4 ships of the line, which we daily harass with our praams and our flotillas.[32]

On the 14th he wrote to Lauriston, who still remained on board Villeneuve's flagship, saying:—

> We are ready everywhere. Your presence in the Channel for 24 hours will suffice.[33]

On the 22nd of August the courier who had been despatched with the news of Villeneuve's having quitted Ferrol, arrived at Boulogne. The Emperor and the Minister of Marine were quartered some distance apart, and each received separate letters from Vil-

---

31. *Consulate and Empire,* vol. v., p. 222, *et seq.*
32. Ibid., p. 243.
33. Ibid., p. 242.

leneuve's flag-ship. The Emperor heard from Lauriston, expressing full confidence that the fleet was on its way to Brest. The Minister Decrès, received a letter from Villeneuve, which gave him strong reason to believe that Villeneuve would never appear at Brest.

Before he saw Decrès, the Emperor wrote to Ganteaume and to Villeneuve, supposing both would be at Brest when his letters reached. To Ganteaume he said, "Set out, and come hither." To Villeneuve he said, "I hope that you are at Brest. Set out; lose not a moment. Bring my united squadrons into the Channel, and England is ours! We are all ready; everything is embarked. Be here but for 24 hours and all is ended." [34]

But presently Decrès waited on him with the expression not only of his doubts about Villeneuve, and his conviction that he would next appear at Cadiz, but of his own view that the whole plan was a mistake—"horribly dangerous." Napoleon, apparently furious, pondered for twenty-four hours, and then accepting as certainty the Minister's belief, sent for his Secretary, Daru, and enacted with him that scene told with such dramatic effect by Thiers and Alison, from a paper left by Daru himself; but over which Alison makes such a strange mistake. Daru being sent for, found the Emperor in his cabinet in a transport of rage, rushing up and down in a fury, and breaking out into exclamations: "What a navy! What sacrifices for nothing! What an admiral! All hope is gone! That Villeneuve, instead of entering the Channel, has taken refuge in Cadiz. He will be blockaded there! Daru, sit down and write——." What was written there and then were the preliminary directions for the Campaign of Austerlitz, and the final abandonment of the design of invading England. [35]

In reviewing the nature and prospects of this last and apparently gigantic and complex effort of France, we are met by a very strong sensation of difficulty resting on the doubt—which I may own to operate with much force on my mind—whether Napoleon ever really meant to try the hazard of invasion. M. Thiers is quite satisfied that he did fully mean it, and he certainly seemed to do so. But with a mind such as Napoleon's, so firmly persuaded of the value of untruth, we never know where we are. Anyone reading the "Pièces

34. Ibid., p. 245.
35. Alison's mistake is that he makes this scene occur on the 11th instead of the 23rd of August; and that he substitutes Ferrol for Cadiz. He was probably misled by his knowledge that Villeneuve was forbidden to enter Ferrol, not understanding that this only meant the *harbour* of Ferrol, not the roadstead, and that the objection rested solely on the difficulty of getting out again except with a north-east wind.

Justificatives" given by Dumas in the eleventh volume of his *Précis des Evénemens Militaires,* where are set out in a continued series Napoleon's orders and observations on the movements and combinations of the Franco-Spanish fleets up to the 26th of June, cannot fail to be struck with the very large space which is given to the West Indian arrangements, and the small space which the notion of command in the Channel occupies.

And then the changes in the plans and their want of completeness require some explanation, if the Emperor was really earnest in that which, ostensibly, he was full of. It was only, apparently, when the impossibility of the Brest fleet's putting to sea became manifest that the ultimate plan of Villeneuve's combining with the forces at Ferrol and Rochefort, and then passing up Channel to release Ganteaume at Brest was finally adopted.

And then we have two statements by Napoleon himself: first, that half the flotilla was sham, and then, that the whole of it was sham. In his note on the flotilla, dictated after his return from Boulogne, he says the whole provision of armed vessels, praams, gun-boats, flat boats, and *peniches,* were perfectly useless; they were a mere blind, to deceive the English into the belief that he meant to attempt to cross without the cover of a fleet—a thing which he very well knew could not be done.[36]

Prince Metternich, in his autobiography, says: "By far the greater part of the political prophets, the camp at Boulogne was regarded as a preparation for a landing in England. Some better instructed observers saw in this camp a French army held in readiness to cross the Rhine, and that was my opinion. In one of my longer conversations with Napoleon in the journey to Cambray, whither I accompanied the Emperor in 1810, the conversation turned upon the great military preparations which he had made in the years 1803–5 in Boulogne. I frankly confessed to him that even at the time I could not regard these offensive measures as directed against England. 'You are very right,' said the Emperor, smiling. 'Never would I have been such a fool as to make a descent upon England, unless, indeed, a revolution had taken place within the country. The army assembled at Boulogne was always an army against Austria. I could not place it anywhere else without giving offence; and, being obliged to form it somewhere, I did so at Boulogne, where I could, whilst collecting it, also disquiet England. The very day of an insurrection in England, I should have sent over a detachment of my army to support

36. See *Précis des Evénemens Militaires,* vol. xii., p. 316.

the insurrection. I should not the less have fallen on you, for my forces were echeloned for that purpose. Thus you saw, in 1805, how near Boulogne was to Vienna."[37]

There is another incidental argument in favour of Prince Metternich's view, which is the varied and vague way in which Napoleon spoke of the length of time during which he required command of the sea to get his forces over. In July 1804 he said: "Let us be masters of the Straits for six hours, and we shall be masters of the world."[38] In draft instructions to Villeneuve, of May 8th, 1805, he says: "If your presence makes us masters of the sea for three days off Boulogne, we shall be able to make our expedition, composed of 160,000 men in 2,000 vessels."[39] In the second draft on the same day, the time is four days and the number of men 150,000.[40]

But, on the other hand, these direct statements, and these loose expressions seem to be outweighed by the distinctly anxious attitude of mind which Napoleon displayed as the time drew near when the arrival of Villeneuve off Brest was to be expected.

But if we are to believe that Napoleon was as much in earnest in the matter of a descent on the shores of England as he was in the matter of a concentration upon Ulm, then we must, I think, say that, confused by the double issue of a command of the sea, which was, after all, to be but an evasion of the enemy, Napoleon lost himself. The plans were too complex, too varied, and too indeterminate to have presented any real prospect of success. We are very generally accustomed to hear it said that Napoleon "decoyed" Nelson to the West Indies, and we seem generally to suppose that Collingwood exactly fathomed the Emperor's drift. But the West Indian Expeditions were no feints; nor do we gather that though, as a general principle, the idea was to draw the enemy's forces abroad, Napoleon distinctly contemplated that his admirals would be followed to the West Indies. Moreover, supposing it were otherwise, the idea of strategy would be somewhat lacking if we suppose that Villeneuve's main object in going to the West Indies was to draw Nelson after him. The fact proves it, for we see Nelson outsailing Villeneuve on the return voyage. If the main object had been to draw a British squadron away, the voyage to the West Indies should have been a

37. *Memoirs of Prince Metternich*. Translated by Mrs. A. Napier. 1880.
38. Napoleon to Latouche-Tréville. *Précis des Evénemens Militaires*, vol. xi., p. 200.
39. Ibid., p. 249.
40. Ibid., p. 251.

pretended one, and Villeneuve, taking care that Nelson was duly informed of his supposed West Indian destination, should have turned
back on the limited Ferrol blockading squadron and annihilated it,
while forming his junction with the ships in the port. It was the
same with Missiessy's squadron. If command of the Channel had
been primarily aimed at, a rendezvous at sea with Villeneuve would
have been properly appointed, and not the distant one at Surinam.

On the whole, I think that in some way or other, failure might
have been predicted for designs which were too great, too complex,
and too full of risk. The mere embarkation of bodies of troops on
board the ships was against success in the supposed ulterior design,
for it meant sickness and short supplies in the ships. Nor can we, in
forming a calm judgment, omit to notice that Napoleon seems to
have been acting all along in the very teeth of his naval advice. We
know that both Villeneuve and Decrès remonstrated with him, and
the strong language of the Minister of Marine on the 22nd of August is not to be forgotten:

> And to speak the whole truth, a Minister of Marine, subjugated by
> your Majesty in naval affairs, serves you badly and becomes useless
> to your arms, if not actually injurious to them.[41]

Thus once more, but finally, we seem to draw the lesson from this
last effort of France that it is unavailing to attempt to obtain the
command of the sea by any other means than by fighting for it, and
that that is so tremendous an undertaking that it will not bear consideration side by side with any other object.

41. *Consulate and Empire*, vol. v., p. 247.